THE BLIND MAN SEES

THE BLIND MAN SEES

Freud's Awakening
and Other Essays

Neville Symington

KARNAC
LONDON   NEW YORK

Extract on pp. 12–13, from "The History of the Psycho-Analytic Movement", in *The Standard Edition of the Complete Psychological Works of Sigmund Freud, Vol. 14*, pp. 12–15 (London: Hogarth Press, 1957), reproduced by permission of A. W. Freud et al./Paterson Marsh Ltd., London.

First published in 2004 by
H. Karnac (Books) Ltd.
6 Pembroke Buildings, London NW10 6RE

British Library Cataloguing in Publication Data

A C.I.P. for this book is available from the British Library

ISBN 1 85575 984 5

10 9 8 7 6 5 4 3 2 1

Edited, designed, and produced by Communication Crafts

www.karnacbooks.com

This book is dedicated to
Balvant Parekh

Who Knows the Truth
Who Knows Himself
And Is Faithful to Both.

CONTENTS

INTRODUCTION   ix

CHAPTER ONE
Freud's awakening   1

CHAPTER TWO
Was Freud influenced by Brentano?   22

CHAPTER THREE
An exegesis of conscience in the works of Freud   30

CHAPTER FOUR
Freud's truth   45

CHAPTER FIVE
The relation between the determinist
and the religious model of the mind   48

CHAPTER SIX
The unconscious as an amoral construction   54

CHAPTER SEVEN
Religion and science in psychoanalysis   72

CHAPTER EIGHT
The nature of reality   85

CHAPTER NINE
Religion and consciousness   100

CHAPTER TEN
The true god and the false god   112

CHAPTER ELEVEN
Natural spirituality   124

CHAPTER TWELVE
An enquiry into the concepts of soul and psyche   137

CHAPTER THIRTEEN
Religion and spirituality   150

CHAPTER FOURTEEN
Is psychoanalysis a religion?   159

CHAPTER FIFTEEN
The murder of Laius   165

CHAPTER SIXTEEN
Psychoanalysis and human freedom   174

CHAPTER SEVENTEEN
Failure of internalization in modern culture   186

CHAPTER EIGHTEEN
Anti-Semitism: another perspective   197

REFERENCES   211

INDEX   217

INTRODUCTION

Psychoanalysis: a scientific religion

This book is made up of a series of papers, written over a period of fifteen years, relating to the proposition that psychoanalysis is a scientific religion. Religion is concerned with the relationship between one human being and another.[1] Many a reader may throw his hands in the air at this and say that everyone knows that religion is concerned with the worship of God.

There are two notions of God that are profoundly different, and I address this in two of the chapters: "Religion and Consciousness" (chapter 9) and "The True God and the False God" (chapter 10). What I refer to as the true god is the ultimate being of which we and the whole universe is constructed and is the genuine rationale for humane and loving treatment of our fellow human beings, but also of animals, plants, and the inanimate world.

There are also two ways in which we interact with our fellow human beings: practical and emotional. All the great religious teachers and mystics have stressed the emotional—that invisible inner activity that links one human being with another. They have all taught that there are two emotional activities that govern our relations with one another—love and hate—and that it is the former that brings peace, harmony, and happiness and the latter only war, distress, and disaster.

The former is the outcome of an acceptance of all that is in us. More accurately, self-awareness and love are both manifestations of an emotional state that is truth.

There are within human beings two emotional patterns, one of which manifests itself in hatred, war, and disaster and the other in love and self-awareness. Self-awareness and love are partners. Self-awareness and hatred are antitheses. When I am in hating or blaming mode, I am not self-aware. When I am unaware, I am, in psychoanalytic discourse, *unconscious*. Freud declared that the goal of psychoanalysis was to make the unconscious conscious. This means that psychoanalysis aims to transform a pattern centred around hatred, blame, and revenge into one that centred around love and self-awareness. This is a achieved through a scientific understanding of how different elements in these two patterns inter-relate. I understand science here in terms of the definition given by R. G. Collingwood: "a body of systematic or orderly thinking about a determinate subject matter" (Collingwood, 1969).

The psychoanalyst examines scientifically the emotional pattern in himself and the other. He can only do this to the extent to which he is self-aware. As what is he is exercising is the inner pattern of his and the other's relationship, then, according to my definition, what he is engaged in is a religious activity. As he is doing it in an orderly way about a determinate subject-matter, he is acting as a scientist. Hence my claim that psychoanalysis is a scientific religion.

Most of the papers here are concerned with this central issue. They were written at different times, and as I have only reached this conclusion through a slow matching of experience to ideas at the same time as ditching those that do not fit the experience, the reader will be able to see the course of development that has led to this conclusion. Four chapters at the end: "The Murder of Laius" (chapter 15), "Psychoanalysis and Human Freedom" (chapter 16), "The Failure of Internalization in Modern Culture" (chapter 17), and "Anti-Semitism: Another Perspective" (chapter 18)—consider how the failure of religious values is responsible not only for individual pathology but also for social *malaise*. Because religion has been a powerful motivating force in human culture, as Tolstoy forcibly argued, its effects in society are enormous, and these last papers all derive from this perspective.

Note

1. I base much of this position on the argument put forward by John Macmurray in his book *The Structure of Religious Experience* (1936).

THE BLIND MAN SEES

CHAPTER ONE

Freud's awakening

When the young Freud was a research student in Brücke's physiological laboratory, he walked home earnestly and, after giving a cursory glance at his sisters, went straight into his small office to continue studying. He was 26, and one day he walked home deep in thought and entered the house with the usual earnest intent upon his face. He was moving directly towards his study when he saw his sisters talking with an attractive girl of about their age. He stopped in his tracks, and, to his sisters' surprise, he started talking to this attractive visitor. That moment signalled a momentous change in the life of Freud. "Ha, ha, he fell in love—that's all", I can hear you say. True, for Freud but falling in love had consequences that were to be momentous in the history of our culture.

Two thousand five hundred years before this event there was another, which occurred in a remote part of Northern India. A young nobleman, named Siddhartha, ventured forth one day out of his father's palace under the guidance of Channa, his charioteer. He had until that day never been out of the palace, we are told, but lived a life enclosed within the bosom of his family, living intimately with his wife and son. On this eventful day Channa pointed out to him an old man, a sick man, a dead man, and a wandering ascetic. He was rudely awakened, as if out of a trance, and that night he slipped out of his father's palace, cast off his nobleman's garb, donned the clothes of a

1

beggar, and set forth on the life of a wandering ascetic. That event was also momentous in the history of culture both in the East and later in the West.

Both these men were religious leaders of enormous significance. I think most of you would accept that Siddhartha, known to us as the Buddha, was the founder of a religion, but I can imagine that you might ridicule me for putting Freud into the same category; yet I do so in all seriousness. I can only ask you to be patient while I try to explain myself.

Stages in the development of the religious leader

Those great religious leaders who have fashioned our world have, in their religious development, passed through six distinct stages:

1. blindness;
2. awakening;
3. struggle;
4. enlightenment;
5. the gathering of followers;
6. the founding of an institution.

In some cases these stages are clearly differentiated, whereas in others there may be a coalescence of two or more of them, but I believe that it is always possible to recognize them in the life of great religious leaders. I am taking as my model of the religious leader the life of Siddhartha Gautama or the Buddha—the Enlightened One in whom these stages stand out with particular clarity.

Blindness

Until the age of 20, Suddhodana, Siddhartha's father, who was Raja of the Sakya clan in northern India, kept his son within the confines of his palace with explicit instructions that he was not to venture into the outside world and in particular that he was not to see those aspects of life which Teilhard de Chardin has called our *diminishments*: illness, old age, death, corruption, suffering, sin, injustice, malevolence, and so on (Chardin, 1964). We hear that Prince Siddhartha had lived through his childhood and adolescence in this state of naive innocence and that it was achieved through his father placing a protective barrier around his first-born. We hear that Siddhartha married, had a son, and yet still lived within this aura of primeval innocence. Then, on that eventful day, he rode out in a chariot with Channa, one of his father's equerries, and there on his journey Channa pointed out to him first an old man, then a sick man, and then a dead man, and at the sight of each he asked his charioteer the meaning of what he saw. His servant answered him that this comes to all men. The Prince was troubled that such was the effect of birth. Then he saw a recluse with shaven head and tattered yellow robe. Again he asked Channa to tell him what sort of man was this, and he was told that it was someone who had gone forth into the homeless life. He returned to the palace, pondering deeply all that he had seen, and then that evening he bid farewell to his wife and baby and in the silence of the night went out again with Channa, his chariot-eer, who left him on the edge of the forest where he exchanged his princely clothes for those of a beggar and went forth into the homeless life, alone to seek liberation from *dukkha* or suffering.

This stage of blindness can also be seen in Mahavira, a contempo-rary of the Buddha in India and the founder of Jainism. It was at the age of 30, on the death of his parents, that suddenly his eyes were opened, and he renounced the noble life of a *kshatriya*. It is also very clear in the account of St Paul's conversion. As Saul, he was blindly persecuting the newly formed Christian religion when on the road to Damascus he was struck off his horse and saw a bright light and heard the words of Jesus: "Why persecutest thou me?" He was taken, blind, to a house in Damascus, and then after three days scales fell from his eyes and he was able to see. His state of blindness is symbolized in this story. There are also condensed in it the stages of struggle and enlight-enment.

In the Christian tradition the conversion experience is always asso-ciated with The Call, Vocation, or *Das Ruf,* and this has tended to obscure its essence that lies in an awakening out of blindness to a clear seeing of death and destruction. The new-seeing is also of the presence of these forces within the circumference of the individual's own life. An illustration of this same blindness can be seen in contemporary times in the life of Leonard Cheshire VC. He led the successful Dambuster bombing raids over Germany during the Second World War. He had led over a hundred such raids without the full impact hitting him; then, when the war with Germany had ended, he was asked to witness the bombing of Nagasaki from an observation plane. He had been told that this was an especially big bomb, but he was somewhat cynical about it—after all, he had dropped many huge bombs over Germany. But when he saw the nuclear bomb explode, he was shaken to the core. He realized that what he had witnessed was of a totally different order to what he had been accustomed to. Then the full force of the destruction of which he had been an agent hit him. He was shaken out of his blindness, and he was gripped by a determination to live the rest of his life dedicated to construction rather than destruction.

In all these cases the person in question has been blind to some important aspect of life. In the case of the Buddha, he has been blind to death, disease, old age, and voluntary ascesis. The latter means that he was blind to the realization that there are people who decide to live their lives in this particular way, who decide to reject the luxuries of life in pursuit of a higher knowledge. The particular blindness here is to a psychic principle of action related to a new vision of life. It is blindness to that inner power that is the source of action. The realization of this power has been a central focus in the teachings of great religious leaders. It is the power of inner action that exists in all and is capable of mobilization. The Buddha had been blind to this.

Mahavira, the founder of Jainism, was awakened at the time when his parents died. He had been blind to the reality of death. St Paul had been blind to the fact that these followers of the Way (Christians) were people with feelings. "Why persecutest thou me?" he is asked on the road to Damascus. In other words, there is a person with feelings in each of these Christians whom you are persecuting. He had been blind to the reality of personhood and to his own destruction of real people. He had been blind to the consequences of his own actions. Leonard Cheshire had been blind to the destruction he was perpetrating when dropping bombs over Germany.

Can we sum up what this blindness is about? It is ultimately a blindness to what we do and also, more importantly, to what we don't do. And this psychological blindness to our own inner psychic acts is accompanied by a psychological blindness to human susceptibility: susceptibility to death, to old age, to pain. The blindness to knowledge of inner psychic acts and to human susceptibility form together into a single psychological reality. They are only logically distinct, but phenomenologically they are one. In the absence of a word for this phenomenon I propose to call it *vital realization*. It is the living realities of the world suffused with personal emotional meaning. The state of blindness, then, is *inert reality*. I use this term because it refers to realities that are present in the mind, but they are just there—there is no emotional relationship to them. This, however, needs some qualification.

The state of blindness is not an existential fact but a psychological one—that is, one that is created and maintained through inner psychological action.

Awakening

I prefer to use the term *awakening* to the word *conversion*. Conversion means a turning to God, and whereas the awakening I am talking about is frequently accompanied by a turning towards God, it is not necessarily so. In the case of the Buddha, he, like Freud, explicitly rejected any belief in God.[1] Also, conversion is frequently associated with unconscious guilt, and it is not necessarily accompanied by an awakening from a state of psychological blindness.

What, then, are the elements that go to make up this awakening? There is a psychological move from blindness to *vital realization*. What are the elements that bring it about? It seems to be twofold: there is an exposure to a bigger and more intense stimulus, most clearly illustrated in the case of Leonard Cheshire, but this is preceded by a procession of increasingly powerful inner acts. These inner acts cannot burst into birth without the external catalyst. What we know is that a combination of inner acts with the external catalyst brings about this transition from blindness to wakefulness or from *inert reality* to *vital realization*.

I call this new state of affairs *vital realization*, because the individual has, through an inner act, created a new relation to reality. What has been created is a personal emotional relation to an aspect of reality. We must take the legend of the Buddha's awakening as a mythological expression of what I am talking about. It strains credibility to believe that the Buddha had never seen an old man or someone ill. In a palace with numerous attendants, servants, and their children there must have been many old people, sick and deformed people, and deaths would have occurred many times. So what the myth describes accurately is an inner reality. There was knowledge of these realities in his mind, but there was no personal emotional relation to them. There are, therefore, two ways in which a reality can be present in the mind—either it is just there as a piece of baggage, or it is something that is a personal creation of the mind. Either the mind is crushed by the external reality, or the mind creates the reality out of its own resources. The human mind does not create *"ex nihilo"* but out of the material that it is surrounded by, as the potter fashions a pot out of an amorphous mass of clay. Working as an analyst, I have frequently had communications from patients demonstrating a changed relation to a fact. A patient said, "I have often heard it said that trust takes a long time to build up, but I had never realized it before", or "I have often talked about concern for people but never realized what it meant before", or "I know that for the last two years you have been speaking to me, but I only *felt* it for the first time yesterday", or "I have often talked about abandonment but only yesterday experienced it and understood it for the first time."

The examples that I could adduce of this could be far more numerous. In the above quotations the word "realize" is crucial—that is, I had never made it real before. These two mental phenomena—*inert reality* and *vital realization*—have been described by Bion as *beta elements* and *alpha elements*. I want, however, to use my two terms, as they give emphasis to the subjective aspect of the experience. Awakening occurs when there is a transformation of *inert reality* into *vital realization*. It is a mental transformation that is more radical than any miracle. I believe that the miracles that frequently accompany the accounts of such change in the lives of saints and mystics are, again, a mythological expression of this seemingly miraculous mental transformation.

I once had an experience of this in the consulting-room, where I made an interpretation and the patient had a staggering realization. For a few moments I felt like Jesus curing the blind man. I am happy to tell you that I did not feel very comfortable in this new identity and was glad that it was only transitory. I mention this, though, because, had I wanted to relate this experience to a child, then I should have used the story of Jesus and the blind man as a symbol. I believe that the miracles in the life of Jesus (and other holy people) are themselves symbols of this inner mental transformation. Of Jesus, the gospels record people as saying, "No one else has taught as this man . . ." (John 7: 46). In other words, he has seen and understood the law and the Prophets of the Old Dispensation in a uniquely new and personal way. They were encapsulated within a *vital realization* for him, whereas for others they were simply an *inert reality*. Before departing from this section on awakening, I want to see if we can get some more psychological understanding of it. Are there any precursors to the moment of awakening? What are its psychological accompaniments? I believe that prior to the moment of awakening, the person is frequently ill. This illness is the manifestation of an inner state of crisis. It is for this reason that Winnicott, who was a psychoanalyst and paediatrician, said that illness is a normal concomitant of development, and he makes the surprising statement, "it can be more normal for a child to be ill than to be well" (Winnicott, 1958, p. 4). In the paper from which this quotation comes, he describes how a child called Joan became ill when a new baby arrived. He then says: "had the new baby not arrived . . . Joan would have remained in robust health, but the value of her personality would have been to some extent diminished owing to her having missed a real experience at the proper age". What I am saying, therefore, is that the transformation from *inert* to *vital* mental reality is always a psychological crisis for the individual, the external manifestations of which are often illness, either physical or mental. A Buddhist told me of a new psychological awakening that occurred in her twenties, but it had been preceded by a severe depression, together with pneumonia.

Prior to the final moment of awakening, there have always been signals that have given the person a start, like flashes of lightning disturbing the peace of the night. Saints describe having tried to push these flashing thoughts aside. This is beautifully expressed within the Christian symbolism by Francis Thompson in his poem "The Hound of Heaven".

> I fled Him, down the nights and down the days;
> I fled Him, down the arches of the years;
> I fled Him, down the labyrinthine ways of my own mind;
> and in the midst of tears I hid from Him, and under running laughter,
> Up vistaed hopes I sped;
> And shot, precipitated,
> Adown Titanic glooms of chasmèd fears,
> From those strong feet that followed, followed after.
> But with unhurrying chase,
> And unperturbed pace,
> Deliberate speed, majestic instancy,
> They beat—and a Voice beat
> More instant than the Feet—
> "All things betray thee, who betrayest me."
> [Thompson, 1913, pp. 107–113]

How are we to understand that which he is fleeing from? Whom or what does the Lord Jesus symbolize? From what is he turning away? He turns to outer distractions, to concreteness. "He" then represents a seeing of the same objects, but in a new way. So, at the end of the poem, "He" says:

> All which I took from thee I did but take,
> Not for thy harms,
> But just that thou might'st seek it in My arms.

In other words, he sees in a new way. Why is awakening resisted so severely when, once it has been overcome, the neophyte gives potent expression to joy—a joy for having reached this new reality? In analysis, this question confronts me continually. Why all the resistance when the patient declares feeling more fulfilled once that bridge from *inert* to *vital* has been crossed? Two answers readily come to mind: the person has to face the wasted years and effort, and it is a challenge to take up new responsibilities. I have spoken of these matters with patients, and yet they seem only partial explanations. They are not explanations that bear the ring of authenticity. At root, resistance is a violent refusal of personal life, and this is deeply embedded in the psychic drama of human life. *Vital realization* brings with it pain, so it is mixed blessing. It is of the very essence of being human that we have this conflict of opposites writ into the deepest strata of our being. Self-analysis is nothing else than an ever plunging deeper into new layers of this ancient conflict, and in this it resembles very closely the inner search and ascesis of the mystics. I would like to quote to you a passage from Teilhard de Chardin's *Le Milieu Divin:*

> And so for the first time in my life perhaps (although I am supposed to meditate every day!), I took the lamp and, leaving the zone of everyday occupations and relationships where everything seems clear, I went down into my inmost self, to the deep abyss whence I feel dimly that my power of action emanates. But as I moved further and further away from the conventional certainties by which social life is superficially illuminated, I became aware that I was losing contact with myself. At each step of the descent a new person was disclosed within me of whose name I was no longer sure, and who no longer obeyed me. And when I had to stop my exploration because the path faded from beneath my steps, I found a bottomless abyss at my feet, and out of it came—arising, I know not from where—the current which I dare to call *my* life. [pp. 77–78]

This was part of the process by which Teilhard established his personhood. It also gives some idea of how frightening a journey it is and how we all shrink from it. It seems a paradox that when he reaches what is that deep current of life, it is precisely there that he discovers what is personal in him. This is the struggle that we shall be considering shortly.

In the story of the Buddha's awakening it is ushered in by the charioteer, Channa, pointing out the dead man, the diseased one, and so on. He represents, I believe, the outer figure who speaks the inner promptings that have until that moment been so rudely pushed away.

The speech of the outer figure (who can be another human being or some piece of arresting evidence) enters into a marriage with the inner thoughts, and communication occurs. It gives permanent form—structure—to the strivings of the inner act to make a new creation. The potter's clay goes into the kiln and is baked hard. Freud said that when a patient says at the end of an analysis that he has known this all along, then it is a sign that it has been a successful analysis. We need now to pass on to the struggle.

The struggle

The awakening represents an inner decision. However, the different parts of the personality have to be won over to it. Awareness of the consequences of this decision for all areas of human functioning can take many years, and when I say all areas of human functioning, I mean from thinking to defecating. The inner act of decision constitutes awakening, and this then has to take possession, by slow struggle, of the whole territory of the personality.

Again, this period of struggle is epitomized in the history of the Buddha. After that initial awakening, he spent several years—about seven, it is said—in a struggle to become free of *dukkha*. It reached a climax of intensity just before he achieved Enlightenment. Prior to that he had practised intense ascesis, together with some other ascetics. He finally left them when he realized that such extreme asceticism constituted in itself an attachment. It was, I believe, an attachment to what we psychoanalysts would call a narcissistic self-image. The final relinquishment of that (accompanied by contempt from his fellow ascetics, whom he left) ushered in his Enlightenment. It is the destructive forces within the personality that sustain the presence of *inert reality* within the mind. The achievement of that transformation from *inert reality* to *vital realization* is through a continuous battle at ever deeper levels against a violent assault on the individual's attempt to achieve an ultimate *vital realization* that endows the personality with a supreme level of personhood. Shortly before Siddhartha achieved Enlightenment, he had a violent confrontation with Mara, the Evil One, and this is a feature that characterizes the period just before Enlightenment. Jesus also passed through that final assault in the episode known as the Temptations in the Desert. St Benedict threw himself into bramble bushes at Subiaco when he was assaulted by powerful desires to return to a life of the flesh in Rome. The word used to encapsulate these destructive forces varies according to the mythology that you adopt.

"Mara" is the term used with Buddhism, "the Devil" in Christianity, or the "death instinct" in psychoanalysis. This concept is essentially a religious one. When Freud re-cast his instinct theory in 1920, he did so in terms that were essentially religious. It was, I believe, for this reason that many psychoanalysts rejected his later instinct theory, and why even Melanie Klein, who adopted it as the hallmark of her psychology, still clung to his positivistic scientific model and, indeed, why Freud himself could never reject entirely his positivistic framework for fear of ridicule from the scientific establishment. The only Freudian who boldly swept aside the homeostatic theory was Fairbairn, who fearlessly adopted a religious mythology.

Enlightenment

Psychological growth is not an even climb to the top of the hill but, rather, a very slight incline, rudely interrupted by quite sudden thrusts upwards—sudden bursts of new development. This is frequently observable in an analysis when a patient has, in modern parlance, a break-through. The line of the graph would go along at a level, and then there is a sudden upward swing. During seven years of struggle, the line on the Buddha's graph would have only crept very slightly upwards, and then, at Enlightenment, it shoots up vertically in a quite dramatic way.

At Enlightenment, the saint experiences a new possession of himself/herself, combined with a vision of human life infused with personal understanding. What has occurred is a final transformation of *inert reality* into *vital realization*, which is inextricably linked, interwoven with an integration of the personality, which overcomes the compartmentalized state that has characterized it before. Personal vision is the subjective expression of the integration of disparate parts of the personality.

The moment of Enlightenment is seen in all great religious leaders and mystics. It is the central moment in the spiritual drama of the Buddha—Buddha means the Enlightened One. In the life of Jesus it is portrayed in the Transfiguration. It is a turning point in the lives of mystics and saints.

The gathering of followers

Shortly after the Enlightenment, which has been preceded by some years of isolation—this is the significance of the desert (psychologi-

cally experienced as despair or depression)—the religious leader desires to re-join the human family and communicate his new understanding to a group of followers. In the case of the Buddha, it was the
monks, or Sangha, who gathered around him, and with Jesus it was the
call of those disciples who became the Apostles. This movement of
heart arises out of a desire to communicate what is felt to be a rich
understanding to human beings, and it arises out of a compassion for
his fellow men. In this matter we come to the tricky question of the true
and the false mystics, both of whom gather followers around them.
The true mystic feels himself to be the servant of a higher truth and
distrusts visions and sensually satisfying experiences. No one was
more insistent on this point than St John of the Cross. There is no sense,
with the true mystic, that he is on an ego trip, which, however, does
characterize the false mystic.

The founding of an institution

Again, religious leaders have done more than just gather followers.
They have moulded these disciples into an institution and given it a
structure. This was so with the Buddha, with Jesus, and with all spiritual leaders throughout history. These people had usually been endowed with good practical wisdom and knew that if their teachings
were to live on, it was necessary to embed their newly found vision of
reality within the structure of society. I do not want to dwell further on
this feature but pass on now to consider whether it is fair of me to say
that Freud embodied all these features in his own person.

Freud

The thesis of this paper is that Freud went through all these six stages,
which are, I believe, classic to the lives of those who have founded a
religion. I want now to see how these stages apply to Freud.

Blindness

Sulloway, in his book, *Freud, Biologist of the Mind* (1980), when discussing the matter of infantile sexuality, points out that, contrary to what is
popularly believed among psychoanalysts, in the last half of the nineteenth century there was an explosion of scientific literature on sexuality and a great deal about infantile sexuality, and that the remarkable
thing is that Freud was completely unaware of it. Even more than that,

it seems that he was encapsulated within a precinct of naïveté. In order to illustrate this point, I will quote quite a long passage of Freud's from "The History of the Psycho-Analytic Movement" (1914d):

There was some consolation for the bad reception accorded to my contention of a sexual aetiology in the neuroses even by my more intimate circle of friends—for a vacuum rapidly formed itself about my person—in the thought that I was taking up the fight for a new and original idea. But, one day, certain memories gathered in my mind which disturbed this pleasing notion, but which gave me in exchange a valuable insight into the processes of human creative activity and the nature of human knowledge. The idea for which I was being made responsible had by no means originated with me. It had been imparted to me by three people whose opinion had commanded my deepest respect—by Breuer himself, by Charcot, and by Chrobak, the gynaecologist at the University, perhaps the most eminent of all our Vienna physicians. These three men had all communicated to me a piece of knowledge which, strictly speaking, they themselves did not possess. Two of them later denied having done so when I reminded them of the fact; the third (the great Charcot) would probably have done the same if it had been granted me to see him again. But these three identical opinions, which I had heard without understanding, had lain dormant in my mind for years, until one day they awoke in the form of an apparently original discovery.

One day, when I was a young house-physician, I was walking across the town with Breuer, when a man came up who evidently wanted to speak to him urgently. I fell behind. As soon as Breuer was free, he told me in his friendly, instructive way that this man was the husband of a patient of his and had brought him some news of her. The wife, he added, was behaving in such a peculiar way in society that she had been brought to him for treatment as a nervous case. He concluded: these things are always *secrets d'alcove!* I asked him in astonishment what he meant, and he answered by explaining the word alcove (marriage-bed) to me, for he failed to realise how extraordinary the matter of his statement seemed to me.

Some years later, at one of Charcot's evening receptions, I happened to be standing near the great teacher at a moment when he appeared to be telling Brouardel a very interesting story about something that had happened during his day's work. I hardly heard the beginning, but gradually my attention was seized by what he was talking of: a young married couple from a distant country in the East—the woman a severe sufferer, the man either impotent or exceedingly awkward, *"Tachez donc"* I heard Charcot repeating, *"je vous assure, vous y arriverez"* ("go on trying! I promise you, you'll succeed"). Brouardel, who spoke less loudly, must have expressed his astonishment that symptoms like the wife's could have been produced by such circumstances. For Charcot suddenly broke out with great animation: *"Mais, dans des cas pareils c'est toujours la chose genitale, toujours . . . toujours . . . toujours"*. ("But in this sort of case it's always a question of the genitals, always, always, always"); and he crossed his arms over his stomach, hugging himself and jumping up and down on his toes several times in his own characteristically lively way. I know that for a moment I was almost paralysed with amazement and said to myself: "Well, but if he knows that, why does he never say so?" But the impression was soon forgotten; brain anatomy and the experimental induction of hysterical paralyses absorbed all my interest.

A year later, I had begun my medical career in Vienna as a lecturer in nervous diseases, and in everything relating to the aetiology of the neuroses I was still as ignorant and innocent as one could expect of a promising student trained at a university. One day I had a friendly message from Chrobak, asking me to take a woman patient of his to whom he could not give enough time, owing to his new appointment as a University teacher. I arrived at the patient's house before he did and found that she was suffering from attacks of meaningless anxiety, and could only be soothed by the most precise information about where her doctor was at every moment of the day. When Chrobak arrived he took me aside and told me that the patient's anxiety was due to the fact that although she had been married for eighteen years she was still *virgo intacta*. Her husband was absolutely impotent. In such cases, he said, there was nothing for a medical man to do but to shield this domestic misfortune with his own reputation, and put up with it if people shrugged their shoulders and said of him: "He's no good if he can't cure her after so many years." The sole prescription for such a malady, he added, is familiar enough to us, but we cannot order it. It runs: *"R. Penis normalis dosim repetatur!"*

I had never heard of such a prescription, and felt inclined to shake my head over my kind friend's cynicism. [Freud, 1914d, pp. 12–15]

I think from this quotation you may get the sense of what I mean. We see a picture here of this man in his early thirties quite insulated from something that was common knowledge among all his colleagues. The comrades around him were in possession of what Polanyi calls either tacit or inarticulate knowledge. What Freud describes in this passage is the way in which he was peculiarly insulated from this common knowledge—just like the unawakened Siddhartha in his father's palace.

Awakening

I am drawing a parallel between Siddhartha and Sigmund. There is no doubt that in the story of Sigmund, Siddhartha's palace is Brücke's laboratory. While the rest of his contemporaries were hurrying on with their medical training, Freud was behind a microscope, studying the gonadic structure of eels. He was involved in an atmosphere of research that was isolationist in the extreme—quite cut off from the domain of human feeling. Ernest Jones has given us a good pen-sketch of this man who was the professor of physiology and creator of the institute and laboratory in which Freud worked. I will just give you two vignettes to give you a flavour of the character of Ernst Brücke. A student of his, who had written in one of his papers, "Superficial observation reveals . . ." had his paper returned with the objectionable line violently crossed out, with Brücke's comment in the margin: "One is not to observe superficially." When in 1872 his much-loved son died, he forbade family and friends to mention his son's name, put all the pictures out of sight, and worked even harder than before. So here was Freud working in this scientific hothouse from which all feelings and emotions were banned and in which was demanded total dedication to positivistic science, and yet a few years later he had left Brücke's laboratory, was dabbling in hypnotism and studying with such suspect characters as Charcot and Bernheim, who were thought of as charlatans in the scientific world at the time. They were tinkering around with such antiquated ideas as purpose and intentionality. Was this Freud the same man as the dedicated Sigmund whom we all knew in Brücke's laboratory?

The reason given why Freud left Brücke's laboratory is that he had met Martha Bernays, fallen in love with her, and in order to be able to afford marriage, he had to get himself into private practice, which was better paid than his position as an assistant in the physiological laboratory. But is this convincing to a psychoanalyst? What we know of Freud is that he was a man of determined character. Had he been determined to pursue his physiological research, he would have done so. Even if we were to accept the argument that he needed to leave and start private practice in order to make marriage financially possible, it does not explain the entirely new direction that he began to take and the enormous trouble he took to get the grant to go to study under Charcot in Paris. What Freud came to understand through Charcot's influence was that conversion hysteria could be explained according to the mind's ideational content. This was heresy to the *Physicalische Gesell-*

schaft of which Brücke was a founder member. This was, on Freud's part, a radical departure from his previous commitment. It was, I believe, an awakening just as dramatic as that of Siddhartha. Although Ernest Jones was well aware of this, yet he passes over its immense significance, and more recent biographers, such as Clark and Gay, treat it with similar inattention. It is surely also significant that this change coincided with falling in love. As far as one can gather, Freud had been almost insulated from girl-friends until that point. The passion for Martha took his personality by storm, and his emotions, until that point screwed under the hatches of repression, burst into life. Martha was for Sigmund what Channa was in the life of Siddhartha. These two different catalysts took these two men in quite opposite directions. Whereas Siddhartha, who was married and had a child, cut all married ties and adopted the life of a wandering ascetic, Freud came out of emotional isolation and bonded passionately with the woman of his choice. I will return to the significance of this difference later. I want here to highlight again the enormous change that took place in Freud—from a natural scientist dedicated to finding physical causes to a pioneer who chartered the little-known territory of human desires and purposes. This was, I believe, an awakening typical of religious leaders.

Struggle

After this radical awakening, there followed 15 years of struggle. It was a period where Freud was searching for a personal understanding of the psychological phenomena that he was encountering in his patients, and one where he felt the psychological isolation of the lone explorer. Ernest Jones interprets this in a somewhat concrete way, implying that Freud was actually cold-shouldered by the medical and academic establishment, whereas Ellenberger demonstrates convincingly that this was something that was not actually so, but, rather, something that Freud experienced. Preoccupied as he was with intense personal and intellectual dilemmas that he was trying to solve, he felt isolated and not understood by those around him. His inner quest and preoccupation were not understood. The only person who had some inkling of what volcanoes were rumbling inside him was Wilhelm Fliess, and Freud's letters to him give us some idea of this emotional and cognitive development.

I want to dwell a while on the nature of that psychological struggle that was going on in Freud. Ellenberger has named it "creative illness" and believed that certain intellectual innovators had been through the sort of experience typified in Freud. He specifically mentions Gustav Fechner, the founder of psychophysics, and Jung. I believe that the sociologist Max Weber went through a similar illness, as did Wittgenstein. The person is psychologically ill and is wrestling to find a meaning to his inner state, there being no theories or explanations to hand that make sense of inner experience and outer observation. The searcher is compelled to find a solution for his own sanity and psychological integrity. This is why Ellenberger believes that Jones is wrong in eulogizing Freud for undertaking his self-analysis. Ellenberger says that Freud *had* to do it. He had no option. Finally, when the searcher bursts forth in enlightenment, he comes out of his illness but also provides a meaning that has a significance for many others. In other words, the problems that crystallize within his breast are society's deepest concerns.

I do not want to say more here than that Freud went through this struggle for many years, and the story of it is still best told in Ernest Jones's classic biography of Freud (1953). You can all read it there. I want just to indicate that this epic struggle is also a phase that is typified in the life of every great religious leader. I want now to pass to the next phase.

Enlightenment

In the year 1897 Freud had a great burst of understanding. He had been working away at dreams, at neurotic symptoms, and had for two years been engaged in his personal self-analysis. In a short time he had the key that unlocked the mysteries of dreams, that gave him an understanding of the symbolical nature of neurotic symptoms, and from this same constellation of insightful understandings he suddenly saw the fact of infantile sexuality, the Oedipus complex, and also the significance of jokes. It was a great burst of new insight for him, which penetrated a whole range of spheres: the sphere of inner psychic life, the locus in which inner psychic life is symbolized, significances in micro-social life as instanced in jokes and in macro-social organization as instanced in his speculations in *Totem and Taboo* (1912–13) and in his later papers, like *Civilization and Its Discontents* (1930a [1929]. This whole explosion of insight flowed from some centrally constructed constructs: repression, resistance, transference, and symbolism.

The most important aspect of this was that all this insight flowed not essentially as the result of academic research and scientific observation, but from a deep and sustained investigation into himself—

known as his self-analysis. It was the fact that these insights were informed by personal emotional comprehension that gave them their extraordinary power. It is this power that lead Freud to attract disciples around him.

I believe that biographers have tended to gloss over this enlightenment although the facts are there to be picked up if the reader is not seduced away by cautious qualifications. So, Ernest Jones says that Freud did not have a sudden "Eureka" experience but only gained his insights bit by bit and by slow progression, but then he also says that 1897 was the acme of Freud's career, that the insights that he achieved in that year were roots of which all future speculation was an elaboration. Biographers who miss the depth and extent of the 1897 experience have done this, I believe, because they have wanted to obscure, just as Freud did, the religious nature of these psychological phenomena.

The gathering of followers

On this section and the next I want to spend less time, as I believe most students of psychoanalysis are familiar with it. It was soon after 1897 that Freud completed *The Interpretation of Dreams,* and it was shortly after that that he began to collect his first followers: Stekel, Reitler, Kahane, and Adler, who became the founding members of the Wednesday Psychological Society. Max Graf said about these meetings: "The last and decisive word was always spoken by Freud himself. There was the atmosphere of the foundation of a religion in that room. Freud himself was its new prophet who made the heretofore prevailing methods of psychological investigation appear superficial" (in Gay, 1988).

Quite a few of these early followers—Ferenczi and Jung, for instance—sought out acquaintance with Freud from having read the *Traumdeutung.* It was the sense in these early followers that here they had a leader who understood unconscious phenomena from his heart. The compelling quality in the leader that attracts is that these things are felt to be personally and emotionally understood in that person. It is this that attracts them and is a consequence of the enlightenment that he had experienced.

The founding of an institution

It is the knowledge that here is a valuable body of new insight that inspires these followers to found an institution: that is, an organization that will live on beyond their own lives and continue to impart the insights of their leader for the future benefit of humanity. It is precisely this that occurred. The early disciples who formed the Wednesday Psychological Society in 1902 became the Vienna Psychoanalytical Society in 1908 and a couple of years later the International Psychoanalytical Society had been formed.

* * *

I have set out the stages that Freud passed through. These stages are classic to founders of religion. It has frequently been said that Freud founded a new religion, but it is usually uttered in a mocking tone. I wish now to put forward the thesis that he did found a new religion, but one that I have called secular.[2] In order to pursue this line of thinking, I want to approach it from a different angle.

To be holy, to lead the devout life, the only path was to enter a convent or a monastery. This statement is certainly true until the beginning of the sixteenth century, when Protestants protested against the vow of chastity that was integral to Catholic Christianity. Protestantism brought the spirituality that had been enclosed within the walls of monasteries and convents out into the marketplace of the world, as Max Weber described so lucidly in *The Protestant Ethic and the Spirit of Capitalism* (1971). The Counter-Reformation within Catholicism attempted, like the Protestant Reform, to adapt a spirituality for the layman, and one of the most significant attempts was set forth by Francis de Sales in his *Introduction to the Devout Life* (1608). Nevertheless, this and other attempts to bring the holy life within the scope of the average man and woman failed, and I want now to examine the reason for this.

The spirituality that had been current in Western and Eastern civilization for over two millennia was infused with the spirit of *"fuga mundi"*—flight from the world. The great religious leaders had turned their back on sexuality and intimate relationships. Their holiness was not in the sphere of intimacy. Siddhartha left his wife and child and went off and embraced the life of a wandering lonely ascetic, and Jesus said unequivocally: "If anyone comes to me and does not hate his own father and mother and wife and children and brothers and sisters, yes, and even his own life, he cannot be my disciple" (Luke 14: 26).

This was not true of Muhammad, but his followers have tried to make it so, and when Salman Rushdie points it out, he is threatened with execution. Mahavira, the founder of Jainism, also embraced the life of a lonely ascetic. St Augustine left his mistress and son, Adeodatus, to cleave to the holy life. The examples are numerous down through the ages in the traditional religions. There is no doubt that Luther and Calvin revolted against this, and both took wives in determined defiance of Rome. Protestant spirituality was a revolt against this *"fuga mundi"*, and yet there is something childish about Calvin's taking a wife, as if this move proved that he was free of the bonds of Rome. What I am saying here is that the renunciation of sex in traditional piety is a symbol of something much deeper: emotional intimacy. Sexual intercourse is the symbol of emotional engagement between two people. I must stress that when I say that sexual intercourse symbolizes this, I mean that the emotional incorporates a bodily interaction that radically differentiates it from what might be called an intellectual friendship. When we understand sexual in this sense, then it makes sense to say that the child sucking at the breast is engaged in a sexual activity. What I am saying here is that the *"fuga mundi"*, which was symbolized in a renunciation of sex, was much more deeply a renunciation of intimate emotional life between one human being and another. (It was for this reason, I believe, that Freud was so insistent on keeping sexuality at the centre of psychological understanding.)

I believe, therefore, that the revolt against traditional Christianity as instanced in the Reformation was only an infantile rebellion and not a mature challenge to the spirituality on which Christendom was based. This applied to the spirituality both of the Reformation and the Counter-Reformation. These reform movements attempted to bring the spirituality of the cloister into the family hearth, but in a fundamental way it was a failure, because it did not address the renunciation of emotional intimacy on which Eastern and Western spirituality had been based for two millennia in the West and two and a half millennia in the East. Francis de Sales, who was recognized by Catholics and Protestants as being a compassionate man, was nevertheless the person who encouraged Jane Frances Chantal to leave home and go into a convent, although she was a widow at the time and had a young teenage son living at home with her. This teenager protested against his mother's departure, and as she left the house to go off to the convent, he lay down across the lintel of the door, so she had to step over him on her passage from domestic life to that of the cloister. Francis de Sales also demanded in his book that when a married person was planning to receive Holy Communion, he or she should abstain from sexual intercourse with the spouse for three days prior to that event. It remained a spirituality where the person kept his secrets between himself and God and the emotional self remained closed off from all except God.

Emotional intimacy brings to consciousness aspects of the self that remain unknown when the person is in a state of emotional isolation. Emotional intimacy removes the veil of the ideal self and reveals the attitudes of heart that otherwise remain hidden: greed, self-centredness, cruelty, hatred, possessiveness, jealousy, envy. It is for this reason that traditional piety acted as a cloak for so much hypocrisy. Traditional piety was based on the *"fuga mundi"* and this applied in Western and Eastern religions alike. Emotional intimacy is possible in the degree to which the individual is detached from "sinfulness". I use the term "sinfulness" as an umbrella word to cover the vicious inner habits just mentioned.

Psychoanalysis offers a setting of personal intimacy with a goal of coming to know oneself. It is the old command of the Delphic Oracle, but with the proviso that it is to be sought in the context of emotional intimacy. Freud was the first religious leader who reversed the ancient pathway to holiness via the *"fuga mundi"*. It is when he took the step towards emotional intimacy with Martha Bernays that his pathway towards psychoanalysis began. Martha Bernays was his Channa.

You may say that this thesis is absurd because Freud's atheism is such a well-known fact. What is less well known is that theism is not an essential component of religion. The Buddha was just as atheistic as Freud,[3] explicitly denying the concept of a transcendent god or a transcendent self within the personality. It needs to be stated with some vehemence that to be religious is not synonymous with theism. Siddhartha was a religious man, but he was an atheist. What is it that makes a person religious, then? I prefer to put it this way rather than to ask the question, what is religion? It is my preference to examine what it means to be kind rather than discuss what kindness is. The former is existential, and the latter is metaphysical. So when someone is religious, what do we mean? It is that a particular value is put above others. What is the value? It is, in essence, that the non-tangible, the not-seen, the unpractical is put first, and this value guides and organizes all the others. The particular way in which this had been pursued had been by the *"fuga mundi"* method. The Reformation and the Catholic Counter-Reformation was a revolt against this particular method in the West. What I have said is that the Reformation was a first step away from the *"fuga mundi"* and towards rooting religion in the flesh of the world. This is why I use the term a "secular religion". The Latin *saeculum* means "the world". The term "secular religion" is not a con-

tradiction in terms if you understand religion in the way I am concep-
tualizing it. The person who has interpreted religion according to the
principle of *"fuga mundi"* is what I would call following "traditional
religion", and, as we know, Freud was bitterly opposed to it. He
opposed it because it was contrary to the secular religion to which he
was dedicated. This is, I believe, why he insisted on publishing *Moses
and Monotheism* (1939a), which was so offensive to religious Jews,
especially in 1939, when they needed all the moral support they could
get. Freud, however, felt that he had to do it: he had to make a stand
against traditional religion and so differentiate his own secular religion
from it.

Judaism has been free from this *"fuga mundi"* spirituality. It is a
spirituality rooted in family life and relationships. Unfortunately,
however, because of its seclusion within Christendom and the failure
of Christianity and Judaism to come into fruitful interchange, it has not
substantially influenced the *"fuga mundi"* mode of religious life.

I would like to conclude with a quotation from Freud's paper on
narcissism: "A strong egoism is a protection against falling ill, but in
the last resort we must begin to love in order not to fall ill, and we are
bound to fall ill if, in consequence of frustration, we are unable to love"
(Freud, 1914c, p. 85). If this is not a religious sentiment, then what is it?

Notes

1. This is what is believed by the Theravada School of Buddhism.
2. What I call "secular" here is what theologians have called "natural"; I
discuss this in greater detail in chapter 9, this volume.
3. Certainly according to the Theravada tradition.

CHAPTER TWO

Was Freud influenced by Brentano?

I wrote this paper in 1975, when I was still a student at the Institute of Psycho-Analysis in London; it was published in the *Bulletin
of the British Psycho-Analytical Society*.

I had read Brentano's *Psychology from the Empirical Standpoint*
(1973) and was immediately convinced that he had defined the
contours of psychology in an accurate way. When I learned that
Freud had attended his lectures for two years at Vienna University, I thought it likely that he would have been influenced by
him. As I say in this chapter, Freud does not mention any debt to
him, but I have noticed over the years that it is often the
unmentioned figure that is the most influential in a person's emotional and intellectual life. I believe this was so for Freud. His
stress in later life on an active subject in relation to internal objects seemed to have come right out of Brentano's psychological
schema.

The fact that Brentano did not believe in the unconscious should
not deter us from thinking that he could have influenced Freud.
This sphere of activity from a psychically active subject in relation
to inner representations is frequently unconscious. This was not

the case for Brentano, but only because he had given it all his psychic attention. For the majority it remained unconscious, just as Freud became conscious of areas of the mind that are unconscious to most of us.

As I read this paper now, thirty years after having written it, I think there is enough in it of importance to be worth reproducing.

It may seem strange to claim that Freud was influenced by a psychologist who rejected emphatically the concept of the unconscious. It is also worth asking the question why Freud makes no mention of such an influence in any of his writings. Rancurello (1968), in his book on Brentano, says: "Though he had been a student of Brentano, Freud offered a conception of man which in general was much less personalistic, and in particular much less aligned with this author's orientation than the conception of either Jung or Adler." Yet, I argue in this chapter that Freud was influenced by Brentano in one very important respect, which will emerge shortly.

Brentano came from a brilliant German family (although originating from Italy), who were also devout Roman Catholics. Franz Brentano himself was ordained a Catholic priest in 1864, and he taught philosophy at Würzburg until he left the priesthood in 1873, when he also resigned his post at the university. He then had a year with no academic post and during that time he wrote his *Psychology from the Empirical Standpoint*. In 1874 he took up a post as *dozent* at Vienna University, where he remained lecturing for twenty years. Freud attended his courses in philosophy from 1874 to 1876.

There was great antagonism towards Brentano when he was *dozent* at Würzburg, both from philosophers and from scientists. The former were mostly idealists under the influence of Schelling, whom he opposed. Schelling had said that there was a world soul that was incarnated in various material forms, and that the mind derived its knowledge from contact with this demiurge rather than from contact with the external world. Brentano, following Aristotle rather than Plato, taught that the mind is in touch with the external world and builds up its ideas through direct contact with it. Students, attracted by this new approach, flocked to him and left other lecturers with empty auditoria. On the other hand, natural scientists from liberal circles viewed him as a mystic and one-sided Aristotelian. He was therefore very unpopular in academic circles, because he challenged the idealist position but also did not espouse the realism of the anti-vitalists. His unpopularity was aggravated when he left the priesthood. To leave the priesthood at any time is viewed with suspicion and disapproval, but this was much more so in 1873 than it is today. In Vienna, as well as in Würzburg, he came in for a lot of suspicion and criticism. At this time, the physicalist tradition was the only respectable orientation in the scientific community. Helmholtz, du Bois-Reymond, Ludwig, and Brücke had made an anti-vitalist pact in opposition to the great physiologist, Johannes Muller. Boring (1950) defines vitalism as "The view that life involves forces other than those found in the interaction of inorganic bodies."

At the time when Brentano was lecturing in Vienna, anyone who claimed to be a scientist while holding a vitalist position was scorned as an anachronism. Brentano tried to prove the immortality of the soul philosophically. It was this, as well as his suspect background as a priest, that led academic circles in Vienna to view him with extreme suspicion. His own rather intolerant personality did not help to assuage people's feelings. His claim, however, to be called one of the founding fathers of psychology in the nineteenth century is every bit as good as Wundt's. For him, the observation of facts had to be methodical, painstaking, and detailed, and it was this that made a piece of work scientific rather than just popular or literary. He wanted to establish a psychological laboratory at Vienna University but was prevented from doing so by his antagonists. Had he been able to do so, his laboratory would have been contemporaneous with that of Wundt's in Leipzig and would no doubt, have also attracted eminent psychologists, such as William James. Still today, when Brentano's name is mentioned, people tend to say, "But, oh, I thought he was a philosopher". It is true that he was *dozent* in philosophy, but it must be remembered that Wundt's Chair at Leipzig was also in philosophy and not in psychology. It is the physicalist tradition, still so powerful a force in many psychology departments to this day, plus the fact that Brentano did not manage to establish an experimental laboratory that has led psychologists worldwide to relegate Brentano to a secondary position in the history of psychology.

It is the same attitude that rejects Freud also as unscientific. What Brentano repudiated was the observation of facts *alone* as being data proper to psychology. For him, it was the mind in relation to those facts that was the true subject of psychology. Brentano remained unpopular and suspect to the end of his life. He has today, however, become more acceptable through his pupil, Edmund Husserl. Via the latter's phenomenological philosophy, Brentano's thought is creeping into psychology under a variety of names.

Freud would have been attending Brentano's lectures at the age of 19 to 21—important years in his intellectual formation. It is not known whether the young medical student had any personal contact with the famous philosopher, but Ernest Jones (1953) has this to say:

> The Editor of Mill's collected writings in German was Theodor Gomperz, a philosopher and historian of high standing in Vienna. When fifty years later his son Heinrich was preparing a biography of his father he asked Freud how he came to be the translator of the twelfth volume. Freud replied, in a letter dated June 9, 1932, that Gomperz had inquired at a party for someone to replace Eduard Wessel, the young translator of the twelfth volume who had died suddenly, and that Brentano had given him Freud's name. Freud had for a couple of years attended Brentano's lectures, as indeed had half of Vienna since he was a very gifted lecturer, but whether Freud's name was passed on to him by one of their mutual friends—Breuer, for instance, was Brentano's family physician—is not known, nor does it seem of any importance. [pp. 61–62]

It is a fair assumption that there was some personal contact between the two men. If there were so many students at Brentano's lectures, then, if he nominated Freud as a translator for one of Mill's books, it is highly likely that he knew him. Also, Rancurello (1968) recounts that after the formal lecture Brentano would go for "walks" with some of his students and go on discussing the topic he had been speaking about. Jones (1953) also says that Freud stated many years later that he knew very little of Plato's philosophy. He would have known some of Aristotle's thought through attending the lectures of the "one-sided Aristotelian". It is difficult to imagine that Freud was not influenced by Brentano at this time, so it is a puzzle why Freud never acknowledged him. I think there are three reasons. In the first place, Freud was most anxious to present psychoanalysis as scientifically respectable. For years Freud twisted and turned to try to keep his theory within the physicalist tradition, and even when he abandoned what was a hopeless task, he never candidly admitted that he had done so. He continued to couch his language in the scientific formulae of the physicalists. Secondly, Freud was very ambitious and wanted to be respected within the scientific community. He reveals his ambitiousness in his interpretation of the dream about "my friend R". He alludes to the fact that his ambition was founded on his fantasy that he was destined to be a great man. It would have been too damaging to have conceded intellectual parenthood to an unscientific Aristotelian. Lastly, Brentano did not believe in the existence of the unconscious—at least, he did not believe in subliminal perception. What was in the mind had been processed through conscious activity. It is arguable that he did not hold this rigidly, as he made some statements that would seem to indicate that this was not the case. For instance: "In an autobiography we should pay attention not so much to what is reported, as to what is involuntarily revealed" (Brentano, 1973). Yet Brentano was among those, in opposition to Nietzsche, who denied the existence of the unconscious. Freud preferred to acknowledge people like Charcot and Bernheim, who did recognize the existence of the unconscious.

Brentano is remembered today in the history of psychology for his notion of "intentional inexistence". By this phrase he meant the relationship that the active subject has with an internal object. Brentano followed Kant in believing that there is an external reality but that man does not know it as it exists but, rather, interprets it. Man has an image of the external world, but the latter does not exist as man sees it. Observation—the business of making internal images—is a process belonging to the subject whereby he interprets reality. The image is the product of observation and cannot be its subject. An image cannot be observed. For this reason Brentano rejected the introspective analysis of Wundt, which was based on observation of an image that can only lead to another image and so on, in an infinite series—therefore, a self-indulgent, sterile process. Brentano assumes that man is in contact with the external world. Kant had founded the science of epistemology in an attempt to prove it. Brentano takes it as proven and goes on from there to state that the external world is a mass of stimuli that, through observation, man experiences in the form of images. He converts the external stimuli into internal images. All the natural sciences are working with these internal images. Fechner's psychophysics, therefore, is within the domain of natural science. Ordering and formulating laws about man's internal images is the work proper to natural science. Psychology studies the relationship of the active subject to the internal images: "We found that the intentional *in-existence*, the reference to something as an object, is a distinguishing characteristic of all mental phenomena. No physical phenomena exhibit anything similar" (Brentano, 1973).

All the physicalists, especially someone like Brücke, under whom Freud studied, held that observation was the stuff of science, and therefore if psychology was a science then it was also concerned with this. Brentano pointed out that, although observation was essential and was a prerequisite for psychology, yet its subject of study was the relationship of the active subject to the product of observation: the internal images. This is what Brentano meant by "intentional inexistence". By "intentional" he meant that quality by which the subject has a reference to an object: "We can, therefore, define mental phenomena by saying that they are those phenomena which contain an object intentionally within themselves" (Brentano, 1973).

Objects are not neutrally existent within the subject's consciousness. They call forth a relationship from the subject. This meant that Brentano opposed the associationist understanding of the human organism and demanded that scientists take account of the psychically active subject. In present-day terminology, Brentano was describing the ego's relation to internal objects.

The associationists are known for two main views, one dependent on the other. One was that the subject builds up a total perceptual field from a mass of minutiae, and the other was that the human personality was itself built up from a whole series of different elements. Those following James Mill held that each part could be isolated and discovered as a component on its own, whereas those following the mental chemistry of John Stuart Mill thought that the different parts came together to form a new compound that could no longer be reduced to the original elements, but—and this is the important point—the personality was to be understood as the relationship between the parts. Those following John Stuart Mill, like Wundt, did hold that there was some cohesive unity so that it was meaningful to refer to a concept such as "the personality", but it remained essentially passive and just a victim of the forces that might drive it hither or thither. It was the Cartesian view of man but without the soul: that the human organism could be explained by a mechanical model, just as an internal combustion engine could. Only theologians held anything different. Brentano, obviously influenced by Aristotle and Aquinas and the Scholastic tradition as taught in the Roman Catholic Church, opposed most fiercely the common view of these scientists. As Rancurello (1968) says: "Brentano's life long intellectual battle against phenomenalistic systems shows that he himself never intended to write a psychology "without a soul"—that is, a psychology as the science of psychic phenomena, or psychic acts, without a 'psychically active' subject".

He believed in the sensory contents as an object of study, as Wundt did, but he refused to say that this was the totality of the subject of psychology. There was a substrate beneath the individual components that *bore* them and underlay them. This substrate is not just passive, or his position would have effectively been similar to that of John Stuart Mill. Rather, this substrate is an active force. His disagreement with Fechner, for instance, is that a measurement of intensity must take into account other factors in the personality. Differences in the intensity of sensation are due not only to the increased magnitude of the external stimulus, but also to the internal psychic act—attention, for example. It can be understood that his understanding of the true subject of psychology—that is, the relationship of the subject to his internal objects—would have no meaning without his understanding of the psychically active subject. We are going to argue in a moment that Freud changed his view from that of Wundt to that of Brentano in the last phase of his life. It is important to realize how fundamental a change this is. I think it is one that has not been fully appreciated. Lastly, a word about Brentano's methodology. His conception of the "method of the natural sciences" was to be applied by analogy, and not univocally. He was quite explicit on this point and said that within the natural sciences, method has to change in accordance with the specific nature of objects being studied. He opposed vagueness in the sphere of science, and he tried to work out a coherent system based on induction—that is, to establish general laws starting from the observation of particular facts. Deduction, on the other hand, was a position arrived at by logic prior to verification by facts. Most scientists agreed that deduction was necessary, but Brentano went further and held that it must be given primacy of place. He said that induction only has value to the extent that it partakes of deduction. Unlike the usual position taken by scientists, he said that absolute truth of "mathematical certainty"—to use his terminology—was only possible in the deductive sphere. This was a departure from Kant, who thought that apodictic certainty was possible in the inductive sphere. A statement like "The whole is greater than the part" or "The shortest distance between two points is a straight line" compelled the mind to acceptance. He called it mathematical or apodictic certainty; inductive laws had "physical certainty". It could only be a certainty by analogy. To subject the data of observation to deduction led to a system that he called "inductive metaphysics". He aimed to produce a unified psychology out of the many psychologies existent at the time, and this, he said, was only possible through the aid of metaphysics, which is propaedeutic to the natural sciences. He held that philosophy was necessary for the sciences of the mind, as Rancurello (1968) states: "He has always emphasized that the ultimate solution of the problems confronting these sciences is dependent upon broad guidelines laid down in philosophy".

Initially Freud tried to anchor mental phenomena to the nerve centres of the brain, but, shortly after writing the "Project for a Scientific Psychology" (1950 [1895]), he gave up the attempt, which he expressed clearly in his metaphysical paper on the unconscious. He then devised a mental topography, where he cut up the mental apparatus into three systems: the unconscious (*Ucs*), the pre-conscious (*Pcs*), and the conscious (*Cs*). In this model he implicitly identified the system *Cs* with the ego, though he did not elaborate it. In "Mourning and Melancholia" (1917e [1915]) he spoke of the ego and also an intrapsychic object. In *The Ego and the Id* (1923b) he elaborated still further and spoke of an inner structure the essence of which was the relation between the ego (or the self, in Brentano's terminology) and the internal objects. In the structural model, the superego is an object with which the ego has a relationship. This is almost an exact replica of what Brentano had taught. Of course, Freud still held on to the pleasure principle and the principle of constancy, but they lay side by side in an incompatible marriage with his structural model, and it was the latter that was central in his clinical work and has been adopted wholeheartedly by his followers, both ego psychologists and object relations theorists. In the structural formulation, Freud had moved from a physicalist position to something that today we would call phenomenological. He had become a true psychologist. In this aspect of his thinking, it is difficult to think that he was not profoundly influenced by Brentano.

It is quite common for a thinker to encapsulate his discoveries initially within the framework of the presuppositions that are legitimated by the scientific community of his time and only later to establish them within an alien paradigm. I believe that Freud first planted his discoveries within the canons dictated by the *Physicalische Gesellschaft*, and only in later life did he begin to graft these, instead, into a vitalist–intentional structure. This became possible for him as he developed more self-confidence. It is at this point that he was then able to draw upon what he had learned and internalized as a young man from the lectures of Brentano.

CHAPTER THREE

An exegesis of conscience in the works of Freud

When we discharge elements that are within hatefully into the bodily outer world, we are violently reproached. This condemnation, which can be very violent, is what Freud came to call the superego. When we cease to discharge elements out of our inner selves but hold them instead within an encompassing membrane, then the superego becomes transformed into conscience. This chapter is an exegesis of Freud's use of the word "conscience". Very often his use of the word is synonymous with what he later termed superego. This chapter distinguishes Freud's use of the word from the one that became current at the time of the Enlightenment. Conscience here is understood to be a free invitation within the personality to act in a way that will ennoble both the self and the other. It is very important not to confuse conscience with superego, as they are entirely different things.

The first mention of conscience is in Freud's 71st letter to Fliess, written on 15 October 1897, where he quotes the celebrated line from Hamlet: "Thus conscience does make cowards of us all" (Freud, 1950 [1892–99], p. 266), and Freud goes on to ponder why it is that Hamlet did not avenge his father by killing his uncle when he kills Laertes and his courtiers without scruple. Freud suggests that Hamlet had himself meditated the same deed against his father (out of passion for his mother). And then he says: "His conscience is his unconscious sense of guilt" (p. 266).

So Freud here equates conscience with guilt for a deed that has been done, but when guilt is unconscious, the form of it is in acts—that is, the killing of Laertes and his courtiers as displacement from the uncle because of guilt: that if he killed the Uncle, it would bring him too close to the intent to kill his father, awareness of which would be too shameful.

In the *Studies on Hysteria* Breuer refers to conscience as something that strikes the person subsequent to the event:

> A very sick woman suffering from pathological conscientiousness and full of distrust of herself, felt every hysterical phenomenon as something guilty, because, she said, she need not have had it if she had really wanted not to. When a paresis of her legs was wrongly diagnosed as a disease of the spine she felt it as an immense relief, and when she was told it was "only nervous" and would pass off, that was enough to bring on severe pangs of conscience. [Freud, 1895d, p. 243]

In other words, when the diagnosis suggested that she had some part in it, she was conscience-struck, whereas once it had been pronounced a "disease of the spine", she felt relief. The implication here is that a pronouncement from on high smothers guilt by an omnipotent act of obliteration. Actually it is not obliterated but goes into displaced acts. Both in this case of Breuer's and the previous use of conscience by Freud, the sense of it is of condemnation for an act already committed. Conscience is always used in this sense by Freud.

In his paper on "Obsessive Actions and Religious Practices" (1907b, p. 119) Freud notes that qualms of conscience occur when neurotic or religious ceremonials are neglected. It suggests that these religious practices are attempts to ward off punishment. The sense of it is not that something bad has necessarily occurred, and so the qualms of conscience are neurotic. This came 16 years before the formulation of the structural model, but the sense of conscience is of a declaration from the superego that the ego is bad. As we shall see, Freud later assimilates conscience to one of the functions of the superego where reproaches from the superego are equated with conscience.

In *Totem and Taboo*, Freud (1912–13) devotes a couple of pages to the subject of conscience. A taboo is an external prohibition, and Freud refers to a taboo conscience being the inhibition in us against breaking the taboo. He makes the distinction here (p. 67) between conscience and guilt, with the former operating prior to the act and the latter subsequent to it. This is the only place where Freud assigns to conscience this function of operating prior to the action.

He then notes the connection between conscience and consciousness manifest in their linguistic similarity, and so he defines the former thus: "Conscience is the internal perception of the rejection of a particular wish operating in us" (p. 68).

Here Freud sees the operation of conscience as referring to an accomplished act, but in particular to the rejection of a wish, so at this stage conscience is the internal perception of this rejection. So Freud sees conscience as a faculty functioning in three modes:

a.   operating prior to the act;

b.   observing the act;

c.   castigating the ego for the act that has been committed.

However, the first and second functions of conscience appear only here and in his paper on *The Question of Lay Analysis* (1926e). To say this in Freud's own language: throughout the works of Freud, conscience is seen as something ego-dystonic and harmful to the ego. The only instance where conscience appears as ego-syntonic is in *The Question of Lay Analysis*. Even here, where conscience is defined as the observer, it is not difficult to see how this slides easily into that part of the personality that observes the ego and is soon castigating it. He goes on to say that there is no reason for the condemnations of conscience. It is just certain and obvious, and he implies that the condemnation is not open to rational enquiry. It has therefore to be ego-dystonic. What comes from conscience is like a dictate from God, who cannot be questioned.

He believes that conscience probably arose from the opposition between two different feelings, one unconscious and the other conscious, where the latter dominates the former: "kept under repression by the compulsive domination of the other". In other words, he here equates conscience with a force that is compulsively dominating, and it is for him the installation within of a taboo. This becomes Freud's established formulation: that conscience is the internalization of an external authority.

He also defines anxiety as a dread of conscience: "we cannot help being struck by the fact that a sense of guilt has about it much of the nature of anxiety: we could describe it without any misgivings as a 'dread of conscience'" (p. 69).

At this stage Freud thinks that anxiety occurs when wishful impulses are repressed. He later came to think that anxiety is the repressing agency itself. He says that the act of repudiation to which he refers in his definition of conscience is unknown—so the reason for this repudiation is unknown.

In his paper "On Narcissism: An Introduction" (1914c), Freud sees the ego-ideal as a narcissistic construct, and conscience becomes the agency that watches to see when the ego fails to measure up to the goals set by the ego-ideal. Conscience, therefore, becomes part of the narcissistic setup. What he describes here is a very familiar picture of the narcissistic structure, where the personality is split into an idealized self and a degraded self, with conscience aligned with the idealized part in the role of watcher, but now it is clear—which it was not in *Totem and Taboo* (1912–13)—that this watching is for the purpose of condemnation. In a schizophrenic illness or in paranoid delusions this demonic watcher is projected into outer figures that may be phantasy ones or real ones (1914c, p. 95). In this paper Freud gives another definition of conscience: "The institution of conscience was at bottom an embodiment, first of parental criticism, and subsequently of that of society" (p. 96).

So it is the idea that that part of the self called the "ego-ideal" or "idealized self" looks down upon the part that cannot measure up to its superiority and makes a judgement of contempt, and that it is this judging agency that is called "criticism". He has changed his definition, so that now conscience is clearly the internalization of an outer critical authority. It has become an exact equivalent of what he came seven years later to name the superego. In this paper he also equates conscience with the dream censor (p. 97)—that is, that which prevents tabooed wishes from emerging directly into consciousness.

The equation between conscience and what was to become the superego is even clearer in the following quotation from "Mourning and Melancholia" (1917e [1915]): "Our suspicion that the critical agency which is here split off from the ego might also show its independence in other circumstances will be confirmed by every further observation. We shall really find grounds for distinguishing this agency from the rest of the ego. What we are here being acquainted with is the agency commonly called 'conscience'" (p. 247)

It is not difficult to see from this that Freud was moving towards his formulation of the superego and his equation of this with conscience. That he saw conscience as a proactive force preventing life-enhancing movements of the emotions is clear in his paper "A Case of Paranoia

Running Counter to the Psycho-Analytic Theory of the Disease" (1915f), where he tells of how a girl's mother, to whom she was jealously attached, played the part of the "conscience" as soon as she made a move towards a member of the opposite sex. It is clear that conscience is an anti-developmental force. Its role here is not to condemn but to prevent movements of emotional development. It is clearly ego-dystonic in the extreme.

In his paper "Our Attitude towards Death" (1915b), Freud equates conscience with a prohibition: "The first and most important prohibition made by the awakening conscience was 'Thou shalt not kill'" (p. 295).

In his paper on "Those Wrecked by Success" (1916d), Freud says that the success of people who achieve in external reality what they had imagined in internal reality provokes an outbreak of disease, and this is due to the "forces of conscience which forbid the subject to gain the long hoped for advantage from the fortunate change in reality" (p. 318). Here again conscience is seen as a punishing tyrant within the personality.

Later in the same paper he discusses the case of Rebecca, the character in Ibsen's play "Rosmersholm", who causes Rosmer's wife Beata to commit suicide so she can marry Rosmer. However, when Rosmer proposes to her, she refuses and gives the reason: "This is the terrible part of it: that now when all life's happiness is within my grasp—my heart has changed and my own past cuts me off from it". Freud comments: "That is to say, she has in the meantime become a different being; her conscience has awakened, she has acquired a sense of guilt which debars her from enjoyment" (1916d, p. 325).

It is clear, however, from Freud's commentary on what has awakened conscience that we are talking of a rigid superego-like structure that condemns her. Yet in his whole commentary this is not entirely the position, because it is conscience that awakens her guilt—that is, brings it to awareness.

In the Editorial Foreword to *Beyond the Pleasure Principle* (Freud, 1920g, p. 4), Strachey refers to a special self-observing and critical agency in the ego as the ego-ideal, the censor, and the conscience synonymously.

In *Group Psychology and the Analysis of the Ego* (Freud, 1921c) he equates conscience with "social anxiety": "It has long been our contention that 'social anxiety' is the essence of what is called conscience" (pp. 74–75). It is the notion that it is based on fear of disfavour from those outside—that were it not for fear of punishment by society, we would murder, rape, or kill. If it were not for this external restraint, that is what we would do, so conscience becomes fear of the external constraint. It fits in with Freud's oedipal drama, where we fear castration from the father. Father becomes generalized to society and its norms, and conscience becomes the voice of father's reproaches. Freud specifically makes this point in *Inhibitions, Symptoms and Anxiety* (1926d): "the father has become depersonalized in the shape of the super-ego" (p. 128).

In *The Ego and the Id* (1923b), Freud says explicitly that the origin of conscience is intimately connected with the Oedipus complex. It is clear, especially in Freud's later works, such as *Civilization and its Discontents* (1930a [1929]) and *The Future of an Illusion* (1927c), that it is the external threat of punishment that deters members of society from rape, murder, and pillage. Conscience is, therefore, within the personality, the fear of the authority that will punish if any of these misdemeanours are committed. It is worth noting that there is for Freud no place for the possibility of transformation of desire, and therefore the ego-syntonic role of conscience has virtually no place in his system.

Conscience is the repository in the personality for the authority of the group (Freud, 1920c, p. 85). Its power can be put of out action by an intensification of emotion brought about through the pressure of the group. I think he means here a smaller group within the larger society. In this paper Freud defines a couple as a group, and therefore the sexual passion between two people or the hypnotic phenomenon in a couple or small group can temporarily obliterate conscience. Thus Freud says that conscience, as the critical agency, is totally silent when someone is in love, because the loved object has been set up in place of the ego-ideal (1920c, p. 113) and no criticism can be tolerated about the loved object. In a similar way he says that in the hypnotic trance the moral conscience may show compliance.

In this paper he defines conscience as that part of the ego which behaves cruelly to the other part. He later came to name it the "super-ego". So here it is not just an observer but the cruel actor.

Freud says that moral conscience (1920c, p. 110) as the repressor is the heir to an original narcissism. He is here reiterating what he said in his paper on narcissism (1914c)—that is, that the ego-ideal is part of the narcissistic setup, and therefore, as conscience is either synonymous with the ego-ideal or one of its functions, it is a consequence of narcissism. Conscience, then, is part of a pathological organization. Freud makes the following very insightful remark about narcissism: "[It] gradually gathers up from the influences of the environment the demands which that environment makes upon the ego" (1920c, p. 110).

It is therefore because of the narcissistic structure that a person is capable of being exploited by an external person, and it is because of this structure that conscience becomes a castigator. Freud recognizes here that it is the narcissistic structure that scoops the external world into an object of persecution to the ego. In other words, it is not society or culture in itself that is repressive of the instincts, but the repressiveness depends upon whether the outer environment has been internalized according to narcissistic principles or according to healthy ones. It is for this reason that I believe that Freud reached the climax of psychological understanding in his papers "Mourning and Melancholia" (1917e [1915]), "On Narcissism: An Introduction" (1914c), *Group Psychology and Analysis of the Ego* (1920c), and *The Ego and the Id* (1923b), where he formulated the idea of narcissistic identification and the way this affected internalization of figures in the outer world and of society generally. In his later "sociological papers" he seems to have forgotten this and reverted to the idea that society is repressive in all circumstances; he has lost thereby the hold he had on the differential processes of internalization. Had he continued his study of narcissistic identification, he might have examined the question of how conscience differs in narcissistic internalization and in internalization that is normal. The question we should like to ask Freud is: what does the personality structure look like when the narcissistic structure has dissipated?—when the individual psyche is largely freed of these processes?

Freud says that a persecuting conscience can be got rid of by projection. He says, in "Some Neurotic Mechanisms in Jealousy, Paranoia and Homosexuality" (1922b), that a person who projects his jealousy into another becomes acquitted of his conscience and so avoids feeling persecuted from within (p. 224). Of course, he will feel persecuted by the outside person, but this is less painful. However, Freud does not go into this at this stage because it goes counter to his theory that persecution comes about as the result of the internalization of an external critical authority. It makes one ask whether Freud's theory of the internalization of an external authority is itself a projection? Later, in *Civilization and its Discontents* (1930a [1929]), he says that the severity of the superego is not only because of the severity of the external authority, but because the subject's own desires to attack that authority have been incorporated into the superego; I think this is the only passage where his insight into the influence upon the outer figure by narcissistic identification comes into play again. It is an aspect of his view that it is the narcissism that sweeps up the external world that makes the inner world persecuting. However, he does not apply the consequences of this theory of narcissistic identification in his "sociological papers" as a whole: it only appears in one passage in *Civilization and its Discontents,* where it is at odds with what he says in the rest of the paper; in *The Future of an Illusion* (1927c) it disappears altogether. There was in Freud the dawning of a different theory, which is not consistent with the dominant one in these papers and would have required an overthrow of his more general position. I do not think that it would have been against his nature to overthrow his theory and replace it, as he had done it about three times before; but for some reason he did not do this when he came to write the "sociological papers".

In *The Ego and the Id* (1923b), Freud says that the conscience and self-criticism can be unconscious (p. 26). He does not say exactly how this is, but I presume he means that when a person is criticizing from the outside, he does not realize that he is criticizing himself from within. He says that "The tension between the demands of conscience and the actual performances of the ego is experienced as a sense of guilt" (p. 37). The implication is that the ego cannot obey the demands of conscience, and therefore it is a guilt-producing agency. It is a consequence of a broken ego. The idea that the structural model with the severe superego is a consequence of a broken ego is not something that Freud explores directly, though it is implied in some statements that he makes, such as when he says that "reproaches of conscience" (p. 53) are typical of the obsessional neurotics, therefore clearly implying that this harsh conscience is pathological.

Fear of castration by the father is primary, and fear of conscience and death follow from it. In this formula, however, the fear of castration is if parental or societal laws have been disobeyed (pp. 57–58). Does he mean here that conscience can punish with death? That suicide occurs through guilt is frequently the case, and perhaps he means that it is the unconscious determinant in other deaths as well.

In "The Economic Problem of Masochism" (1924c), Freud says: "We have attributed the function of conscience to the superego" (p. 166), and, a little further on: "The ego reacts with feelings of anxiety (conscience anxiety) to the perception that it has not come up to the demands made by its ideal, the super-ego" (p. 167).

Freud attributes guilt—pangs of conscience—to the idea that society has proscribed some behaviour, that this proscription has been internalized in the superego, and that guilt arises if the ego disobeys this command. As we shall see later, this is at variance with the view that conscience may prompt an individual to act contrary to the injunctions of a particular society.

Freud's view rests on the assumption that the individual is made up of untamed impulses, it is an external authority that imposes restrictions, and when this authority is internalized, it becomes responsible for "domesticating" the individual.

Freud was struck, especially in his later years, by the severity of the superego, and he tried to account for it. He suggests that the superego arises through an identification with the parents (1923b, p. 30; 1924c, p. 167). Identification occurs concurrently with a desexualization or sublimation, and it takes place after the erotic component no longer has power to bind the destructiveness that was combined with it. The destructiveness defuses into the superego and makes it harsh. Hence, in "The Economic Problem of Masochism" (1924c), he says: "As I have said elsewhere, it is easily conceivable that, thanks to the defusion of instinct which occurs along with this introduction into the ego, the severity was increased. The super-ego—the conscience at work in the ego—may then become harsh, cruel and inexorable against the ego which is in its charge. Kant's Categorical Imperative is thus the direct heir to the Oedipus Complex" (p. 167).

Kant's categorical imperative does not have the support of rational enquiry. The categorical imperative is the voice of the God of Abraham, Isaac, and Jacob, which is an object of belief without rational support. It is this God whom Durkheim considered as responsible for binding society into a cohesive organization, and Freud saw the superego as the habitation of this harsh figure within the structure of the personality. What this god particularly requires is the renunciation of the sexual instinct. This is why Freud thinks that: "Conscience and morality have arisen through the overcoming, the desexualization, of the Oedipus complex" (1924c, p. 169). It is through this desexualization that the harshness of the superego gains its force (p. 169). Freud came to think that the sadism of the superego is to be explained by the cultural restriction of the aggressive instincts (p. 170). In *Civilization and its Discontents* (1930a [1929]), Freud posits that in any human culture there is a superabundance of aggression, and society copes with this by demanding, as it were, that the individuals in that culture suck in this poison for the sake of the wider group. This sadistic poison is then channelled onto the poor ego of each individual, instead of being discharged outwardly in war and savagery.

It is worth noting here that Abraham, one of Freud's most insightful followers, did not think that the individual human being was of necessity at war with society. He believed that the state of antagonism between the individual and society such as Freud described was true only of individuals who were stunted in their emotional development, and that the mature individual overcame in himself this dichotomy (Abraham, 1925, p. 410). This accords with the view that it is the narcissistic currents that create the opposition between the individual and society that Freud implies in the passage quoted from *Group Psychology and the Analysis of the Ego* (1920c).

In *The Question of Lay Analysis* (1926e), Freud uses conscience in a different sense from his use of it both before and after this paper. He thinks of it here in its ego-syntonic function: "If a patient of ours is suffering from a sense of guilt, as though he had committed a serious crime, we do not recommend him to disregard his qualms of conscience and do not emphasize his undoubted innocence; he himself has often tried to do so without success. What we do is to remind him that such a strong and persistent feeling must after all be based on something real, which it may perhaps be possible to discover" (p. 190).

This passage gives a contradictory message. He is saying here that conscience is about something real that needs attention. So Freud believes that qualms of conscience are based on some real action the person has committed, which he intends to unearth. This is in contradiction to the idea that is dominant in his other papers: that the person has just internalized a cultural injunction. The other anomaly in this paper is that in all other places Freud refers to conscience as a function of the superego, but here it is the other way around (p. 223). He seems to imply that conscience is the prime faculty. This would allow for the possibility that he thought of the superego as a deformation of conscience. I think this anomaly could only be resolved through textual criticism of the original German, but that is something that I neither have the training nor the knowledge to be able to do.

That conscience is the fear of being found out either by an outer authority or an inner one is enunciated most clearly by Freud in *Civilization and its Discontents* (1930a [1929]) in the following passage: "This . . . is the reason why it makes little difference whether one has already done the bad thing or only intends to do it. In either case the danger only sets in if and when the authority discovers it" (p. 124). "Thou shalt not be found out" lies at the heart of this morality. Taken on its own, this is almost a psychopathic position. The following statement a bit further on makes it clear that he does not consider that such a position deserves the name of bad conscience: "This state of mind is called a 'bad conscience'; but actually it does not deserve this name, for at this stage the sense of guilt is clearly only a fear of loss of love, 'social anxiety'" (pp. 124–25).

Conscience is a signal fear of punishment. Then there is a transition, he says, whereby the external authority becomes internalized in the superego. He says here that the reason the superego torments the ego is that the latter's role is to pass on the tradition to the next generation. This social necessity is driven by the instinct for survival.

The fact that Freud considers reward in eudaemonic terms is also clear from the following passage: "it is precisely those people who have carried saintliness furthest who reproach themselves with the worst sinfulness. This means that virtue forfeits some part of its promised reward" (1930a [1929], p. 126).

What he says here is only partly true. Saints and holy people do reproach themselves, and some are given to excessive statements about their sinfulness, which would suggest the operation of the superego, but the consciences of people who have dedicated their lives to the pursuit of virtue are more refined; they also derive peace and contentment from following it, and there are many passages from mystical writings that illustrate this.

As has already been said, it is here, in *Civilization and its Discontents* (1930a [1929]), that he believes that the severity of the superego is not only because of the external authority but because of the ego's own attacks on that authority (pp. 129–130). Also unlike in *The Question of Lay Analysis* (1926e), he maintains here that conscience is a function of the superego: "This function consists in keeping watch over the actions and intentions of the ego and judging them, in exercising a censorship" (1930a [1929], p. 136).

Freud equates the need for punishment with masochism. The general tenor he adopts is that the operation of conscience and the anxiety it provokes is a pathology to be cleared up. The notion of a healthy conscience, except in *The Question of Lay Analysis* (1926e), seems to be absent. Obeying the superego prevents happiness for the ego (1930a [1929], p. 143).

In "Dostoevsky and Parricide" (1928b), Freud says that the normal processes in the formation of conscience must be similar to the abnormal ones. He goes back here to describing the superego/conscience as the internalization of a severe, harsh father, which is what he calls abnormal; he seems to be saying therefore that normal conscience is also pathological in nature (p. 185).

In Lecture XXXI of the *New Introductory Lectures* (1933a), he says that the persecution of being watched, and so on, comes from a projection of the critical superego, and that being observed is a precursor for being punished (p. 59). He also talks of conscience not *allowing* the ego to do something. Conscience *forbids*. It is clear that by this time he has thought out the functions of the superego more clearly. The superego has three functions: self-observation, conscience, and maintenance of an ideal (pp. 60, 66). Self-observation is a necessary preliminary to the judgement of conscience. Whereas in *Totem and Taboo* (1912–13) Freud defined conscience as this self-observing function, he now sees this as separate, and conscience as the critical judge in the personality. In *Lecture XXXII* (1933a) he makes the point that conscience lives in the unconscious, and in his paper "Why War" (1933b [1932]) he says that conscience is the internalization of the death instinct (p. 211).

In *An Outline of Psycho-Analysis* (1940a) Freud refers to the judicial function of the superego, which is called conscience (p. 205). In the same paper he refers to the torments caused by the reproaches of conscience, which correspond to the child's fear of loss of love. This is the idea that runs through Freud's works: that the fear of loss of love of the parents becomes transferred to conscience. Fear of loss of love from the superego is what causes the torture when a "sinful" act has occurred.

We must conclude that in all of Freud's works—with the exception of that passage in *The Question of Lay Analysis* (1926e)—the assumption is that conscience is bad: a persecutor and something pathological in the personality. It remains now to see whether this is the accepted meaning of conscience among moral philosophers, scholars in religious studies, and moral theologians and, more generally and most importantly, whether Freud's use of the word is what is understood by the educated public what great writers and poets have understood to mean by conscience.

* * *

What starts as a small investigation frequently turns out to be a matter that requires hours, weeks, months of scholarly research. What I thought would be an easy matter to dispose of becomes something much more complex and requiring considerable historical enquiry. My brief investigation into this is as follows: that conscience (being the translation of *suneidesis*) appears rarely in classical Greece, but Socrates, for instance, says of those who had perjured themselves at his trial: "Let their consciences punish them." It was not, however, a common concept in the Greco–Roman world. The person who launched the concept into the currency of our language was St Paul. He alone of the New Testament writers pioneered the term. His use of it accords with that of Freud: it is the inner accusation for a deed that has been committed. This is the usual meaning of it in St Paul's letters, and it continued to be the meaning of conscience within Christendom.[1]

In more recent centuries conscience has acquired a broader meaning. I cannot say exactly when this occurred, but I surmise that it was with the emergence of the Enlightenment within European thinking. Rousseau certainly emphasized that conscience, not reason, was our guide to action: "Conscience does not tell us the truth about objects but the rule of our duties; it does not tell us what we must think but what we must do; it does not tell us right reasoning but right action" (Rousseau, *Nouvelle Heloise*, quoted in Hampson, 1971).

With the secularization of social institutions, was there to be no foundation for ethical thinking? Conscience, as used by St Paul and by Freud, remained, but two important dimensions accreted to its use.

Conscience came to be used as that faculty in us which invites the individual psyche to do what is right. In other words, conscience came to be used as the faculty that guides the individual towards righteousness and also points to the path where that is to be found. Bertrand Russell (1974) puts it thus: "The orthodox view is that, wherever two courses of action are possible, conscience tells me which is right, and to choose the other is sin" (p. 190).

Therefore it acquired the meaning of a guide that pointed the individual psyche in the direction of righteousness. The word "righteousness" has such appalling connotations for us today because it suggests a right path ordained from above by a superior power—most frequently either God or a god-equivalent. However, the modern sense of it is the faculty that points to a path that is inwardly right for this individual. The other sense of it is that conscience indicates the right path for the individual, with the implication that it may require the individual to repudiate the sanctions of outer authority. So Hannah Arendt said of Eichmann that he was not a hater of Jews, but his conscience told him to obey the orders of his Nazi superiors (Arendt, 1964). In other words, a bad conscience is one where the dictates of external authority are internalized. It suggests that a good conscience is something freed of such external injunctions, where it may invite the individual psyche to act in opposition to an outer command.

In his *History of European Morals*, Lecky says: "Conscience, whether we regard it as an original faculty, or as a product of the association of ideas, exercises two distinct functions. It points out a difference between right and wrong, and when its commands are violated, it inflicts a certain measure of suffering and disturbance" (1913, p. 62). So, in addition to the function that Freud attributes to conscience, in post-Enlightenment thinking it has acquired two other functions: that of an inner guide to what is right and that it is a function that is individual and not an internalization of the injunctions of external authority. The post-Enlightenment idea of conscience as a *personal* guide is absent in Freud.

Paradoxically, no one emphasized this personal status of conscience more than did John Henry Newman. I say "paradoxically" because he was a leader of the Oxford Movement in the Anglican Church and then, on conversion to the Roman Catholic Church, went on to become one of its cardinals. Yet, despite his devotion to the Catholic faith, he said that if he had to choose between obeying the Pope or his conscience, it would always be his conscience. Like Hannah Arendt, one presumes that for him automatic obedience to an external authority would be a sign of bad conscience. Newman describes the faculty of conscience in this way: "Conscience is a personal guide, and I use it because I must use myself; I am as little able to think by any mind but my own as to breathe with another's lungs. Conscience is nearer to me than any other means of knowledge" (1888, pp. 389–390).

The conclusion seems to be that Freud sees conscience as the condemnation for a crime committed and as the internalization of external authority. It seems that, according to post-Enlightenment usage, Freud's definition of conscience is too limited. He has reverted to the Pauline use of the word conscience and does not allow for conscience as an inner guide to right action. If, such as in the extreme case of Eichmann, conscience functions as the internalization of the dictates of external authority, then this is what has been declared to be "bad conscience". What Freud describes as conscience is then "bad conscience" or a pathological conscience. The question that then arises is: does Freud's psychology incorporate what is called 'good conscience', and if so, by what name does it appear in his works, or is the concept absent in Freud?

A harsh conscience, the internalization of an external authority, occurs through narcissism. It is a property of the narcissistic setup that it sweeps the external authority into its internal psychic sphere. What Freud describes is the pathological emotional activity that arises as a consequence of narcissism. A healthy conscience, a sane conscience, escapes his attention.

I want to add a final footnote, which requires more investigation. What I refer to as "good conscience" or the post-Enlightenment meaning of conscience can, I believe, also be understood as a judgement upon an act committed. If this is the case, then what differentiates a conscience that is ego-syntonic from one that is ego-dystonic? I believe it is whether the act committed is believed to be reparable or irreparable. I put this in as a final aside because the question of how these two are to be differentiated will take us upon another trail.

Note

1. St Paul's use of conscience requires the same detailed analysis as does Freud's. Just as with Freud, there is his general position, yet it is contradicted in certain passages. This has been traced to some extent by Vereecke (1997, pp. 75–101).

CHAPTER FOUR

Freud's truth

I wrote a review of Richard Webster's *Why Freud Was Wrong* (1995) for the *Sydney Morning Herald* in 1995 (30 December). I decided to include it in this book because there has been so much ill-informed de-bunking of Freud, and Webster's book seems to epitomize this philistine deluge. Rather than concentrate upon Freud's thinking, the author does what psychoanalysts are often accused of: reading a motivation into the author of the theory rather than examine the theory unsullied by this personalist bias.

This is a long book, consisting of 528 pages of text and a further 100 pages of appendices and notes. If the reader, relying on the publisher's credits, believes he is embarking on a work of originality and scholarship, he is in for a disappointment.

The classic biography of Freud is the three-volume masterpiece written by Ernest Jones, his devoted disciple. For its detail and understanding of psychoanalysis, Freud's brainchild, it is unsurpassed. However, Jones was a fanatic who failed to differentiate clearly the good from the bad in Freud, and Webster fairly quotes some of Jones's worst excesses. Probably the best corrective account is to be found in Ellenberger's *Discovery of the Unconscious* (1970), where in a long chapter on Freud the author places him soberly in context and unidealized.

Webster relies on Ellenberger and also on Sulloway and Thornton, but, surprisingly, makes no reference to Ricoeur, whose philosophical treatise on Freud still remains the most comprehensive cultural evaluation of Freud that we have. Webster believes, though, that the critique of Ellenberger and others needs to be taken further.

Webster's critique of Freud rests upon two premises: that Freud saw psychogenic origins in everything and that Freud was a self-inflated egoist determined to fashion an empire that would be a permanent monument to his name. This latter position is similar to that espoused by Frederick Crews, whose article in the *New York Review of Books*, 18 November 1993) created such a storm of protest and counter-protest in America. Webster is at pains to show, through a careful tracing of those patients treated by Charcot, that the diagnosis of hysteria as a disease entity is unsustainable. Webster supplies evidence to support the idea that some of these patients were suffering from closed head injury and temporal lobe epilepsy. I think Webster is right to challenge the idea that hysteria is a disease entity, but he is incorrect to suppose that this disproves psychogenic origins for some of the observed phenomena.

Elizabeth von R was one of Freud's early patients, and he attributed her organic symptoms to disappointment in love. That people become physically ill through emotional traumata was well known among common folk in Freud's day as it is today, and there are countless references to it in literature. So Freud's general statement was unexceptionable in folklore but was scorned within the medical establishment. What Freud did was to import into the medical establishment truths that were well known in folklore and literature and attempt to give them scientific respectability. Webster is quite correct in pointing out that Freud frequently resorted to aetiological elaborations of symptoms that were fanciful, but his understanding that emotional traumata had consequences visible in a variety of symptoms and his determination to make doctors listen to such explanations was well overdue. But Freud did more than that: he produced a model of the mind that was acceptable to physicians trained in the physicalist school, which was dominant at that time. Thus he fashioned a hypothesis that gave a plausible account of how emotional traumas became transformed into neurotic symptoms.

Today we know and understand a great deal more about how this transformation takes place, and a psychoanalyst would try to defend neither Freud's antiquated hypotheses in all their elaborate detail nor some of his—for us today—rather naive methods of treating his early patients. Freud was at the very beginning of a new procedure and methodology, which has developed enormously since his day. In psychoanalysis Freud did discover a new method for investigating the mind.

Webster's greatest fault is his failure to analyse the object of his critique. Is he attacking Freud, or is he attacking psychoanalysis? His ignorance of psychoanalysis as it is practised today is alarming. For instance, he quotes Ernest Jones's absurd statement that the analyst is a dispassionate observer who displays no part of his personality but believes, evidently, that this is a belief held by analysts today, which is entirely false. He also draws a parallel between the psychoanalyst and the priest in the confessional, saying that whereas the priest can point out and instruct his penitent regarding his sinful behaviour, yet the analyst has to be dispassionate and is forced to validate self-destructive behaviour. There are several schools of psychoanalysis today that base many of their interpretations on the understanding that self-destructive emotional acts lead to severe anxiety states.

However, the kernel of Webster's error lies in something more subtle and more insidious. Ellenberger understood that Freud, like Janet and Jung, were trying to elucidate the mind's emotional functioning. Ultimately what is important is that we grow in our understanding of the mind. It matters not a whit who contributed to that understanding, whether it be Freud, Jung, Shakespeare, or Tolstoy. In Freud, as in all great thinkers, there are new insights of great value, but also a great deal of rubbish. There is a crying need in the present day for a study of Freud that illuminates his lasting insights and separates these from much of the mistaken formulations in which they are embedded. This book is yet to be written, and Webster has not produced it for us.

One last word. Creative understanding never emerges from studies whose central aim is the demolition of a *person*, but it does emerge from elucidating those *tendencies of thought* deriving from a thinker that are destructive to society and distinguishing them from those that are constructive. Webster contributes to the personality cult that he abhors. And, oh, what a waste of study, of scholarship!

CHAPTER FIVE

The relation between the determinist and the religious model of the mind

In the determinist model all human action is explained by efficient causes. In this model a person's actions are all explicable in terms of stimuli to which the person reacts.

In the religious model the human being is called to account for his own actions. This implies that the individual is the source of his own activity. In the religious model a judgement is made upon the individual on the basis of his behaviour.

* * *

In the determinist model everything that a human being does is caused entirely by an external agent. There is no essential difference between the theory of action for an inanimate object and for an animate one. I have been pushed either by an object outside that has bumped into me or by an object inside. In psychological discourse the outer object is referred to as a *stimulus,* whereas the inner one is called either a *drive* or an *instinct.* I cannot therefore be held accountable for my actions. Now, as we have seen, in the religious model of man the individual is held accountable for his actions and, in particular, for the way he treats his fellow human beings and also his own self. This latter point is also central in the major religions.

If I can be held accountable for an action, then it is not possible to attribute that action to an efficient cause. Therefore in the religious model there are actions the source of which is to be found in myself. In essence, it seems to me, this is what differentiates the religious view from the determinist one.

Are we to say, then, that one is wrong and the other is right? But before we go on to address that question, I want to look at psychoanalysis and see in which theory the discipline is grounded. Let us start with Freud.

I think it is clear that Freud rooted himself in the determinist model. His teacher and mentor, Ernst Brücke, together with Helmholtz, Karl Ludwig, and du Bois-Reymond, were the founding fathers of the *Physicalische Gesellschaft*, the Physicalist Society. These four men had signed the anti-vitalist pact, which stated that all action was to be explained in terms of the physical forces of attraction and repulsion. Freud spent nine years in Brücke's neurological research laboratory and was a faithful member of and believer in the physicalist tradition. In *The Project for a Scientific Psychology*, Freud (1950 [1895]) attempted to explain human motivation in terms of these forces of attraction and repulsion within the neurological system.

However, Freud abandoned the attempt to tie down psychological processes to the neural pathways and the forces of attraction and repulsion. When he did this, however, it was not that he thought that the psychological processes could not be so tied down, but that scientific research had not gone far enough to achieve it, and he always believed that one day it would. From that time until the early 1920s, Freud worked within the paradigm of the topographical model. In this model human motivation is explained in terms of efficient causes, along the classical lines of the determinist theory. The clearest exposition of this model is to be found in what has become known as Freud's metapsychological papers. In all these papers the source of action lies in instincts reacting to stimuli.

It is not difficult to see that this model does not fit the unconscious intentionality that is the central theme of *The Interpretation of Dreams* (1900a). As Marie Jahoda has pointed out in *Freud and the Dilemmas of Psychology* (1977), there are in Freud not one metapsychology but many, jostling around without any inner coherence. Jahoda considered that this was a constituent of Freud's genius. However, intellectually this is not a satisfactory state of affairs, and, I believe, we must make the attempt to achieve coherence. It is the thesis of what I am saying that the intentional model and the determinist one do not fit as they stand at present. If we were to take Jahoda's approach, we could just say that most academics have selected the determinist theory, and clinicians work on the intentional model. This would be to say that the differences that have emerged in this group find their origin in Freud's own inconsistencies. The present attempt at reconciliation would, then, represent an attempt to unify two theories within Freud.

So, from the early 1900s to 1920, the topographical model ran alongside the intentional model. As we know, in the early 1920s Freud developed his structural model. In this model there is an attempt to combine the determinist and the religious model. Instinctual action finds its origin in the id and intentional activity finds its source in the ego. (The superego need not detain us at the moment, as Freud understood this to be "fed" from the id directly.) Although this model attempts to combine the instinctual and the personal, it is not successful, because the coexistence of these two is not a possibility if we consider, as Freud does, that the two operate at the same level. I believe, however, that the solution to the problem is to be found in the psychological fact of a transformation of instincts within the emotional field of action. However, before tracing this, I want to look at object relations theory and to see how this develops Freud's theory further.

To understand the theoretical leap that occurred with the advent of object relations theory, I think we can understand it best if we turn to Fairbairn. Melanie Klein maintained Freud's inconsistency, which Fairbairn tried to resolve. He said that libido is object-seeking. We know that Freud had also said this in his *Three Essays on Sexuality* (1905d). However, there was this crucial difference between the two: in Freud's schema the object was the means of reducing tension in the organism, and therefore the object had a subsidiary function, whereas with Fairbairn libido sought out the object, and its means of doing this was to pass through the erotogenic zone, this being the path of least resistance.

* * *

So Fairbairn said that the libido is object-related and that this is its primary orientation. How this is so, Fairbairn does not investigate, nor does he try to work it out philosophically. He makes it clear, however, that, for instance, sexual activities such as thumb-sucking in a baby or masturbation in an adult are compensatory activities, and they are the external correlates of an inner attachment to bad objects. The point is here, then, that in Freud's theoretical schema libido is satisfied equally by masturbation or sexual intercourse, whereas Fairbairn says that masturbation or thumb-sucking in the adult or in the child are expressions of frustrated libido. For Freud, the link between human beings is in the sexual; for Fairbairn, however, it is in the emotional.

Although Melanie Klein did not spell out a theoretical base in the same way as did Fairbairn, nevertheless her clinical observations lead her to define pathology in terms of relations to objects. A person is either dominated by a part-object relating, violent projection and introjection and projective identification, or by whole-object-relating concern for the object and awareness of guilt. The foundation of mental health is directly correlated with the individual's capacity to manage the guilt inherent in the depressive position.

In both these theories pathology is the consequence of damage to the object and also to the ego, and the one reflects the other. Also—and this is a crucial point—that guilt is experienced. This guilt arises from the feeling that I have *done* something to bring this about, that I have been an active participant in this disaster. There is, therefore, at the basis of these theories the understanding that I can be held accountable—not totally, but in part—for this state of affairs. If my ego is in a shattered state, I am partly responsible. This view is not compatible with the determinist theory.

Are we, then, to throw out the determinist model? Or are we to reject what I have referred to as the religious model? I believe that it is a mistake to throw out either one or the other. The determinist model arose out of the scientific thinking of the last century. It was borne out of a determined repudiation of a mythological cosmogony believed and preached by the major religious systems existing in the West. The causal explanations of Christendom were to be replaced by an explanation that did not look outside physical bodies for their cause. We have therefore to explain the whole world of movement and change in terms of the discoverable physical laws of the universe. The idea that God created the world or mankind with some specific purpose or intention in mind is ruled out. Clinical evidence seems to show that shame, guilt, and anxiety result from that component in a psychological event that originates in the ego. My clinical experience confirms the view of Husserl, who said that the ego is active even in receptivity. Anxiety will be present in the degree to which the ego contributes to the fragmentation of its own reality. It seems, therefore, that accountability is a central concept, necessary for the comprehension of anxiety. Accountability means that the ego is its own source of action, so that in the behaviour of the individual there is at least a quantum of activity that finds its source here—in the ego. The object relations theory of

Melanie Klein and her school have this accountability as an inherent assumption of their theory. I think that Fairbairn's theory implies it, but other aspects of his theory contradict it.

The question I now want to address myself to is how it is possible to hold the determinist theory and yet at the same time allow for accountability.

* * *

I am walking in the country, I come to a large open expanse, and I see before me a great crowd of people. My friend, who is with me, asks, "Why are all those people standing there like that?" And I reply, "They are standing there because of the gravitational pull of the earth—if it were not for that, they would be whirling about in space." My friend gives me a wry look and says to me, "You know what I mean!" And I reply, Oh, so you are in search of meaning, are you!" I then say to my friend, "Oh, I did not realize that it was meaning that you were after; I thought you just wanted explanation. However, if you want meaning, I can tell you that all those people have forgathered here in order to witness an air show, which is about to start in a quarter of an hour's time". Now we have here two answers to the same question, but one of them is at the level of explanation and the other is concerned with meaning, purpose, or intention. I believe that the determinist theory operates at the level of explanation, and what I have referred to as object relations theory or the religious model operates at the level of meaning, purpose, or intention.

Freud borrowed the concept of the id from Groddeck. As you know, id is the Latinized translation of "das Es". The German Es means "it". Groddeck used the word to mean a principle within the organism that determines the specialist axes in a person's life in the time sphere, in the sphere of extension, and in the sphere of colour. In other words, a principle that determines when the foetus will be born, when the organism will die, the person's height and shape, and also the colour of his hair, eyes, and so on. Groddeck had almost a mystical or romantic idea of the id, but shorn of this, he meant by it the organic substrate that determines the life contours on those axes that I have just described. Freud adopted Groddeck's term and meant by it this organic substrate.

This time my friend and I noticed John, aged 17, taking Jane out to a disco, and he asked me, "Why is John taking Jane out?" And I answered, "He is taking her out because he has reached the age of puberty." Again my friend looked at me wryly and said, "I knew that—you know that is not what I mean." And I, annoyingly, say again to my friend, "Oh: so it's meaning you want." And so, then, I answer, "John is in love with Jane—that is why he is taking her to a disco".

So there are two levels of explanation: the determinist and the religious. Both are true, but the one with which psychoanalysis is concerned is the latter.

CHAPTER SIX

The unconscious
as an amoral construction

This paper was the keynote address at a Psychoanalytic conference in Melbourne in 1992. The chapter sets out to demonstrate
that the unconscious is constructed in order to hide from the individual his own immoral activity. The title may be misleading unless one realizes that the chapter challenges Freud, who tried to
construct a metapsychology on principles derived from natural
science and therefore *amoral.*

> Each man must look to himself to teach him the meaning of life. It
> is not something discovered: it is something moulded.
>
> Antoine de Saint Exupéry, *Wind, Sand and Stars,* p. 37

Socrates' principle

Socrates said that if I know that what I plan is evil, I cannot do it.
He said that therefore the key to good living, to moral action, lies
in knowledge. I cannot know that something is evil and yet do it.
It is, said Socrates, a psychological impossibility. He believed that if it
was possible to show to someone through rational argument that a
project or way of behaving was wrong, then the person would be
unable to do it.

It may surprise you to hear me say that I think Socrates' proposition is correct.

"I am an aircraft mechanic, and my job is to service light aircraft. When I do a 100-hour service, I do not flush out the channels to the engines' carburettors because I believe it is not necessary; then a senior mechanic shows me that planes landing on dusty airports can over time clog the airflow into the carburettor, and this can cause engine failure. From that day I cannot *not* flush out the channels to the carburettors."

"I am a pederast, and I have sexual relations with young children. I enjoy it, and the children seem content in the activity; then a child psychologist comes to me and gives me incontrovertible evidence that this activity of mine is damaging to the children. He explains it to me so clearly and lucidly that I give up this sexual proclivity."

At this latter example you will, I know, smile wryly; the reason is that as seasoned men and women of the world you know that a sexual disposition of this nature is not given up so easily, and, as psychoanalysts know, a rational explanation from a child psychologist would rarely be sufficient to break a habit of this nature. How, then, is it possible for me a psychoanalyst to maintain Socrates' proposition that if I know that an action is evil, then I cannot do it? Socrates' principle is upheld if, when the child psychologist has explained to me the bad consequences of my sexual activity, I give it up, but it can also be upheld in another way. The child psychologist has explained to me the bad effects of my behaviour, yet I continue doing so. Socrates' proposition, however, holds good because when I continue my behaviour, I obliterate the knowledge imparted to me by the child psychologist. I say to myself that child psychologists are notoriously unreliable in their propositions. I have to discount the knowledge often with a "I know that child psychologist is right but . . ." and then a host of plausible reasons. There are, of course, more primitive methods of obliterating knowledge. I can wipe out altogether what the psychologist has told me, so that I have no memory of it.

I once twice interviewed a man who had dragged a 10-year-old girl by the hair around her house, raped her, and then killed her. I interviewed him about two weeks after the event. The memory of the event was quite blotted out. When I saw him, he was on remand, and a couple of months later he came up for trial at the Old Bailey and was found guilty and given a 25-year prison sentence. Shortly after that he hanged himself in Wandsworth Prison. My surmise is that the memory of what he had done flashed back to him, and the guilt was insupportable. This is an extreme example, but less obvious examples walk into our consulting-room every week. I was once seeing a man who was pestered by a fierce condemning voice inside. As he was engaging with me in the session, its strength diminished. However, he realized that when he went out and shut the door of my room firmly—in that very moment he obliterated me from his mind, and then into that vacuum hopped that fiercesome voice again. Socrates' proposition stands, therefore, because either I cease to do what is self-damaging,[1] or I continue with the activity but destroy knowledge. This latter alternative was not ever formulated by Socrates.

Contradictions in Freud's explanatory schema

I want to take the matter a little further, and say that this is the only reason why I destroy knowledge: to hide from myself that what I do is destructive or damaging, both to myself and to others. Later I shall examine what the core of this is. Therefore the only reason why I obliterate knowledge of what I do is because what I do is damaging. Psychologically the obliteration of knowledge produces that state of mind which we call unconscious. Freud differentiated between two types of unconsciousness: that which he called the true unconscious or the system Ucs, and what he called the preconscious or the system Pcs. The difference between the two is that the former has a moral dimension, whereas the latter does not. He says that an acknowledged wish— in other words, a wish that is known—is localized in the system Pcs, whereas a repudiated or suppressed wish is localized in the system Ucs (Freud, 1900a, p. 551). In Freud's examination of the stimulus for dreams (ibid.), he makes a distinction between a physiological stimulus, such as thirst, bladder pressure, or day residues, and a wish that is contrary to civilization's requirements. The Interpretation of Dreams is full of examples of such suppressed wishes. Freud held that an unfulfilled wish is the cause of dreams. Therefore even when a wish is not apparent in the manifest content of the dream, it is always present in the latent content and must be looked for. Freud (1900a, pp. 152–154) tells of a woman who dreamt that her nephew, Karl, was dead, lying in a coffin. The woman says that she could not possibly wish for the death of her nephew, especially as Karl's elder brother, Otto, has already died. Freud unmasks the fact that the woman cherished romantic wishes towards a man who last came to the house to pay his condolences when Otto had died. Therefore her wish that Karl would die makes sense, because in such an event the woman would again have a chance to have contact with the man who is the object of her desire.

In his interpretation of this dream, Freud isolates the woman's wish to see the man she cherishes from the means of achieving it: that is, the wish that Karl would die. Freud, in fact, bends over backwards to reassure the woman that no such wish is present, and yet the meaning of the dream is clear. There is the shocking wish that Karl should die, because then she will be able to see the man she desires. Her passion is as desperate as that. It seems clear that this is the reason why the wish is suppressed. The woman suppressed knowledge because her passion is so great that she could even wish for her nephew's death in order to obtain it. This was not a conclusion reached by Freud, though it stares one in the face. The intensity of such a passion is missed by Freud. If one equates *intensity* with *psychosis*, then Freud's view that psychosis cannot be treated by psychoanalysis means that the more intense passions of the soul are not the subject of analytic investigation for Freud. This type of enquiry was to come later in the person of Karl Abraham and those influenced by him. You may wish to say that these were not doings but just a thought or a wish, but this suggests that thoughts and wishes are not doings. This point needs further examination.

The nature of psychic activity

A person's behaviour can be analysed into his motor activity and his psychic activity. The two can only be separated logically; in reality they are inseparably bound together. The man who firmly closed my consulting-room door was performing a motor action, but included within its structure was a psychic action. A table is made up of colour and shape, but colour cannot exist without shape, and shape cannot exist without colour. They are existentially inseparable but logically distinguishable, and thus it is with motor activity and psychic activity. When that man obliterated me from his mind, it was a psychic act, but it could not occur divorced from a motor action. The psychic act is like the shape of the table, and the motor act is its colour. This simile is not exact but aimed at directing the mind to an act of comprehension that stretches further than the exactitude of the simile.

The view I hold is something like this: that in the mind's sphere there is a basic foundation of psychic activity, and then slowly there are transformations up a scale, so that towards the top we get concepts and finally mathematical symbols; as you go up the scale, there is increased variation. We describe this mental variation as desire, thought, judgement, understanding, and so on. Palaeontologists think that all life derived from heterotrophic bacteria and at the same time as there evolved more complex forms, so concurrently there was a burgeoning variety of living forms (White, 1986, pp. 20–21). In a similar way the personality is founded upon basic forms of psychic activity, which evolve into these varied mental acts of a higher category. This phylogenetic level is recapitulated at the ontogenetic level by Bion in the Grid (Bion, 1977, pp. 9–39).

The most difficult things to describe are these fundamental activities of the mind. I want to define these activities according to their effects, and therefore as either destructive or constructive. To illustrate first the destructive, I will use the following example:

A colleague in London was taking a sabbatical year and asked me if I would be prepared to see any of his patients who required treatment while he was away. I assented to his request, and in due course, six months after his departure, a lady rang me in some desperation. She had had two love affairs with men who turned out to be impotent and at last had found Michael, with whom she had an active sexual life, and then, all of a sudden, he had become impotent like the others. I offered her 20 sessions once weekly, by the end of which time my colleague would have returned.

In the first four sessions she told me about her parents, her job, her lovers, and other facts that made up the outer contours of her life. I made various innocuous comments, but I had seen nothing that illuminated the conflicts of her inner life. Then, towards the end of the fourth session, a light dawned in my mind, and I started to gather it into an interpretation when I was aware that it had fluttered away. I had lost what I had in mind to say. I noted it vaguely with a dim perception. The next session, again I saw something clearly and was about to put it into the words of an interpretation when it faded from my mind. This time I noted it with a new acuity and made the connection in my mind between her lover's sexual impotence and my mental impotence. I changed the object of my focus[2] from the details of what she was telling me to this disturbing occurrence in my own mind. So, early in the next session, something began to crystallize, and I was emotionally determined that this time it would see the light of day; sure enough, I delivered the interpretation, as I intended. The following week she returned with a smile on her face and told me that last Thursday night—Thursday being the day of the session—she had made love to Michael, and he had been potent. She added that she thought it was connected with last Thursday's session.

The inner structure of evil

The connecting link between the crystallization and the delivery of my interpretation and her lover's potency was her own psychologically constructive act. However, I want to zoom in on the activity of hers that was disrupting my own mind.[3] As analyst, I represented a part of her own mind—that part which was being savaged by a domineering tyrant within. The part that is being thus savaged I will call the *embryo mind*. In each of us there is an *embryo mind*: it is that emotional centre in the mind that is capable of developing into an autonomous source of mental action. The *embryo mind* does not grow into an autonomous mind by a natural instinctive progression but through cumulative acts of personal insight. Whereas physical growth occurs through the organism's instinctive activities, mental growth only occurs through acts of personal appropriation. In her mind, then, she was divided against herself, and there were two sets of activities: the tyrant attacking and the emotional *embryo mind* consenting to this ravaging dismemberment.[4] I reach this formulation of mental events not only from the treatment of this one woman but from the examination of the minds of many others, including my own.

What I am describing is, I believe, the core neurosis. It is the seat of madness in the personality. Freud called the Oedipus complex the core neurosis. The savage attack from the tyrant one can think of as an assault from a vengeful father. Then the *embryo mind* or child has been "sleeping with mother", but what does this represent in this case and others like it? I think it is attachment of a "comfort zone" kind that is safeguarding to the individual.

The activities of this inner mental configuration are extremely powerful, and they are not contained within the framework of our own minds. When the atom is split, radiation implodes into the surrounding objects. The mental configuration I have been describing is known through its implosion into the human minds inhabiting the micro-social and, at times, the macro-social environment.

Listening to my account of the woman with impotent lovers, you may say that her treatment with me was successful, yet I believe that it was not so. The problem arises when it comes to elucidating to the patient the activity from within that has been the source of the trouble. My experience is that it is enormously difficult for the patient—indeed, for anyone—to realize that he or she is responsible for such mental savagery. So, although to the observer it may look as if I had worked a bit of magic with this patient, it was no more than a temporary palliative. It takes, I believe, a long analysis for an individual to become possessor of those violent mental onslaughts that I am trying to describe. After the Big Bang it took a long time before the radiation had consolidated into atoms and molecules; it takes a long time before this primitive mental activity becomes encradled into permanent structures.

The question is, "Why is it so difficult for me to become possessor of my own psychic activities?" and I must stress that I mean psychic activities operating at the level that I have described in the clinical vignette. There is no difficulty in acknowledging the damage that has been done *to* me—by my mother, my father, my brothers and sisters, teachers at school—but to own that *I* have done and continue to do such damage myself, to those in my emotional circle, and, even more, to my own mind is something from which I shrink with nothing short of panic. What happens is that I continue to act in a damaging way and manage it by pushing awareness of it away. We return now to the dictum of Socrates: that I cannot do evil and know it, so I do the evil, do the damaging activity, but destroy awareness of it or, more accurately, prevent it reaching awareness.

You may object to my using the word "evil" for the psychic activities of the configuration that I have described above. This needs some examination. Evil is, of course, the opposite of good, and both entities are products of a value judgement (see chapter 8, this volume). When I make the judgement that something is good, I mean that this reality has worth to it. It is worth my energy, it is worth sacrificing time and pleasure on its behalf, and so on. When activity destroys life, prevents creative development, we call it bad. When it comes to ourselves, we have the greatest difficulty in seeing the truth of these matters, and psychoanalysis has developed a technical vocabulary for those psychological methods we employ to maintain blindness. We call these stratagems "defences" and Freud, in his later formulation, said that we are not aware of these even—that is, we are not aware of the activities that prevent the emergence of awareness. What I am saying here is quite simply that we pull out these strategies so as to remain blind to our self-damaging activities, which are judged to be bad. The reason is that when we are damaging our minds, we cannot bear to know it. What I am saying is that this and this alone is the reason why I fashion unconsciousness.

I want now to summarize this core activity that I must needs hide from myself. It is that my mind is divided into a tyrant and an *embryo*, and the former attacks and savages the first fumbling attempts of the embryo to develop personal thought. A toddler is just beginning to walk when a savage dog pushes it over. The toddler gets up again, and the dog pushes it over again. Analogies of this kind always fail at some crucial point, as does this one. In this parable the toddler does not invite the dog to do this, but the *embryo mind* does just that. Now, what I am asserting is that when I am acting in this savage way within, I *must* rub it out. What I do is so appallingly destructive. If you saw an assassin attacking a young child, you would cry out in horror. This is exactly what I am doing to my own *embryo mind*, but I have to silence what I do. One thing you have to remember: the worse the savagery, the better hidden it must be. In order to hide the savagery, it is frequently necessary to hide the whole of oneself.

The obliteration of knowledge

The first point to note here is that I make myself unaware. I fashion the unawareness, the unconsciousness *of what I have done, what I am doing, and what I intend to do*. This is in contrast to Freud's conceptualization of unconsciousness. Freud has a mental map of "the unconscious" as a pre-existing locus of the mind into which memories, wishes, and thoughts are relegated. What I am saying is that there is no unconscious separate from the memories, wishes, and thoughts, but, rather, unconsciousness is a quality of the memories, wishes, and thoughts. The question is, how is the state of unawareness fashioned?

The first matter to get absolutely clear, however, is this: that the self-mutilation of the mind is the primary state of affairs upon which unconsciousness is a necessary consequence. This throws a different light upon the lifting of unconsciousness. If we take it as a principle that if I am self-mutilating within and I fashion unconsciousness, then the only way in which unconsciousness can be lifted is if my inner actions change. As my inner emotional activity changes, so the need for unconsciousness falls away. Back to Socrates: to the extent to which my emotional activity becomes invested with good quality, exactly to that extent I can know it. The change can only take place through my own free action. You may ask what the role is, then, of interpretation: it is quite simply to illuminate the inner emotional activity, but the interpretation does not in itself change the inner state of affairs—only free inner emotional action changes it. So now to return to the question: how do I fashion unawareness?

Let me start by making some existential observations. The first is this: that disintegrated parts of the mind and unconsciousness are partners in crime; they always go together. I think I am right in saying that all psychoanalytic theories hold that the mind is a construction of parts—the mind, as well as being considered as a whole, can also be viewed through the prism of the parts out of which it is composed. The parts are in relation to each other. This relationship between parts can be either *antagonistic* or *harmonious*. When I use the phrase "disintegrated parts of the mind", I mean parts that are in antagonism to each other, and, therefore, that parts in antagonism to each other and unconsciousness are the partners in crime.

What I am saying here will have a familiar ring to all well-bred analysts. In *Beyond the Pleasure Principle* (1920g) Freud enunciated his theory of two instincts that course through mankind: the death instinct and Eros, later named Eros and Thanatos by his followers. Eros is that instinct which joins individual entities up, whereas Thanatos disrupts them. Looking at what I have said through this lens, then, you might say that the mind in a disintegrated state is the product of the death instinct; but here it is necessary to make a second existential observation: that "disintegrated parts of the mind" and unconsciousness always co-exist with a third psychological element—guilt. The guilt is not explained by Freud's theory of the death instinct. Melanie Klein's theoretical model of anxiety was that the infant fears annihilation from the presence of the death instinct within. I believe that this is wrong, because it makes logical sense of the fear of annihilation but does not explain guilt.

I am guilty when I have *done* something. When I do something, I do it to something or somebody. When I mutilate my own mind, I am doing something to somebody. The somebody to whom I am doing this thing is myself. Now, how do we explain guilt here? Am I not entitled to destroy my own mind, if I wish? It may be stupid, may be foolish, may be crazy, but why shouldn't I, if I wish? People often become sloppy and unscientific on this point and say things like, "Well, you shouldn't feel guilt", or "There is no need to feel guilt", and so on, yet the "hard and stubborn fact" (William James, quoted in Whitehead, 1925) remains that I am guilty. There is so much wishy-washy therapy that attempts to encourage an individual by saying that he or she has no need to be guilty. Integral to psychoanalysis is scientific observation. A well-attested observation is that when I mutilate my own mind, I am guilty, and my behaviour demonstrates it. So what have I done?

The Kleinians are, I am sure, right when they say that I do things *in phantasy*. There is a great danger of contrasting *phantasy* with *reality* and thereby thinking that when I say I do something in *phantasy*, I am not *really* doing it. The word *phantasy* with a "ph" describes a particular sphere of reality: the mental and emotional sphere. When the Kleinians talk of attacking the breast in *phantasy*, I prefer to translate it as the mutilation of my mind. However, in the example of the woman with the impotent lovers, the mutilation of her own mind was enacted symbolically (but really) upon my mind. She was in *phantasy* attacking my mind. I hope that I have made it clear that she was really doing so with my cooperation. The action towards my own my mind symbolized the mutilation of her own. Therefore I have destroyed my own mind, *and* I keep this up with sustained activity. But coming back to my question: why am I guilty? Am I not allowed to destroy my own mind? It is mine, after all? Analytic observation testifies that I am guilty when I do this. So how are we to understand this guilt? It would suggest that when I say that my mind is my own, this is not quite right. It would suggest that others have some claim on my mind.

Mankind has survived on this planet through his creative inventiveness. He has survived through inventing tools through which he fashions the environment so that it can provide a home for him. If it had not been for this, we would still be living in that restricted area of the world, mostly Africa, where our cousins, the great apes, reside. When I discover how to make a stone axe that will fell an antelope, my comrades in the tribe demand that the product of this discovery become the possession of all. My mind is not for myself, it is for all. If I mutilate, I experience intense guilt—more intense even than if I steal my neighbour's cow. It is a much more serious attack on the resources of the tribal group. Sociologically this is a functionalist analysis of the phenomenon of guilt and comes within the parameters of a Darwinian model. It sounds all right and the explanation is scientifically respectable, but the guilt that can be observed through the psychoanalytic lens is so enormous that, I think, a functionalist model is insufficient to explain it.

The problem with a functionalist explanation is that the mind is analysed in terms of its usefulness, but the mind is the source of activities that cannot be reduced to a utilitarian schema. What of art, for instance? It was a mind that created the Mona Lisa, a mind that created Beethoven's Fifth Symphony, a mind that wrote Hamlet, a mind that sculpted the marble statue of David in Florence, a mind that designed and fashioned the Taj Mahal. Although all true art has been fashioned to serve the designs of man, yet it simultaneously transcends all utilitarian purpose. When some years ago a vandal attacked Michelangelo's Pietà in Rome with a hammer, a groan of horror travelled like shock waves through people of culture in all the civilized world. This is like a universal consent to a sublime art that it is sacrilege to traduce. So also to mutilate a mind that is able to raise man's spirit to a new eminence is a desecration that is universally chronicled in the phenomenon of guilt. When we observe guilt, we know that desecration has occurred and is occurring.[5]

The nature of knowledge

We have now to return to our question: "How does the mind fashion unawareness, unconsciousness, of what it does?" Our existential observations are threefold: parts of the mind are in antagonism to each other, the intrapsychic presence of self-mutilation and the concurrent presence of guilt. The answer is, I believe, startlingly simple: it is that consciousness is the *product* of parts in harmony, and unawareness is the *product* of parts in antagonism. This seems to be so, and I feel confident in stating it with all definiteness. But why? To answer this, we will have to examine the nature of knowledge.

The psychological concomitant of knowledge is certainty. The object of knowledge is the being of that which is known. This contrasts with the object of the senses, which is the manifestation of being. The senses are the instruments through which this manifestation is registered. These senses are sight, hearing, smell, taste, touch, and, most important of all, feelings. The senses can register incorrectly. They give access to a wide variety of manifestations. The object of knowledge is simply the being of things. These two mental faculties are unified through a synthetic act. Now I want to say something that you will find unsatisfactory, and that is that I do not know the answer to the question that I have posed—that is, why do I only *know* when the parts of my mind are in harmony with each other? It is, I believe, because there is, then, co-naturality between the object known and the knower. When the parts of the mind are in antagonism to each other, a fundamental quality of *being* is being repudiated—that is, its unity, which is an intrinsic quality of *being*. The principle of co-naturality is that there is, between the knower and the known, a constant: the unity of its being. The sort of mutilation of the mind that I have tried to describe in this chapter removes from one of the two terms—the knower—that element through which knowingness is possible. An eye without a retina is unable to see. Therefore this break-up of the mind is the cause of unconsciousness. The action whereby I smash up my mind is the archetypal evil, and this action of its nature fashions unconsciousness. The principle of co-naturality is, I believe, a foundation stone in our conceptualization of our human world. It is a given that cannot be reduced further to some more basic principle. It is, therefore, one of the building blocks of the human sciences.

The defects of Freud's theory

I want now to turn our attention to Freud. At its most simple, what I have been saying in this chapter is that unconsciousness is constructed in order that I shall not know the self-damaging evil that I do. We are concerned here with a moral order—the very foundation upon which our human values are constructed. This is the reason, I believe, why psychoanalysis is violently repudiated by positive scientists and traditional religions. The former repudiate it because they attempt to understand human nature outside any moral order, and to encompass it entirely within the conceptual framework of the natural sciences and traditional religion repudiates it because it is a moral order that overturns its own. It is a moral order existing at a more fundamental level that makes that of traditional religions irrelevant and out of touch with where the action is in human relations.

What I need to do here is to demonstrate the way in which Freud showed us that we hide from ourselves those wishes of which we are ashamed or guilty. *The Interpretation of Dreams* (1900a) is full of examples of dreams the manifest content of which hides the latent wishes because the individual feels badly about those wishes. What such an account would require is a scholarly demonstration of the intentions that we humans hide from ourselves and of how Freud shows that we hide these shameful wishes from ourselves, and then how his theory of the mind contradicts that which he is most keen to show us. The dream I have quoted is a good example of a wish of which the dreamer is ashamed, and therefore it is hidden from awareness. Our whole analytic work is concerned with the unveiling of the way in which we deceive ourselves about our own psychic actions. Bill Blomfield, in answer to the question "Can a liar be analysed?" says: "Has there ever been a real analysis that did not involve a struggle with lying in some form?" (1992, p. 23). This is what Freud worked with—it is what every analyst works with—but Freud tried to fit this into the theory of constancy. This theory, first propounded by Fechner, proposes that the living organism seeks a state of non-excitation so that when a state of tension arises, the organism seeks immediately to discharge it. Stimulation from outside is deflected through motor activity: if a swarm of bees descend on me and start to sting, I take evasive action, preferably rapidly, but if the stimulation is from within, I cannot take flight through motor discharge. I then either hallucinate the satisfying object or bring my mnemic residues into correspondence with the outside world and so reduce the inner stimulation and bring the organism back to a state of equilibrium. In the psychology textbooks of today this is called the "homeostatic theory", named as such by W. B. Cannon. To demonstrate this contradiction in Freud's conceptualization would take a scholarly treatise. This has been done to a very great extent by George Klein in his book *Psychoanalytic Theory* (1976) to which I refer those readers who are interested in examining the way this permeates the Freudian corpus. What I shall do here is to try to demonstrate the matter via a short cut.

My short cut is through the work of Fairbairn. Fairbairn re-cast Freud's libido theory in a way that was simple, yet revolutionary. Fairbairn (1976) said that libido is object-seeking whereas Freud had said that libido sought to re-establish equilibrium. In the *Three Essays on Sexuality* (1905d) Freud had given a place to the object of libido. He said that the sexual drive had a source, an aim, and an object. The aim was the restoration of equilibrium, and the object was simply the object through which the aim was achieved. So, for instance, hunger is a state of disequilibrium, the aim is to restore a state of equilibrium, and it is achieved through devouring a meat pie. The meat pie is, then, the object. Similarly, when someone is sexually hungry, the organism is in a state of disequilibrium. In order to restore the state of equilibrium, the individual has sexual discharge. Again the aim is the restoration of equilibrium, which can be achieved through sexual intercourse with a member of the opposite sex, or with a member of the same sex, or with an animal, or through masturbation. As long as the object reduces the tension of the organism, then what that object is does not matter for Freud's theory.

The difference between Freud and Fairbairn on this matter is that, for Freud, the object is just the means by which the aim is achieved, whereas for Fairbairn what is just a means becomes the end-point. For Fairbairn, the physiological reduction of tension is just the means, the pathway, along which libido has to travel in order to reach its object. For Freud the end-point is the reduction of tension; for Fairbairn the end-point is emotional contact with another human being. Fairbairn has changed the model from the organic to the personal. In terms of Freud's *theory*, I could sit in a prison cell with no window to the outside world. The only contact from outside is a pipe down which some pellets of food and water are ejected every few hours. I sit in my cell, eat, drink, and masturbate, and I am entirely happy. I never see, hear, or talk to another human being, but I am content because I have the necessary equipment to restore me organically to equilibrium. I am content because subjectively the reduction in tension is experienced as pleasure. In terms of the theory, there is no unpleasure at all, and therefore I am the happiest man in the world, living in my prison cell.

We all know that this is absurd, but this theory serves a function: the only good and bad that exist for me in my prison cell are the pleasure every time I eat, drink, or masturbate and the unpleasure when these possibilities are denied to me. If we define morality as the manner in which we behave towards ourselves and others, then what we have here is an amoral theory. Freud constructed an amoral theory. It is not possible to enter into the reasons why Freud did this. At its briefest, it was his passionate hatred of religion. An important function of religion in society is the regulation and codification of the right and wrong ways of behaving towards our neighbour. When we start to talk of how I should treat others, we are in the religious sphere. The thesis of this paper is that unconsciousness is fashioned in order to hide from ourselves the damage that we do to ourselves and others, but especially the damage we do to our own minds. This is something that Freud could not allow. He was forced to explain unconsciousness on a different basis. He had to explain it amorally.

I want to point out something that is surprising. Why is an idea made unconscious? This fundamental question is not answered by Freud. He says that it is an idea that is repressed and therefore becomes part of the unconscious, and he tells us that the idea is the representative of an instinct, but his reasoning as to why something is repressed is feeble. He says that it is because it is in opposition to the dictates of civilization, but this does not do justice to the violence with which memories are repressed. I think it is incorrect to say that an idea is the representative of an instinct. I believe that an idea finds its origin in the ego out of which it is constructed.

In order to explain psychological data amorally, Freud had to squeeze all of human motivation within the parameters of the constancy theory of which the man in the prison cell is an exemplar. Another important pillar of his theory is the division of the mind into primary and secondary process. In the primary process the disequilibrium is restored through hallucinatory wish fulfilment; in the secondary process it is restored through bringing the memory of a past satisfaction into correspondence with an external perception. This perception focuses upon food, water, sex objects, and objects of danger, but all within the constancy theory. But the roots of this theory lie in the belief that psychic action from the primary process does not touch outer reality. The point of that example of the woman with impotent boyfriends is that her psychic wishes were not confined within an imaginary system but, rather, they affected the sexual potency of her boyfriends and the mental potency of her analyst. Reality as opposed to unreality is, then, differentiated according to whether something exists in time and space. I have argued in chapter 8, this volume—"The Nature of Reality"—that reality is to be distinguished from unreality in the human sphere not according to whether something exists in space and time but according to its value.

It is terribly important to realize that I construct the human world in which I live and I am constructed by it. That woman patient was having an effect on my capacity to crystallize inchoate intuitions into interpretations. In the face of that I had to develop greater emotional strength in this sphere, and when I did deliver that interpretation, the patient reconstructed her human world. I will give a simple example. I had an instructor helping me to master a computer programme. He would show me how to do it, and I would promptly do it wrong, whereupon I apologized. Another instructor, this time a woman, had similar difficulties with me. At the end, she said to me, "Go on practising, but next time I come stop apologizing."

I took what she said to heart and thought to myself: "Instead of putting all that energy into apologizing, use your resources into getting it right", and it led me to further thoughts on the matter. Instructor 2 had a positive constructive effect on her pupil, and, I believe, her pupil did change, not just technically but emotionally. Instructor 1 had a destructive effect. Mothers have constructive or destructive effects on their children, and children have constructive or destructive effects on their mothers. I once had a patient who had a constructive effect upon me: she changed me from being a psychotherapist into being an analyst. Of course, I consented to this construction. I do wish we could all grasp this, then there would be no more talk about a mother being really like that or a child being really like this. Personal reality is always a factor of interpersonal construction. In Freud's constancy theory, objects are not persons. Reality is or it is not—that shimmering mass in the desert either is water or a mirage. If it is a mirage, it is not real, but if it is water, it is; but personal reality is not like that. I construct or destruct according to my inner relations between parts.

I have already described how I fashion unconsciousness, but this is quite different from Freud's view. He believed that there was a system *Ucs*, as he called it, and, in terms of his theory, what came to be relegated to that system were unfulfilled wishes that were satisfied through hallucination. But in terms of Freud's theory his wishes are "musts". I will quote to you his definition of a wish: "The accumulation of excitation is felt as unpleasure and that it sets the apparatus in action with a view to repeating the experience of satisfaction, which involved a diminution of excitation and was felt as pleasure. A current of this kind in the apparatus, starting from unpleasure and aiming at pleasure, we have termed a 'wish'" (1900a, p. 598).

I hope no one would feel that this was a satisfactory definition of a wish. Essential to a wish is that I may wish *A* but I may also wish *B*. If there is no alternative, then it is no longer a wish. Freud had to force "wish" into a biological straitjacket. I am a driven creature, according to Freud's model. Once I have to do *A* and can do no other, then it is no longer a wish, and, for Freud, I *have* to avoid pain and I have to seek pleasure. I live in an amoral universe. In his followers, particularly what is known as the British School and even more particularly Wilfred Bion, the bearing of pain cannot be avoided when mental growth is desired.

If I have it firmly in mind that I keep something unconscious because I am damaging my *embryo mind*, my approach to psychoanalytic practice will be different from the view that something is kept unconscious because it produces unpleasure. Freud's schema is wrong on two counts: In the first place, he says that the unconscious is ruled only by the pleasure/unpleasure principle and that it has no contact with reality; but if we take, for instance, the case of the woman with the impotent boyfriends, then her unconscious psychic activity is in contact with reality—both her own inner reality and the reality of my mind. Also, Freud's view that repression occurs because of unpleasure suggests that unpleasure is avoided through repression, but *in terms of the constancy theory* the way unpleasure is converted to pleasure is through the libidinal aim finding satisfaction through contact with the

object, whereupon homeostasis is reasserted. It is, of course, very uncomfortable—unpleasurable, if you like—for me to realize that I am
damaging my own mind and that of others. It is the knowledge of what
I do that produces the unpleasure. Freud says that it is the idea as
representative of the instinct that is repressed, but what sense are we to
make of that? Why should the instinct for food, for drink, for sexual
satisfaction be repressed? Freud does put forward another explanation. In the oedipal drama, a child's libidinal drive towards the mother
is repressed because of fear of father's retaliation, but in terms of
constancy theory, which aims to avoid unpleasure, it would make
sense to know father's retaliation so that I can avoid it.

I could go on and on circling around this issue. The nub of the
matter is that Freud erected a huge, elaborate fabric in order to convert
the unconscious from a moral category into one that is amoral, but if
we look into it with care, it simply does not hold up.

I believe that the confusion generated by this pseudo-construction
of Freud continues to mar our clinical work. I will give you just one
example. Many of our most disturbed patients suffer from the effects
of a tyrannical superego. It is my observation that such a tyrannical
superego always coincides with inner psychic activity that is damaging. The true reduction of the strength of the inner tyrant can only be
accomplished as the individual slowly transforms damaging action
into constructive action, and therefore this is the psychoanalytic aim.
Analytic strategies such as affirmation of the patient's understanding,
empathic understanding of his distress will do nothing *in themselves* to
reduce the violence of the superego. Yet these would be effective if
Freud's amoral theory were right. In fact, however, those analysts
working with psychotic processes who are Kleinian, or influenced by a
Kleinian perspective, achieve the aim of dethroning the superego
through tackling the emotionally destructive processes. Hence, they
espouse a moral view of the unconscious. They need therefore to
articulate the theory underlying their practice and differentiate it from
Freud's amoral theory.

Conclusion

My thesis is simple: that Socrates was right. We cannot do evil; we
cannot do what is damaging to our own mind and to that of others and
know it. We fashion the unconscious so as not to know it. We need to
ditch Freud's explanation of it as an amoral construction if we want to

make progress in the work of helping our more disturbed patients and have a coherent theory supporting what we do.

Notes

1. Psychoanalytic discourse uses terms like *self-damaging, self-destructive* and so on. In religious discourse these would be described as *evil*.

2. When there is powerful emotional effect upon the other's mind, it is a sign of psychotic process. Whenever this emerges, I believe that the analyst needs to focus his attention upon his own inner psychic processes.

3. It was only capable of disturbing my mind to the extent to which she was able to find an emotional lesion in it.

4. Therapeutically it is important to find out the psychological "pay-off" for this consent from the *embryo mind*.

5. It is necessary to add here the ontological insight that integral to our nature is the necessity of being of which we are composed (see chapter 9, this volume).

CHAPTER SEVEN

Religion and science in psychoanalysis

This chapter is an adaptation of a lecture given at the Freud Conference in Melbourne on 2 April 1995.

The crisis within psychoanalysis

There is, I believe, a crisis within psychoanalysis and within the psychotherapy schools that derive from it. Hardly a week goes by when our enemies do not assail us in the media. This is healthy. Criticism and challenge can only sharpen our minds to think more clearly and reflect more deeply upon our practice and its methods. What worries me are the replies to these taunts by our own practitioners, rushing, as we usually do, to our own defence. Many of these criticisms are prejudiced assaults that do not deserve much attention, but there is a common theme running through much of the critique that has some basis: it is that the "talking cure", as it was called by Freud, is not producing any results; that patients visit their analyst or therapist year in, year out, with no visible change in their condition.

I know from my own experience that this criticism is frequently verified. I have heard clinical presentations where a patient has been visiting an analyst or therapist for four, five, six, even ten, years without any change that I was able to detect. I have heard this not just on isolated occasions but frequently. These are the obvious cases where no change has occurred and where a malingering situation has set in, but even in cases where it looks as though change has occurred, it is often a case of subtle accommodation to the analyst or therapist, and the patient remains with the same mental structure within. Most frequently, this consists of a mentality that is paranoid. I am not, here, supporting many of the burgeoning therapies that claim to cure mental disturbance in a quicker, more efficient, cost-effective way. Many of these only give the appearance of cure. The criterion here is if a patient "feels cured" or "feels better". Experienced clinicians know that such feelings are an insufficient criterion. We have all seen the case where such a statement is made with confidence one day, and next day the person has committed suicide. No, I am not criticizing psychoanalysis alone but the whole psychotherapy movement. In fact, I believe that in a sick situation, psychoanalysis is probably the healthiest patient.

So what is the cause of this malaise? I believe that it is twofold: that psychoanalysis is failing to be scientific and failing to be religious and that unless these two axes transect, then the process, the analytic experience, remains sterile. I must now try to explain what I mean.

Omnipotence: the common enemy

Religion and psychoanalysis have one enemy in common. In psychoanalysis we call it "omnipotence", and within the Christian tradition it is called "the sin of pride", or "hubris" in classical language, or "*mana*" in Buddhist psychology. All the great liberationist religions have the aim of rescuing mankind from the condition in which he finds himself. In all these religions hubris is the core sin from which flow all others. In psychoanalysis there is also a core condition from which human beings need to be rescued: narcissism and the bad aspects of narcissism are to be found in a constellation of factors that are interrelated: paranoia, envy, and omnipotence. Psychoanalysis seeks the transformation of these factors in the personality, whereas the great religions seek their obliteration. I do not want to focus now on that difference, important though it is, but to signal the fact that both religion and psychoanalysis judge that human beings need to be liberated from these factors.

There is little doubt that figures like Jesus or the Buddha understood that human beings needed to be liberated from this condition for the sake of achieving inner enlightenment. The reasons largely became lost in their followers, and what remained was condemnation of the condition.

It can come as a shock to realize that a patient has entirely obliterated something in his or her perceptual field.

> In my consulting-room I have a statuette of Madonna and child in
> Copenhagen china straight in front of the couch. A woman had
> been coming to see me four times a week for two and a half years
> when she suddenly saw it for the first time. As she lay down, she
> said, "That's new, isn't it? I've never seen it before."

For two and a half years she had totally blotted it from her field of
vision. It was a case of negative hallucination. It emerged that this
statuette represented myself holding her emotionally, and this was
blotted out. But how is someone, such as this woman, able to blot out
the presence of the other and herself so effectively? My observation
tells me that it is through the presence of omnipotence. In an omnipotent state this woman was able to interfere with the faculty of perception so that it functioned in an aberrant way. Omnipotence, closely
allied to the superego, issues instructions that are then obeyed:

> "Thou shalt not see the statue on the table.
> If thou darest raise thine eyes and see it,
> thou shalt be struck dead."

Where does this omnipotent power come from? To answer this, I resort
to another clinical vignette.

> A patient complained bitterly that his father was very authoritarian
> and then went on to say that his secretary at work would not carry
> out his orders. The analyst pointed out that it was he who was
> authoritarian and gave further evidence for this assertion, where-
> upon the patient went into a massive depression.

It became clear that his controlling authoritarian manner had been to
ward off a depression that the personality was not capable of manag-
ing. It was similar with the woman who blotted out the statuette. She
consented to the situation to protect herself from a depression that she
was not able to sustain. So there is an agreement within the personality
to invest this figure with the power to blot out the perceptual faculty.
This obliteration occurs through the agency of omnipotence. I believe
that the divine figure in religious myths who turns Lot's wife into a
pillar of salt or causes Eurydice to vanish into Hades is an externaliza-

tion of this inner reality, which has power to obliterate our mental faculties.

This begins to make a bit more sense of why psychoanalysis sets out to tackle the presence of omnipotence in the personality. As we have seen, it may function to protect the personality from a severe depression, but this is at the price of destroying the mental faculties. Psychoanalysis is concerned with mental development, and in order to restore damaged faculties, it has the task of integrating omnipotence so that it does not act destructively. The way this is integrated has been well described in a paper entitled "The Survival Function of Primitive Omnipotence" by my wife (J. Symington, 1985). Omnipotence does not disappear but becomes the servant of the ego rather than the other way around. We can see from this, therefore, that psychoanalysis sets out to demote omnipotent functioning within the personality and replace it with a form of functioning that makes full use of the mental faculties. A person can manage by the use of omnipotence, but only at the cost of damage to his or her perceptual and cognitive faculties. Observation also tells me that when this kind of damage is occurring in the personality, then the individual is plagued by guilt.

Through psychoanalytic investigation we discover that omnipotence destroys those mental faculties that are capable of revealing our inner psychic condition. We understand, therefore, that psychoanalysis aims to transform omnipotence so that it no longer has the power to act against the mental faculties. However, we cannot put a full stop there. We still have a question to answer: why does psychoanalysis set itself this task? To answer this question, we have to examine more closely the mental faculties that are attacked by that omnipotent part of the self. I shall go back to the woman who blotted out the statuette in my consulting-room. She blotted out what it represented: myself as separate and herself as dependent. However, what I want to focus on here is the obliteration of me as a separate person. This was done through obliterating part of the perceptual faculty. In this instance it was vision that was interfered with, but by what faculty is it that I apprehend another human being as a person?

It is common for us to hear someone complaining that he or she has been treated as a mere object by another, but the other who has perpetrated this behaviour is quite unaware of it, just as my patient was unaware of the presence of the statuette. It is not perception or memory that is blotted out here, but the epistemological faculty. I apprehend another person not through the senses, but through knowledge. The person of the other is apprehended through an act of knowledge. I see a face and legs, hear a voice, smell perspiration, touch hairy skin, but have no knowledge of a person.

When I say I know a person, is there a synonym for "person"? What do I mean when I say it? What am I referring to? I am referring to the *being* of the other, and ontological reflection tells me that *being* is one and indivisible. It is therefore the reality in which I and the other share, and is the root upon which the concept of transference is based. The patient who blotted out my statuette, who eradicated my personhood, also obliterated her own person. This being is identical with that reality apprehended by the seers whose metaphysical insights have been recorded in *The Upanishads*.

This radical obliteration of our *being* is the source of neurosis, psychosis, addiction, perversion, and psychopathy. The uncovering of the processes that lead to this obliteration is, then, *the* psychoanalytic task. Observing and cataloguing these processes in their intricacy, their subtlety, and their complexity is the scientific activity *within* psychoanalysis. It is the scientific activity *of* psychoanalysis. I will go so far as to say that the criterion of whether a technique or theory is truly psychoanalytical is if they can be registered meaningfully within this straightforward schema, and, contrariwise, all those theories and procedures that cannot be so accommodated are mere dross, only worthy of the dustbin. I believe that if this criterion were strictly followed by the editors of our professional journals and publishers of books, a veritable forest of trees would still be standing unmolested upon our landscape.

We need to stop for a moment to reflect on being and its nature. A human being, a plant, a stone, a dream, friendship, and the universe are objects that have an element in common. They all exist. Existence is their common denominator. Also all parts of myself exist. When I reflect on the fact that I exist, I realize that I share this with you. My existence, my being, is not *mine*, because once you reflect upon it, you discover that it is indivisible. This is why the seers of the Upanishads, having reflected long and deeply upon this, formulated that time-honoured phrase:

THAT THOU ART.

This realization does not come about through a quick piece of reasoning. In the same way as I may only realize my vulnerability and dependence after several years of analysis, so also the realization THAT THOU ART was only arrived at after years of emotional reflection. Many years ago I studied ontology, the science of being, under the tutelage of a philosopher who only taught what he had personally assimilated. With his help I achieved some insight into existence. I believe that it has been the most important realization of my life. I have neither achieved it deeply, like the seers of the Upanishads, nor have I been faithful to it through all the upheavals of life; but it gave me a glimpse of their vision and what it was about. I shall refer to this reality for the rest of this chapter as our *participated being*.[1]

So, obliteration of *participated being* is the source of neurosis, psychosis, perversion, psychopathy, and personality disorder, and, contrariwise, the unimpeded access to *participated being* is the source of mental health and well-being. Our logical conclusion is that the person who is able to be in relation to *participated being* enjoys mental health and keeps a pathway open to ongoing emotional development.

Participated being does not lie fallow within the personality but exacts an influence. Like all parts of the personality, it is emotionally active, but what are its signals? How do we make contact with its presence? The earth's core lies 3,500 miles into its centre, but geologists tell us that it makes its presence felt at the surface through radiation waves that are responsible, together with particles from the sun, for the phenomenon of *aurora borealis*; it is also believed that the electrical currents it generates are responsible for the magnetism registered on the dial of a compass. In a similar way there is a signal from *participated being*: we call it "conscience". Now we need to spend a little time on conscience.

I think most of us here have been aware of that nasty inner twinge as I am about to move towards an objective. At that moment I have one of two options: obliterate its meddlesome voice or desist from my intent. It is often thought that conscience speaks when I am about to injure my neighbour. It often does speak on such an occasion, but hurting my neighbour is not the reason. If the latter were the case, then dentists would be the most conscience-ridden people in our community. Analysts also often say things that hurt, and in fact that meddlesome conscience might start clamouring if I desist from an interpretation for fear of hurting my patient. I suspect that if a dentist were afraid to drill a tooth because of the pain he would inflict, then again that troubling voice might start to clamour. No, conscience speaks when, wielding an axe, I am about to hack and smash at *participated being*. If I do so, it will affect my neighbours, most especially those who are close to me; but that is a consequence of what I do and not the essence of it. *Participated being* makes demands upon the personality. Just as I experience hunger when the organism needs some more stored energy, so conscience clamours when *participated being* is under threat.

I once came across a criminal who had bashed an old lady over the head. About two weeks prior to this event a forensic psychiatrist had lent him two pounds. Subsequently the criminal felt extremely guilty about not having repaid the two pounds to the psychiatrist, but not the least guilty about having bashed the old lady. The guilt had been displaced. One can imagine that man telling a psychotherapist how guilty he was about not having repaid the two pounds but making no mention of the old lady whom he had bashed. In such a situation it is common for the psychotherapist to miss the displacement. Where there is neurotic guilt or psychotic guilt. there is also real guilt that cannot be borne. Also, in such a case, conscience is stifled and replaced by a savage superego. I point this out so as to make clear the difference between a healthy conscience and a savage superego. The persecuting jabs of a savage superego are not signals from *participated being* but signs that the latter is walled off and not accessible to the rest of the personality. I am sure of this: that many psychotherapists miss the voice of conscience—in fact, they often aid in smothering it, which means that the inner structure of the personality remains unchanged.

Now, having ascertained that the obliteration of *participated being* is the source of all mental disturbance, it is clear that the establishment of *participated being* as the fountainhead of emotional life in the personality is the guarantor of mental health and sound emotional development. However, we realize with some wonder that this is also the source of religious life in mankind.

We often, I believe, get into trouble when we start to discuss science, religion, and aesthetics because we concretize them into things. We *reify* them, to use a sociological term. Science, aesthetics, and religion refer to three different mental vertices. There is a mental attitude that is scientific, a mental attitude that is aesthetic, and a mental attitude that is religious. Let us understand first the attitude that is scientific.

If I plan to make a table to fit into a corner of my sitting-room, I do not just start hacking away at a piece of wood willy-nilly. I judge the size of the table I want and its shape, and then I start to take measurements for its height, the measurements for its width and depth, I measure the thickness of the top and then that of the legs, and so on. All these calculations can be set out on paper before a saw has touched a plank of wood. My purpose in this endeavour is to make something for my use. When I take the measurements and make the calculations, I am being scientific. It is the attitude of mind that I have to adopt when I want to adapt the natural environment to my use. The process necessary for the adaptation of the environment for the use of man is the scientific attitude. There was no science before hominization[2] because other animals adapted themselves to the environment, but man has this power to adapt the environment to himself. As soon as he turns his mind to this end, he is in the scientific domain.

When I decide to shape the legs of my table in a tapering style, I do so because it pleases me. It has no direct practical use. I make it beautiful to please my soul. This is the aesthetic state of mind.

Now, what is the mental attitude which we call "religious"? Whereas in the scientific and aesthetic modes of mentation the environment is shaped to my desire, here something has a claim on me rather than the other way round. This something is what I have named *participated being*. You will note that there are two aspects to *participated being*: it is both me and not me. Remember that motto of the Upanishads: THAT THOU ART. I am it, and, at the same time, I am not it. This dual perspective upon *participated being* is essential to our understanding of religion. In the religious state of mind I act according to the principle that *participated being* has a claim upon me.

You may be saying that this is at a far remove from the work of psychoanalysis in the consulting-room, yet the exact opposite is the case, and I want to give just one example.

A man was in despair that his life was so discontinuous. He had moved jobs umpteen times, in and out of six marriages and no persevering conviction. "Shall I do this or shall I do that? To be or not to be?" There was no cohering centre, and his outer life was an expression of this inner state of affairs. He came for analysis because he wanted, he said, to be a person before he entered the grave. When I made an interpretation that made sense of an array of phenomena, I found that my mind would begin to wander in an aimless manner, and his subsequent speech was dissociated from something that was emotionally meaningful and had a lullaby effect upon me. Something prevented me from remaining connected to meaningful cohesion.

I realized that this something also prevented him from maintaining the cohesion that he so direly wanted. The transference is to be understood like this: *participated being* is not known directly, but its failure to be established as creative reality in the personality is experienced as chronic frustration. *Participated being* is crippled in its expression. What I experience as analyst is what is occurring within the patient's mind, and it tells me how *participated being* is being smothered. It may at first seem a paradox that the source of creative action lies in *participated being*. This is because that is the locus of what is most me within the personality, and yet it is not mine. I believe a great deal of confusion could be avoided if this were grasped. There are two poles within which modern humanity has taken refuge: that of self-surrender to a deity,[3] in the service of which the personal is crushed, and that of surrender to self-expression, which on the surface looks personal but also represents the crushing of the personal. This polarity can easily be observed in social groupings and also in the fluctuations of the psychic life of the individual.

* * *

Let us take stock of where we are. We have made two statements: that the establishment of *participated being* is the foundation-stone of mental health and sound emotional development, *and* that it is the core of religion. The conclusion that we come to is that the establishment of this foundation stone within the personality is the goal of psychoanalysis, which is a religious endeavour.

What we are talking of here is what is called "natural religion"— that is, religion the foundation of which resides naturally in mankind and the dictates of which are mediated through conscience. It is rational—as opposed to revealed religion, which is not. The difference between natural religion and revealed religion needs to be understood. When I act according to the inner principles of natural religion, I act according to the principles of *participated being*—according to this being that is more me than me, and yet it is THAT. When acting according to this principle of natural religion, I act creatively. When I am in accord with the THAT within me, when it is that which acts and which I allow to act, then I act creatively. The THAT is the creative principle within me.[4] Narcissism—me-ness—smothers this creative principle within. The sense of creativity flowing from a non-me principle within is well known to artists and writers. Rudyard Kipling (1970) referred to the Daemon within him. He says at one point that he could not write because the Daemon had left him.[5] Being faithful to the principles of natural religion is a state of mind described by Melanie Klein as the depressive position.

In revealed religion I bow my head to a deity and offer sacrifice to it in fear and trembling. The mental state associated with this is what Melanie Klein named the paranoid–schizoid position. Revealed religion, which is the sophisticated elaboration of primitive religion, is the cultural reification of this primitive state of mind. In this state *participated being* is obliterated. Revealed religion is the enemy of natural religion. This does not mean that all members of revealed religions are necessarily in this state. We have already instanced the mystics, who have, through contemplation, internalized in a deep way the reality of natural religion. There is a constant tension within revealed religion between the primitive and the mature. There are many members of the revealed religions who have managed to escape the strictures of the deity and avoided being crushed, but the message of those who have is nearly always that it has been a severe struggle. I believe that Gerald Manley Hopkins has expressed himself in this sense.

I may stand up and say that I do not see why I should not be sadistic, why I should not harden my heart against friendly gestures towards me, why I should not be bloody-minded if I want to be. Why shouldn't I despise blacks, treat women as sexual objects? There is no convincing argument based on Darwinian principles against such a position. My interlocutor might say that if I proceed in such a direction, I will make a muck of my life, but my answer is that it is my life and I am entitled to make a muck of it if I want to. The devout reader of *The Upanishads* will try to show me that my life is not my own; he will enunciate to me the principle of THAT THOU ART, and I will say "rubbish". This is the place where the Socratic method falls down, because it assumes good will on my part. Each of the great religious movements—Judaism, Christianity, Islam, Zoroastrianism, Hinduism, Buddhism, and Socratic religion—have particular mental attitudes not shared by the others. It is my view that in this era in which values have collapsed, we cannot afford to cling to any one system but, rather, search out the good in each. *The Upanishads* has the primordial vision, but it does not have an elaborated theory of moral action. Buddhism does have such a theory, but it exists in a realm cut off from human intimacy and rational argument. Socrates does exist in the midst of mankind, but he lacks the profundity of vision enjoyed by the Upanishads. Judaism, Christianity, and Islam have a vision of compassion and what constitutes the personal, but are all overshadowed by a deity that demands sacrifice and worship. What we are looking for is a religion that fits mature emotional action in the modern world.

*   *   *

I use the phrase "emotional action" to describe an activity that is differentiated from motor action. I turn to someone and say, "I love you"; I turn to another person and say, "I hate you"; I turn to another and say, "I envy you"; and to another, "I respect you". These statements describe inner psychic action towards the other person. I think you will all agree that these activities are very different: I love, I hate, I envy, I respect, and yet, I believe, we are all hard put to it to describe accurately the inner activity of which these words are the description. It is the job of psychoanalysis to make a scientific investigation of these hidden activities. I am in close association with another person—perhaps my wife, my father, my mother, my children, my colleague at work—and I envy this other person or, alternatively, I respect him or her. The difference between these two activities is enormous. The other person, over time, will have two quite different experiences. I have, of course, only chosen four of these activities but they are numerous and cover a wide spectrum: I suspect, I disdain, I scorn, I adore, I revere, I trust, and so on.

The social change often associated with secularization since the Industrial Revolution has witnessed a shift from extended family patterns to the nuclear family. This, you will understand, is shorthand for a change where personal emotional attitudes are the governing factors in social engineering. In traditional society I could despise my wife, and the social structure would hold the marriage in place. Today it would lead to divorce. These hidden emotional activities, then, are what govern the patterns of living in the world today. This is certainly so in what is known as the Western world, but it is becoming so in many other societies also. It is in the sphere of these activities that the core values of religion are most urgently required. What has happened, however, is that traditional religion has been rightly jettisoned because it cannot do the job that the patterns of modern living require it to do. There have been two general pathways that have resulted from this situation: either a moral decadence manifested in violence, drugs, suicide, depression, and existential despair or a pathetic retreat into fundamentalist sects, astrology, fortune telling, tarot cards, ufology, and an ever widening panoply of secular and pseudo-religious superstition.

My thesis, then, is that the core values—or core value—of religion is necessary in our times, and that it needs to be mediated into the sphere of emotional intimacy between people. What I have referred to as primitive religion and revealed religion, its elaborated successor, has to be ditched and natural religion put in its place.

Every interpretation contains a judgement. This is the religious axis within psychoanalysis. It is this axis that gives an interpretation its cogency, its power to penetrate beneath the surface. However, if psychoanalysis consisted in just this, it would be a secular form of preaching. Of course, it often is precisely this and has been criticized, rightly, for being an agent of social control within conventional society. This religious axis, therefore, easily degenerates into a series of ritualistic, well-worn interpretations that are ineffective. Psychoanalysis is also scientific, and that axis is also essential if the process is to remain alive and potent. We must now examine this scientific axis.

Whereas the religious preacher always *knows* the object of his faith, the scientist does not. The scientist investigates his world; he is on a journey of discovery. To every answer that is arrived at, there is another "Why?" Each answer is another point on that chart to answer the big question: How does the mind function? The answer to this question has a use. It is of direct use to the patient, but its use is wider than this. It stands as a hypothesis for further investigation. I will give an example of this.

A man was in distress over a crisis, and I offered him an extra session. He was initially grateful and felt cared for. Then he had another thought: "He has offered me this session because he wants the money for it." He had an inhibition about voicing this second thought, and the scientist in me asked the question (of myself) "Why is there an inhibition about expressing this thought?" The next day he asked for a change of time. It emerged that this had not been requested for any practical reason but to discover whether I was full of free times, which would confirm the thought about the expression of which there had been an inhibition. With further investigation it became clear that the inhibition screened not a thought, but a delusional conviction.

There was, then, an hypothesis that inhibition is a mechanism to screen delusion. This is an hypothesis that could be tested and seen whether it applies in the wider social context. Also, if this were the case, and a patient in analysis becomes less inhibited, does this represent a transformation of delusion into thought? And if this is the case, how does this occur? This leads to further scientific investigation. As points on this chart become established, it then becomes possible to generate a theory to make sense of these new observations.

Each interpretation—each new judgement—is also the establishment of a psychological fact. The religious axis and the scientific axis intersect. Three factors need to be investigated, then, in an analysis: the religious, the scientific, and the intersection of these two. The religious and scientific axes are necessary to establish a psychological fact. In the emotional sphere psychological facts are established by judgement and by the human thrust to know or curiosity.

It is these three factors that establish the identity of psychoanalysis. It is possible by using these criteria to distinguish between psychoanalysis and that which is not. If it is religious without the scientific axis, it degenerates into primitive religion; if it is scientific without being religious, there is theory detached from emotional reality. In other words, without these three factors the process engaged in is neither scientific nor religious but aesthetic. It may be very beautiful, I may be filled with good feelings, but there is no substance, no knowledge of myself. What I am in possession of is an illusion. This latter condition is the state of affairs in much psychoanalytic practice and in most psychotherapy, and it is the reason for my statement at the beginning that there is today a *malaise* in the psychoanalytic and psychotherapeutic movement. There is, I believe, the genuine article. In this chapter I have tried to establish those criteria through which it is possible to distinguish the genuine from the fake.

Notes

1. *Participated Being* is synonymous with *being*, but the former accents the fact that our *being* is a shared *being*.

2. Except to a minimal extent in the tool-making activities of chimpanzees and gorillas.

3. This deity can be incarnate in an institution, ideology, or person.

4. Now, strange to say, this is how Groddeck conceptualized *DAS ES* = THE IT. Freud adopted this term of Groddeck's in the structural model, but he changed it into an instinctive force.

5. Some will protest that many of the most creative people have been extraordinarily narcissistic. I would not deny it for a moment, but I would maintain that the creative in them does not flow from the narcissistic currents in their personality. The creative moments, even in the most creative of people, are often not numerous. There is frequently a tension between the creative and the narcissistic that becomes the primordial struggle of their lives.

CHAPTER EIGHT

The nature of reality

It is the thesis of this chapter that when we say something is "real", it is a value judgement and not a statement as to whether or not it exists. An hallucination exists, but we say it is not real. We distinguish it from a perception, which we say *is* real. Therefore this distinction is not made according to whether what is perceived exists but according to its quality. What this chapter sets out to examine is what quality in human subjects and objects leads to this distinction between what is real and what is not.

I originally gave this paper at the Freud Conference in Melbourne in 1992. I was excited by what I felt was a new discovery when I gave the paper, but it was muddled with other realizations. With the passage of time I have come to think that the central insight of this paper is of enormous importance for understanding in the social sciences. It seems to be the key concept that separates social science from natural science.

An hallucination comes about through a discharge of a hated element from within onto the outer, whereas a *true* perception comes about through an inner element that is embraced or loved. So what distinguishes the real from the false is whether inner elements are loved or hated. This puts the social sciences upon a different foundation from natural science. I believe this basis revolutionizes our thinking about our human world.

Concepts that are appropriate for the study of the natural world have been imported into the scientific study of the human world. The effect of this has been the reverse of anthropomorphism, which applies what is appropriate when describing human beings to the non-human world. It is an interesting fact that there is no antonym for anthropomorphism in the English language. Isaiah Berlin drew attention to this. Berlin's thesis was that there was a unified system of philosophical and theological thinking in Europe that was Christendom, and in the eighteenth century this was overthrown by the Enlightenment, the scientific principles of which, deriving very largely from Newtonian physics, now governed the understanding of the world. Berlin's thesis was that the Enlightenment, as a system of thought replacing Christendom, was just as monolithic and rigid as its predecessor had been. His book *Against the Current* (1979a) is about those few figures who have stood up against certain presuppositions of the Enlightenment. There is one particular figure, dear to his heart, whom Isaiah Berlin has picked out and elevated into a position of supreme significance: the philosopher, jurist Giambattista Vico, who came from Naples. When I came to read Isaiah Berlin's 1980 treatise on Vico's *New Science*, there was a particular statement that revolutionized my whole way of thinking. This was that you can only know that which you have created. He uses the Latin tag that you can only know *"per caussas"*.[1] Only if you have created the thing—have caused it to come into being, in other words—can you know it. If you have not created it, you cannot know it. Vico said that the only area of human knowledge that can be absolutely known and validated is mathematics. He held the view that mathematics is a creation of the human mind. I know that there is a philosophical debate on whether mathematics is a system that corresponds to attributes and patterns within the natural environment, within nature, or whether it is totally a creation of the human mind. My own view is that mathematics does correspond to patterns within the natural environment, but that it is *also* a creation of the human mind: that the mind creates something that harmonizes with the pattern and structure of the natural environment. Vico's point was that mathematics is the only sphere of knowledge where you can get complete knowledge and truth. But for me it was a very revolutionary thought to come across the notion that you can only know something if you yourself have created it. As psychoanalysts, we are in the work of trying to uncover knowledge that is screened from consciousness. This suggests that the knowledge is there: strip away some resistances, and it will be revealed. This notion is quite different, because what is being said here is that there has to be a creative act first, and only then, when there has been a creative act, can you know. In other words, it was not there until the creative act had occurred. This means that the whole endeavour that I am engaged in is quite different from what I thought. That what one is engaged in is the attempt in an interactive way to bring about the inner creative action, because only then can awareness come about. Consciousness, therefore, is the product of inner creative action. When the full impact of this hit me, I found it mind-blowing: until then, I had a very well set up system of what psychoanalysis is and what the procedure is for uncovering repressions and resistances, and now all this was blown apart.

I will now give you Isaiah Berlin's two quotes. He says:

> If anthropomorphism was falsely to endow the inanimate world with human minds and wills, there was presumably a world which it was proper to endow with precisely these attributes, namely, the world of man. Consequently a natural science of men treated as purely natural entities, on a par with rivers and plants and stones rested on a cardinal error. [Berlin, 1996, p. 96]

Again, he says,

> If following Descartes's rigorous rule, we allowed only that to be true knowledge which could be established by physics or other natural sciences, we should be confined to behavioural tests and this would result in the opposite fallacy to that of anthropomorphism . . . [he has no word for it] . . . namely the uncritical assimilation of the human world to the non-human, the restriction of our knowledge to those characteristics of men which they share with the non-human world; and consequently the attempt to explain human behaviour in non-human terms, as some behaviourists and extreme materialists, both ancient and modern, inspired by the vision (or mirage) of a single, integrated, natural science of all there is, have urged us to do. [Berlin, 1980, p. 23]

Vico lived and died a remote, unknown jurist in Naples, and it was only about a hundred years after his death that the French philosopher, Jules Michelet, resurrected him out of the ashes and pointed to the importance of what he had been saying. That we can only know that which we have created was one of Vico's illuminating ideas; the other was that within the human sphere there is another avenue of knowledge that is over and above the sensory equipment that we have at our disposal for the apperception of the natural world: there is another faculty of knowledge, which he called *fantasia*. I think the best translation for *fantasia* is imaginary intuition through which we understand and make judgements about our fellow human beings.

The idea that our perception of the human world is achieved through a special faculty goes contrary to the view that we have all inherited in the social sciences. Nevertheless it seems clear that we have imported into our understanding of the human world mental categories that are appropriate for our perception of the natural world. The positivist model keeps appearing in all sorts of guises and in many different spheres. It is often thought that within psychology its home is in behaviourism alone, but in fact psychoanalytic theory is full of it. No exegesis has been done on psychoanalytic theories and practice in such a way as to get a model that is appropriate to our understanding of human beings. It has also been convincingly demonstrated that Freud imported this physical science model into his theoretical constructions within psychoanalysis. A certain amount of scholarly work has been done to try to set right this perspective of Freud's which, I believe, was "a cardinal error", to quote Isaiah Berlin.

This has been addressed in a book called *Psychoanalytic Theory* by the American psychologist/analyst, George Klein (1976). Klein says that if you read his clinical papers carefully it is clear that Freud has in them a completely different theory to the one that appears in his metapsychological and other theoretical papers. Klein says that his metapsychological model just does not work, which is why he had a different one, which he used to explicate clinical cases.

There is, however, one concept that has, I believe, managed to escape the notice of those engaged in trying to put matters to rights. I am referring to the concept of reality. I think this is the way in which reality is usually understood within psychoanalysis. When psychoanalysts talk of reality testing, I think they mean: "does this person see the world as it is?" But what is missed in this is the way in which an inner belief structures our perception of the world.

I was treating a girl who complained of the way her boss at work treated her. I shall call her boss Mr Jones, and let her name be Mary. For instance, her working hours were nine in the morning until five in the evening, but this boss, Mr Jones, would frequently keep her back until half past six without any apology, without any extra pay. He was offhand with her, he would not bother to listen to any requests that she made, and so on. He sounded in every way insensitive and exploitative.

So was that reality, or was it not? Now I will introduce you to the next episode in my story.

I noticed that when I spoke to Mary, she didn't listen to what I said. I would speak, and she would continue talking, as if I had not said anything. I pointed this out to her on several occasions, but it didn't seem to have any visible effect. When I spoke, she ignored me; when I damaged my knee and hobbled round on a walking-stick, she ignored the fact. It took me some time to realize that this manner of treating me was similar to the way Mr Jones was treating her. When I did realize it and I pointed it out, she dismissed it and just went gaily on. However, one day I pointed out all the various ways in which she ignored me and drew for her a picture of an interconnecting pattern of attitudes towards me, but with more emphasis and conviction than before. Now, for the first time, I noticed that she paused. I had the distinct impression that whereas before she had brushed all that I had said aside, this time she received it. After quite a long pause she said, in a rather tight manner: "I can see what you mean". For the rest of the session she spoke in a subdued manner.

That was a Tuesday morning. Now I will tell you the next scene of this drama, which was on the Wednesday morning. She came in looking bright and cheerful and said,

"You know, something very curious happened yesterday. When I got to work, Mr Jones smiled at me. When the lunch hour came, he told me to make sure that I gave myself enough time for lunch. And at five o'clock, when he was in the middle of dictating letters, he looked at his watch and said 'oh, it's time we broke off now and went home. I can give you the rest of these letters tomorrow.'"

This incident is no surprise to me today because I have witnessed similar occurrences on numerous occasions. What I want to do, though, is to attempt to understand psychologically what has happened. How is it that this behaviour of Mr Jones changed, and what connection was there between that and what I had to said to her the previous day? And then I want to examine what this means for our conceptualization of reality.

My first step is that I presuppose that what occurred between Mary and Mr Jones was a consequence of what occurred between herself and me. But when I spoke to her on that Tuesday morning and she gave the appearance of hearing me and receiving emotionally what I said, this *caused*[2] the way that Mr Jones had behaved towards her later that morning. You may say that was pure chance, that Mr Jones was in a good mood that morning, that he had just heard that he had won a large sum of money on a horse, or that his daughter got a first at university, or that his wife had at last agreed to sell their London house and move to the country, or some other reason of that nature. The only thing I can say to you is that I have witnessed similar connected events very frequently. I have been led to the conclusion that the emotional occurrence in the session gave rise to the human events in the patient's life later that day, and a human event altered the way that Mr Jones behaved towards her.

That is the phenomenon. Now I want to try to unravel an explanation of it. How is one to understand it? When I say that Mary gave signs on that Tuesday that she received what I had said, it means that she did something. This receiving was something that she did. It was an activity. And in this I follow the philosopher Edmund Husserl (1979):

> This phenomenologically necessary concept of receptivity is in no way exclusively opposed to that of the *activity of the ego*, under which all acts proceeding in a specific way from the ego-pole are to be included. On the contrary, receptivity must be regarded as the lowest level of activity. The ego consents to what is coming and takes it in. [p. 79]

A central point in this hypothesis that I am putting forward is that the ego is active, even in receptivity. In psychoanalytic literature there are numerous expressions deriving from the positivist model such that *B* is the consequence of *A* without any mediation from the ego, but, rather, *B* happens because of *A*, after the manner of one billiard ball cannoning off another. And there is nothing about an ego responding, receiving, and doing something in relation to it. My only point of disagreement with Husserl is that I doubt whether receptivity is the lowest level of activity. My surmise, deriving from clinical experience of resistance, is that receptivity is a high level of activity. Often receptivity is a first step and, as such, often the one requiring the maximum of exertion. I think that activity shaped by habit and ritual is probably the lowest and what we are talking about here, this sort of receptivity, is a high level in the gradient of action.

Therefore this is the argument so far: receptivity is an action of the ego, and so the first thing is that Mary's ego acted on that Tuesday morning. It was an action on her part. We have to analyse this action: we make inferences at this point because we only see the product of the action and not the action itself—a point emphasized by Elliott Jaques: that a true decision is always made at the level below the threshold of awareness, and therefore the action itself has to be the object of an inference. Mary was not aware of her action, but she was aware of the product of her action: I am going to argue that Mr Jones's behaviour, his changed behaviour, was a product of her inner action. I call such inner activity creative communication—a communication that has an inviting, creative effect on the individual. If it is an inner free creative action that brings about change, then one has to alter, in my view, even the way one teaches people about the technical manner of perceiving in psychoanalysis.

We have now to analyse the action; for this we have to infer, and this is something that I had to do as observer in this particular clinical situation. You remember that on the Wednesday she came and she said that a curious thing had happened to her. It was the sense of it having happened *to* her, not something that she had orchestrated—she had no idea of any initiating activity on her part. And that is also, to me, a very interesting clinical point. Because it is as if the natural tendency would be to denigrate an action inside herself. And I just make this observation. It is, I think, an unnerving fact to realize that we are probably not aware of the most important actions of our lives. Realization only comes later.

Some time after this—a couple of weeks later—Mary said, "You know, I don't think Mr Jones is really as bad as I thought him to be. I don't really think he's like that." So she's making a judgement here that "Really, Mr Jones is like I experience him now", whereas before she said, "I don't think this really was what he's like." I draw attention to this because she makes that judgement. So this is the way I perceived the argument. When I say, then, that she received what I said, what was her action? We are talking about an action that occurred—so what was it, what do we infer, what sort of an action are we talking about? I think she gets a glimpse of Mr Jones as a type of figure in her. And it would not be anything as articulate as that, but as if she gets a flash type of image pattern of that. And I think one has to posit that she takes some action in relation to this disagreeable image or patterning and says "No" to it. This is, of course, one of the problems of trying to address and understand these mental realities—it is appallingly crude language that I am using because it is not articulated like that: it is a level of action, and all we can do is put these words to it that would be appropriate conversationally. She gets some glimpse of herself as Mr Jones and says "No" to it.

Mr Jones's way of behaving arouses the very exploitative aspects of him that she resents so much. At the moment of owning this in her, she owns it rather than dispelling it: two quite different inner activities. In the moment of ownership she takes responsibility for this Miss Jones in her; he becomes incorporated into her own pattern of integration and, because no longer disowned, it is modified.

So, then, on the Tuesday, when she walked into Mr Jones's office, she met a more benign figure than she had encountered before, and that is because this other activity whereby she expelled the hated aspect in herself had been lessened and no longer provocatively stimulated Mr Jones.

There are two sources of action in Mary, and the behavioural activity of Mr Jones depends on which is dominant. I refer to these two sources as "creative" as opposed to "discordant". The Mr Jones to whom she reports on the Wednesday is different from the one to whom she had reported on previous days. The question that confronts us is whether it is valid to ask which is the real Mr Jones; and so we just need to go into this business of inner source. I think it is necessary to posit that when Mary glimpses this patterning inside her, in some way she feels bad about it. She feels bad about something. She feels badly about the action in relation to the figure—that is, disowning. In the clinical situation, the me at whom her activity was directed represented what I refer to as the Miss Jones inside her. I was the representative of this inner patterning. The disowning action that flows from this muffles the autonomous source. It is like erasing the speech on an audio tape at the same time as recording over it. She glimpses, then, this activity of hers, and the only thing that makes sense of what occurs outwardly is that an option, a choice, occurs within. There is an option to reverse this activity. And there is some glimpse of the activity flowing from the discordant source. The autonomous creative source is the core of the self: the source of inner creative action. When this is rubbed out—never entirely, but largely—then this source of action is only faintly operative within the personality. It seems that once the discordant source is glimpsed and owned, it in itself ceases to be discordant but, rather, becomes part of the creative core. The very action of recognition, of owning—the only way I can put it is owning as opposed to disowning—itself changes the reality. So it is the action in relation to, that changes within. This change, though, occurs through an option. This, I think, is at the root of our problem with the model that we operate from within psychoanalysis: that it is based on the idea that there is an "it", a drive that occurs within, and not an option. I am sure the drive theory is wrong, as is also Freud's structural model, which derives from it.

Psychoanalysis has had many different theorists. Winnicott comes along with an idea of a true self and a false self, and this theory gets pasted onto Freud's theory, and it does not fit. Melanie Klein comes along with her theory, and it gets pasted on in just the same way: although it is discordant with Freud's theory, it gets pasted on all the same. I think the only two people who tried, in different ways, not to do this were Fairbairn and Bion. Fairbairn challenged the original theory, but although he said that libido is object-seeking, it remained a drive the source of which lay in some unchosen part of the personality. It was not an object that had been opted for.

There was a time when I was interested in those few people who had recovered from being alcoholics, drug addicts, prison recidivists, and so on. The number of such recoveries are not many, and I did a bit of informal research into a few of these. One of these people had been in and out of prison on numerous occasions, on drugs, chronically alcoholic, but at the time when I knew him, he was a journalist; he was married, he had a couple of children, he was a very creative journalist, he had written some books, and, it seems, he had made an extraordinarily good recovery. So I asked him to plot those moments that had led to his recovery. He explained to me that when he was in prison—and, of course, in prison you are not allowed any drink—he would say to himself, "I'm determined when I get out I'm not going to drink again." When he came out, he told me that even when he walked down the street, if there was a pub on that side of the street, he would walk across to the other side and walk down that side and then walk back and so on, tensed up in that way. As you can guess, it never worked. Back he went to prison again, but on this particular occasion he found himself in Wormwood Scrubs and was chatting one day to Klaus Fuchs, who had been imprisoned for 25 years for selling atomic secrets to the Russians. He told Fuchs about his drinking problem, and Fuchs listened to him and said, "If the will and the imagination come into open conflict, the imagination always wins." This was an amazing revelation: he realized then that his activity, his whole activity, was in the wrong sphere.

In the psychoanalytic literature—especially in Kleinian literature—such activity is spoken of as being done in phantasy. When people say it is done *in phantasy*, they imagine that it is not done at all, that it is not a true action—yet it is real action. So it is as if Fuchs might have been saying to this recovered addict that his activity needed to be in this phantasy sphere and not in external motor activity.

Now I want to come to my central point: that the real is the consequence of owning or accepting activity within, whereas what is not real comes about through disowning activity. I am going to correct this later, but I am just going back to Mary's statement that she thinks that really Mr Jones is not like that—she is making the judgement that the activity that was going on inside her before was a disowning one. Therefore disowning activity is judged not to be real, whereas accepting activity is judged to be real. Therefore we also have to say that the perception of the human world around us is governed by these inner emotional activities.

To come back now to the interpretation that I made to Mary: when I pointed out effectively that she was treating me as Mr Jones was treating her, there was contained in that a value judgement. It was not spoken, but it was inferred—that is, the value judgement was that to exploit a person in such a way is bad, certainly not good. The idea of analytic neutrality is an unachievable aim once we reach this level. The idea that it is comes from a failure to reach this level of experience. So I believe that Mary makes a value judgement that to exploit someone in the way Mr Jones is exploiting her is bad, and that if she is doing it, then, it is bad.

The logical conclusion, then, is that there are basic activities within the psyche to which values are assigned. What I am saying here is that disowning actions are judged to be worthless, and that these fashion behaviour or imagery that we refer to as untrue or not real, whereas actions of acceptance generate a behaviour or perception that is judged to be real. The interpretation was taken in by Mary: a change occurred from an emotional activity of disowning to one of acceptance, and the latter structured her perception, which was judged by her to be real, whereas the previous disowning activity was judged to be unreal. So when we talk of reality as opposed to unreality, the differentiation is made according to this inner judgement.

For me, it was a very exciting discovery that the difference between reality and unreality is based on two different inner emotional activities that attract the judgements of good and the bad. However, we need to refine what has been said, because there is a glaring fault in the argument. The weak link in the chain of argument is Mary's statement that Mr Jones is not really as she had thought him to be. Her statement, then, is that his reality is how he appears now, not as he did before. This means that she has a definition of the real within her. What does she mean when she says that after that Tuesday session Mr Jones was real? We are saying that an inner action that proceeds from an owning fashions human reality, which is, then, perceived in a different way from a disowning inner activity. Perception of our human world, then, is governed by basic emotional activities within the psyche.

I want, however, to come back to what was, to me, an exciting discovery: that the difference between reality and unreality, then, is in a moral categorization at this deep level of action, differentiated through the functioning of conscience at the individual level or at a moral valuation at the cultural level. I had already been convinced that reality within the human sphere is not to be defined according to whether or not something exists. When I was training as an analyst, the term "reality" was used in the sense that something existed, and I had an archaic sense that this was wrong. The philosopher who argues it most compellingly is John Macmurray, in his book *Freedom in the Modern World* (1932). I am sure that most professional philosophers tend to look down on Macmurray because he was a popular writer, but for me this is one of the most stunning books I have ever read. It is based, I believe, on the Reith Lectures which he gave in the early 1930s. In it he argues for the view, among other things, that when we talk of the real in the human sphere, what we mean is that which is significant, and he gives many examples. We may say, for instance, that the characters in a novel are very real, by which we mean that they are significant. Now the only thing I would add to this is that they signify the differing emotions of our internal world. Macmurray dismisses the positivistic definition of reality, but I am taking his thesis a step further: what I am saying is that reality is defined according to inner action that is judged to be good, whereas the inner action that is judged to be bad produces unreality. However, there is still a fault in this argument, which we will come to.

It may just be necessary to pause for a moment to establish that it is sensible to speak of unreality. Macmurray makes the point that a fictional character is real. So, he says: so what is unreal? And I will give you just one quote. He says, when a young woman faced with a proposal of marriage asks herself, "Do I really love him?" what does she mean? Macmurray says he does not know, but she is obviously aware that her feelings may be unreal. She is afraid that what she feels for the man may not be love, although she thinks that it is. And, naturally, she does not want to wake up someday to discover that she never really loved her husband but was deceived by her own feelings into thinking that she did. That is Macmurray.

It is similar with my patient Mary: she believed that the post-Tuesday Mr Jones was the real one, and not the ante-Tuesday Mr Jones. What Mary thought was that the real Mr Jones turned out not to be the real Mr Jones. How, though, is this possible, unless one is to posit that there is some judgement as to feelings that are real as opposed to those that are unreal? "Owning" and "disowning" is not quite right either, but they are the best verbs I can lay my hands on.

Do I have any basis on which to make such a judgement? When I disown I say that part of me is not part of me; I pretend that what is me is not me; I perceive myself disowning the nature of my own being. It is a deception, an untruth, a falseness to which we assign a moral valuation. The owning of the self is assenting to what is—that this is the truth—and we assign a moral valuation to that also. So the pre-Tuesday Mr Jones is a product of disowning inner action, and perception is governed by this activity. Before moving on to another point, I want to distinguish conscience from what Freud called the superego. Freud used the superego sometimes in the sense of conscience, but he also used it sometimes in the sense of a harsh tyrant, and my clinical experience is that when there is a harsh superego, it muffles conscience. I am for the moment taking it that it is conscience that judges real from unreal and not the superego.

Something needs to be cleared up in this argument. The more pragmatic readers will, quite naturally, say, "Well, here is this analyst just buzzing around in the inner world, he doesn't live in the real world. Mr Jones—the pre-Tuesday Mr Jones—was exploiting Mary." This is quite true: he held her back, he made her work till half past six without any extra pay, he didn't give her a lunch hour, and so on, and so on. "That is real", the reader will say. It is real. I observed it. It is on videotape. So what is the meaning behind the statement that really Mr Jones was not as she thought him to be? Therefore Mary, as I said, is making a judgement upon her own perception. But we have argued above that perceptions are governed by inner actions. Therefore she makes a judgement upon her own inner actions. These actions, she says, were not real; yet Mr Jones's pre-Tuesday state was real enough, we say. So there is a logical contradiction to be sorted out here. It is similar to the contradiction between Heraclitus and Parmenides 2,500 years ago, when Parmenides said that that which is *is* and that which is not *is not* and therefore there can be no change. Heraclitus, on the other hand, said that all being is in flow. Although Aristotle believed that he had solved the problem, I do not believe he did. The similarity is that what I am saying is: here is non-reality that is not reality, and this is what reality is. And yet, Mr Jones was doing this. So we must find a quality in the post-Tuesday reality that is not present in the pre-Tuesday reality. Just for a moment we might just define this quality and give it an algebraic formula: let us call the post-Tuesday reality X, and the pre-Tuesday reality $-X$. I call it $-X$ because there is the sense, I think, in the judgement that is being made, that this was not really Mr Jones, whereas now this is the real Mr Jones: the post-Tuesday fellow is the real Mr Jones. There is, I think, the judgement being made that this prior state of affairs lacked something, and therefore I call it $-X$. The minus aspect comes from this disowning inner action. This inner state of affairs lacks wholeness, unitedness, inter-relatedness—especially inter-relatedness. In this model there is the notion of parts. Is there one word that would cover all these, so that we can abandon algebraic symbols and return to the world of common discourse? I believe that the simplest word, the word that has stood the test of time, the word upon which Socrates based his moral philosophy, is quite simply—the good. In the human sciences you just cannot get along without a concept of the good. The good means wholeness; the bad signifies a lack. You cannot get along without such a concept. Aristotle tried to solve the Parmenides problem by saying that there was being that lacked something, which he called being that was in potency, as opposed to being that enjoyed fullness, which he referred to as pure act. We judge one thing to be real, another unreal: pre-Tuesday Mr Jones unreal, and post Tuesday Mr Jones real, true or false, genuine or fake. There has to be an underlying concept that carries and supports these meanings. It is very difficult to define and conceptualize, but that does not mean that it is not real. It reminds me of a philosopher who had his feet very much on the ground, who used to say: if you are standing on the kerb of a road and there is a fog, and there is a car coming through the fog, it is just as real as if there were no fog; just because you cannot see the car's outline clearly, it is just as real, and in fact it is more dangerous, if you don't see it clearly. So I make the same point about the good. It is real, although it is very difficult to define it and see it clearly. It is the quality of being that enables us to speak of someone being genuine and another false, a character in a novel being real from one that is unreal, the authentic from the inauthentic.

Therefore –X, then, becomes the absence of good. Plato and Aristotle and also the scholastic philosophers defined the evil or bad as the absence of good. So I come back to this point. It means that when we distinguish reality on the basis of a quality in being to which we refer as good, we are making a judgement about the inner owning activity. This, I believe, is what we mean when we use the term "reality testing": are the inner emotional activities of an embracing, owning nature, or not? That, in a way, is the end of the argument—the main point I want to make—but I am going to add just a couple more things.

I believe that this way of understanding reality testing is very different from what is commonly understood by the term within psychoanalytic discourse. It is usually understood to mean that such and such exists or does not exist. The positivist approach to reality is meaningful if applied to the inanimate world, but it fails utterly when the same principles are applied to the intentional activity of human beings; what I am adding to this is the startling discovery that in the human world the real is distinguished from the unreal according to the quality of the inner emotional activity.

There is, then, of course this very tricky question of how the real is to be determined inwardly by the individual and also by the scientist. The inner indicator, it seems clear to me, is conscience. However, this is not enough on its own. Conscience is the inner structure, but I believe that there are two other elements: time and prophecy. We either have to say that the good is that determined by the opinions of the majority, and God forbid that we should ever let that be our criterion, but then we have to seek another. In what we have been saying, the inner action that is good is difficult to determine. Mary knows it through inference. Frequently a false trail has been pursued, either individually or politically, and it is only over time that its wrongness becomes apparent. In the history of ideas, certain ideas that had been accepted for centuries have been found ultimately to be wrong—and sometimes the consequences have been disastrous. The problem, of course, is to see it at the time. Throughout history societies have thrown up those few individuals who have pointed to a good path for humans to follow. This is what I refer to as prophecy. Karl Jaspers used this term, the *axial era*, for that period from about 800 to 400 BC, when these great prophets appeared on the human scene: Isaiah, Jeremiah, and Ezekiel in Israel, Socrates in

Greece, Zarathustra in Persia, Mahavira and Buddha in India, Lao Tzu in China, and so on. In our own times, I can mention Kierkegaard, Solzhenitsyn, Gandhi, and a host of others. The giants of literature have also been our prophets: Shakespeare, George Eliot, Tolstoy, Dostoevsky, and many others. What I am trying to get at is that this conscience in the individual, this quality of vision that I call prophecy, is proclaimed by one but finds an echo in many, not just at the time of their own lives but throughout history. It is neither the majority of people who hold such views nor the dominant part of the personality of the individual but, rather, a peripheral part of the individual, which finds a resonance in the voice of the prophet.

Time is the other element. Full judgement requires the passage of time. Duration, of which time is the measurement, is an inherent feature of reality. You look out of your window, see an oak tree, and snap a photograph, and you say: "That's an oak tree." It is not. The reality exists from the acorn to its demise two hundred years later. Living things are not static but in movement, and this is also true of human reality. To grasp the real in its wholeness, it is necessary to grasp, in a single act of comprehension, the three elements—conscience, prophecy, and time—and these three give us a window into the unseen reality that lives in the depths.

So when we talk of the pursuit of reality, we mean that which partakes of an accepting emotional process, as opposed to one that repudiates it. The human sciences have, I believe, through falsely aping the natural sciences, failed to comprehend what humans mean when they designate something as real. This is a fallacy that is so basic that it has, I believe, spawned a whole host of misconceptions within the social sciences. I am proposing a radical re-orientation of perspective.

Note

1. Berlin (1980, p. 81) specifically says that Vico used the spelling "*caussas*" rather than the usual spelling, "*causas*".

2. *Cause* is not the right word, because it implies that Mr Jones was not free. Let us say that it *invited* Mr Jones to behave in the way he did.

CHAPTER NINE

Religion and consciousness

I believe that "revealed religion" is antithethical to consciousness, whereas "natural religion" is conducive to it. This chapter is an attempt to substantiate this statement. In order to do this, I need, first, to define the difference between revealed religion and natural religion, then to elaborate my theory of how something comes to consciousness, and, finally, to show how revealed religion prevents it, whereas natural religion favours it. As each of these elements in the argument is in itself a huge topic and each is open to debate, this chapter is necessarily a sketch or an outline that requires considerable elaboration.

When people say that they are religious or not religious, they conceptualize religion according to one particular form of it—the form that has been transmitted into Western civilization through the agency of the Judaeo–Christian community of the faithful. I include Islam in the Judaeo–Christian tradition. The idea that this one particular form constitutes the whole of religion is such a deeply rooted assumption that, I have found it usually takes more than just intellectual argument to open people to the notion of any religion other than this one. I shall try first to outline what is meant by revealed religion.

My easiest path is to take the most extreme example of it. This has the advantage of highlighting the fact that it is rare in the real world to find either revealed religion or natural religion in the pure state.

Within much revealed religion there are traits of natural religion, and within the latter the tendency to degenerate into the former is always present—and I use the word "degenerate" advisedly.

In revealed religion an almighty being suddenly overpowers an individual, who becomes enslaved to this extraneous force. This almighty being is referred to as God. This god is revealed in a moment of ecstasy. The clearest example of this is the way in which Allah was revealed to Muhammad. In the midst of an ecstatic trance, the teachings of Allah were revealed to Muhammad, who dictated them and had them transcribed onto tablets, which became the Koran. Muhammad himself was a slave in submission to the Voice of Allah. It was believed that there were permanent tablets of stone in the heavens, which became transcribed into the Koran through the human agency of Muhammad. Any possibility of thinking, which is an inner creative process, is crushed under the force of such an ecstatic experience.

An authority on Islam has this to say about Muhammad: "From the books of tradition we learn that the prophet was subject to ecstatic seizures. He is reported to have said that when inspiration came to him he felt as it were the painful sounding of a bell. Even in cold weather his forehead was bathed in sweat" (Guillaume, 1976, p. 56).

However, this same ecstatic seizure of the individual—or sometimes a group of individuals—is a re-appearing theme in the Judaeo–Christian tradition. In Judaism one needs only to consider these two passages—the first from the Book of Exodus, the second from Isaiah:

> Now at daybreak on the third day there were peals of thunder on the mountain and lightning flashes, a dense cloud, and a loud trumpet blast, and inside the camp all the people trembled. Then Moses led the people out of the camp to meet God; and they stood at the bottom of the mountain. The mountain of Sinai was entirely wrapped in smoke, because Yahweh had descended on it in the form of fire. Like smoke from a furnace the smoke went up, and the whole mountain shook violently. Louder and louder grew the sound of the trumpet. Moses spoke, and God answered him with peals of thunder. [Exodus, 19: 1–5][1]

> I saw the Lord Yahweh seated on a high throne; his train filled the sanctuary, above him stood seraphs, each one with six wings: two to cover its face, two to cover its feet and two for flying.
>
> And they cried out one to another in this way, "Holy, holy, holy is Yahweh Sabaoth. His glory fills the whole earth."
>
> The foundations of the threshold shook with the voice of the one who cried out, and the Temple was filled with smoke. I said: "What a

> wretched state I am in! I am lost for I am a man of unclean lips and I
> live among a people of unclean lips, and my eyes have looked at the
> King, Yahweh Sabaoth." [Isaiah, 6: 1–5]

Then, within Christianity, one need only to think of the Pentecost
experience, as it is described in the Acts of the Apostles:

> When Pentecost day came round, they had all met in one room, when
> suddenly they heard what sounded like a powerful wind from
> heaven, the noise of which filled the entire house in which they were
> sitting; and something appeared to them that seemed like tongues of
> fire; these separated and came to rest on the head of each one of them.
> They were filled with the Holy Spirit, and began to speak foreign
> languages as the Spirit gave them the gift of speech. [Acts of the
> Apostles, 2: 1–4]

and also, in the same book, the incident that has become known as the
Conversion of St Paul on the road to Damascus:

> Suddenly, while he was travelling to Damascus and just before he
> reached the city, there came a light from heaven all round him. He
> fell to the ground, and he heard a voice saying, "Saul, Saul, why are
> you persecuting me?" "Who are you, Lord?" he asked, and the voice
> answered, "I am Jesus, and you are persecuting me." [Acts of the
> Apostles, 2: 1–4]

These are all shamanistic experiences, where a transcendent power is
believed to have taken possession of the believer and in whose power
the priest, prophet, or shaman becomes the automatic translator of the
godly message. Yahweh tells Jeremiah: "There! I am putting my words
into your mouth" (Jeremiah, 1: 9), and much of the Koran is a record of
what Muhammad said while in ecstatic states.

How is one to understand the psychological process behind these
experiences? I think what I have been describing would be formulated
by a psychoanalyst as a split-off part of the self taking possession of the
whole personality, and it occurs because in the narcissistic part of the
personality a wound has been incurred, and the god arises as an
epiphenomenon of this insulted self. It is, then, the insulted self that
takes over the personality. God is the insulted self. An example comes
to mind from an incident described by a colleague (personal communication):

> The analyst had a moment of deep empathic understanding of this
> woman's deprived childhood. She conveyed this to the patient, and
> there were a few moments of emotional "togetherness" of a deep

kind. Then the cruel event occurred: the session, like an insensate
executioner, came to an abrupt end. The woman was hurt to the
quick. The next day she would not come into the consulting-room;
she declared with emphatic certainty that there were hidden micro-
phones in the room, and no rational argument could dissuade her
from her conviction.

An irrational god had taken over. So the irrational god is the insulted
self puffed up into the full majesty of an awe-inspiring god. I think the
kernel of ecstasy lies in the psychological process whereby one part
of the self inflates and overpowers the rest of the personality. This part
is named "god" in the Judaeo–Christian culture. It is such a violent
marauder to the personality that it is ejected and experienced as outside the self. We know that the voices heard by a schizophrenic are
thought by him to come from outside, whereas they are from within
the personality.[2] This part of the personality that is called "god" is
bribable. If I offer sacrifice to this great power, I may buy his mercy. In
this lies the basis of magic and superstition. This, I believe, is the origin
of the god revealed in Judaism, in Christianity, and in Islam. Although
there are great differentiations through the cultural colourings within
these three great historical religions, yet, I believe, the psychological
origins of the powerful god who dominates all three are as I have
described. I dare to say what I have described is the psychological
explanation for what is known as revealed religion. What makes it so
enduring is that it is always intertwined with natural religion. Disen-
tangling the two is, I believe, an urgent task for our present time.

Natural religion arises out of ontological reflection. Ontology is that
branch of philosophy the sphere of enquiry of which is reality itself.
One might put it that the rest of philosophy and of science are concerned with specifics: the nature of time, the origins of life, the nature
of consciousness, epistemology, perception, cognition, the historical
process, chemistry, physics, astronomy, biology, sociology, religion,
aesthetics, and so on. All these disciplines seek understanding of a
circumscribed section of reality. ontology studies reality itself. Its goal
is to comprehend reality. In the way that Archimedes had a sudden
insight into what we call volume, so the goal of ontology is that the
student of this subject acquire insight into the nature of reality or, more
accurately, have an act of comprehension the object of which is reality
itself. This is something that each person has to do for himself. The
teacher of ontology can lecture upon it, giving perspectives from different angles, using analogies, but the act of comprehension has to

occur within each individual. One thing is certain: this act will never occur if there is some background assumption that there is a powerful Creator responsible for the world we see around us, which is named his creation, or this belief has to be banished to another part of the personality in order for it to be possible. Inner creative acts cannot occur in the presence of a powerful judging god. The doctrines that come out of revealed religion prevent an act that comprehends reality. They lay down a system of belief that interferes with the possibility of that act of comprehension. Banishment of this belief is, I think, a precondition for an unprejudiced inquiry into the nature of reality. Rather in the way that a painter needs to banish his knowledge of the structural forms that are in front of him if he is to represent faithfully the coloured sensations he perceives, so the ontological enquirer needs to banish those beliefs in order to see (in the mental sense) existence itself. Only in this way will a new world of comprehension come into being. These are remarks about what might be called preliminary methodology that is essential for ontological reflection.

In this reflection upon existence itself, the first thing that strikes the mind is its absolute character. One cannot say that existence *is*, but it might just as well not be. The conclusion that existence might just as well not be is derived from belief in a god as is revealed in Judaism, Christianity, or Islam: that such a god could click his fingers and annihilate existence. This belief prevents the act of comprehension that I am talking about. It is very difficult for people to banish such a belief system: to get behind it, as it were, to what immediately confronts the mind. There is another class of thinkers: those who are so keen to alienate themselves from such a supernaturalist belief system that they restrict the sphere of knowledge to that alone which is processed through the senses. This is the obverse side of the same belief system deriving ultimately from revealed religion. But if the ontological inquirer can detach himself from these beliefs, then the mind is able to let itself be confronted with existence in all its starkness. In such an insight it becomes clear that intrinsic to existence is that it is necessary, it is absolute, it cannot not-be. It just is. There can be no explanation for it. The idea of an explanation is that there is something outside existence, but the only such category is non-existence. To suggest that non-existence explains existence is absurd. Existence is its own explanation. This is what we mean when we say that existence is absolute. I am not sure if I am understood? I cannot say it more clearly. The task is to comprehend it.

If, by a fiction, I place my own self outside the object of my scrutiny, then I call what I am doing philosophy. If I abandon this fiction and place my own existence into the melting-pot of the object of my scrutiny, then my endeavour is religious. Philosophy becomes religion at the point when I put my own self into existence. I exist, so it is by a fiction that I remove myself from the object of enquiry. It is irrational, it is an arrogance of mind, an absurdity to extricate myself from existence, as if I could, by some sleight of hand, pretend that I do not exist. I exist: so my own self is in the existence that I comprehend in a simple act of insight. This fundamental act of comprehension is the foundation stone of natural religion. It has been defined by C. C. J. Webb thus:

> Those things in religion, the appeal of which meets a universal response, whether they be statements about the essential and eternal nature of reality, apprehended by the reason as true in their own right, from whatever source they have been learned, or whether they be precepts of conduct, the moral obligatoriness of which, when once propounded, is also perceived, as Kant would say, *a priori*, these will constitute, so it has seemed to some, natural religion. [1915, pp. 33–34].

If this is accepted, then this insight into my nature has consequences for the way I live my life. I am learning something about myself through this ontological reflection. It is not something that is outside myself and therefore of no personal relevance. When people refer to an ethical system that is non-religious, they mean one that is not rooted in revealed religion; I believe that all ethics has a religious basis, but of the kind that I am defining here. Religion has been defined in many ways, but, although restricted and limited to *praxis*, the simplest and the one that, in its simplicity, holds conviction for me is that of Tolstoy: "Religion is concerned with how one lives one's life."

If I live it according to the principles of revealed religion, the overriding principle is that I act in accordance with the ordinances of the god who has revealed himself to me via his representative, be it Moses, Jesus, or Muhammad. I am, of course, able to think and elaborate within the boundaries that have been set me by what has been revealed. I am not free, however, to generate thoughts that are in contradiction to the divine dictates. My belief has limited the scope of my enquiry. In revealed religion the origin of enquiry is in an imposed dictum; in natural religion the origin lies in a rational act of creative insight. The person who passed from being a believer in revealed religion to being rationally convinced in the ontological basis of natural religion was Tolstoy. Having been brought up a devout believer in the Russian Orthodox Church, he came utterly to repudiate it, but he embraced natural religion on the basis of his own rational conviction.

* * *

I want to examine as closely as possible that primordial act of understanding in which existence is comprehended. My contention is that this act, by which a reality becomes a possession of the mind, is a creation. At first sight it may seem impossible that a reality that exists and that has existed prior to the advent of a human mind—before what palaeontologists call *hominization*—could in any way be the object of a mental creation. Yet one has to ask whether the act by which Newton "discovered" gravity was a creative one. Does the fact that the forces that came to be described by Newton as gravity pre-existed him and pre-existed any such formulation gainsay the fact that his insight was a creative act of mind—that he created the form that we know as gravity? I wish to contend that all those forms of reality, from Archimedes' insight into volume to Einstein's theory of relativity, are the creative acts of seminal thinkers. One could think of ways in which this contradiction might be resolved—in particular Hume's and Kant's formulations—but I prefer not to go down that path but to propose that there are certain antinomies in our apprehension of reality that are beyond the capacity of the mind to grasp. I realize that this principle has its dangers: that we might fall back upon this comfortable nostrum every time we encounter a difficult-to-grasp contradiction. However, there is also danger the other way: that we deny a bit of experience because we cannot make it fit the limitations of our minds, which are unable to integrate two pieces of experience that appear to be contradictory. The failure to recognize the limitations of the mind can lead to an arrogance that ultimately distorts our comprehension of reality. Of these two errors, I believe the latter is particularly current among contemporary thinkers. The former was more in evidence in that cultural epoch in Europe known as "Christendom".

You might ask, "On what ground do I state that the act of insight is creative in its nature?" I would define a creation as a reality the origin of which is generated in the mind. There is the view that the mind is a *tabula rasa*, a waxen tablet, upon which reality imprints itself. I cannot refute this view, although I think it is false. Let me correct this categorical statement. I think that there are elements existing in the mind in this form, but that there are also elements that have been created by the mind, and that in every mind there is a mixture of these two elements: the imprinted and the created.[3]

It should be clear that the key elements in the mind deriving from revealed religion are of the imprinted kind. "Does God exist?" Yes. "Why?" Because he has told us so. "Is murder wrong?" Yes. "Why?" Because it is against the sixth commandment. And so on. As I said a while back, there is, concurrent with this kind of mental presence of elements, a dictatorial figure to which the mind is in servitude. The greater this figure's empire over the mind, the more numerous and more dominant are such imprinted elements. So, for instance, in a religious fundamentalist this servitude is almost total, but in what is known in Anglican circles as a "Broad Church" it is much less so. But my contention is that it is the dominant and circumscribing form, the form legitimated by what we know as revealed religion. The presence of a harsh dictator is familiar to psychiatrists in the mental disorder that has been given the name of "schizophrenia", where a powerful voice commands the individual to act mentally and practically in this way or that way. It is my contention that this is present with particular clarity in schizophrenia but it also present in other conditions that are categorized as pathological, such as bipolar disorder, obsessive compulsive disorder, psychopathy, and hysteria. This oppressive dictator forbids thought, forbids the generation of thoughts, forbids creation.

You will see from the way I am developing this argument that I am making an equation between revealed religion and those mental conditions that psychiatry designates as pathological. A discipline that designates this mental condition as pathological in contrast to another that is sane is a very powerful authority in the land. We all know the gross misuse to which this power has been put in certain societies. What we need to ask, however, is what the principle governing the diagnosis is.

There is a judgement that certain mental conditions are pathological. On what ground is the observer who makes this judgement standing? I believe it comes from the standpoint of someone who has had an Archimedes type of insight either in itself or in one of its modes. One needs to think of the huge revolution in scientific thinking that occurred in the epoch that has been named, understandably, the "Enlightenment". That epoch could be defined as the period during which the great insights into the workings of our world were first formulated in a thorough way, and this form of thinking became, in this era, legitimated by society. The names of these thinkers—Copernicus, Galileo, Tycho Brahe, Kepler, Newton, and many others—are known to all. The scientific insights that lay behind these great developments were all creative in nature. The capacity of the human mind to understand the workings of the world through creative insights was the foundation stone of the Enlightenment. It was the core value that structured thinking during that epoch. It is against that backdrop that a series of mental conditions were defined as pathological: that is, because they handicapped the creative mental functioning.

The core scientific insight is the comprehension of reality itself . As this is also the foundation stone of natural religion, science and religion are differentiated according to the principle that in the latter the focus is upon the consequences for the observer, and in the former upon the use to which the insights can be put for the sake of the observer.

I shall need to come back to the relationship between natural religion and revealed religion, but I want now to substantiate my statement that natural religion and consciousness are concurrent partners, whereas revealed religion is antithetical to consciousness.

When I speak of consciousness, I mean consciousness of one's own self—the process whereby I become aware that I am shy, courageous morally but not physically, jealous, a good judge of character, snobbish, patient with young people but intolerant with older people, and so on. In other words, I come into possession of a picture of my own character. How is this possible? It is the outcome of a scientific observation. But how do I manage to be a scientific observer of myself? The Spanish mystic, John of the Cross (2000), has this line in one of his poems: "*Vivo sin vivir en mi* [which translates: I live without living in myself]. What on earth does he mean? I resort to a psychoanalytic piece of understanding to answer this question. Psychoanalytic research is confident that I am able to put myself into another individual, into an ideology, into a group, into my body, into a sexual activity, into an auto-generated ecstasy. For our present enquiry I take just the last of these: that I can put myself into an auto-generated state of the particular type that we call ecstasy. I quote an example of this from Marion Milner's book *An Experiment in Leisure* (1987):

> I was one day driving over the mountain road to Granada in the Spring, the cone-shaped, red-earthed foothills all covered with interlacing almond blossom. Also it was the first sunny weather after days of rain, so that I was filled with exultation as we climbed higher and higher into the clear mountain air. I was full of that kind of exultation which makes one above oneself, I felt powerful and im-

portant, as if it was somehow my doing that the country was so lovely, or at least that I was cleverer than other people in having got myself there to see it—I was certainly thankful that I was not as other men are. Then I noticed the character of the country was changing . . . but as soon as I tried to look back in my own mind, I found there was nothing there, only a rather absurd memory of my own exultation but no living vision of what had caused it. Then I remembered the Pharisee and the publican . . . at once the look of the country was different, I was aware only of it, not of myself at all, and always afterwards it was that bit of Spain that I seemed to possess in imagination. [pp. 208–209]

In this passage she puts herself into her exaltation and then extracts herself from it. When John of the Cross says that he does not live in himself, I think he means that he does not live in an exalted self. The matter to note here is that when Marion Milner was *in* her exalted state, she saw neither the object nor herself. When she came out of her exalted state, she both saw the object and also the state she had been in. My thesis is that the core of the person is reality in its absoluteness, but the comprehension of that is a creative act, and a product of it is awareness of oneself. One could put it that when Marion Milner was in that exalted state, she was mad, but she became sane at the moment when she withdrew herself from the exaltation and observed the state she had been in. Therefore I am drawing a parallel between the ecstatic state as instanced in the cases I have quoted in revealed religion and the act of comprehension inherent in natural religion: that the latter is sympathetic to the development of consciousness, whereas the former is antithetical to it. I would go further than this and say that natural religion is a necessary foundation for the development of self-awareness, whereas revealed religion strangles the possibility of it.

My rationale for saying this is that an inner creative act is responsible for both the presence of the object and awareness of the state of the self: that the two are interdependent: that the object is known through being created, and here it is necessary to formulate my theory as to how objects in the outer world are known. There are, I believe, two independent sources of information. The senses process sensations that are registered as colour, shape, noise, touch, smell, and taste. The act of insight grasps reality in itself. An act of belief—or what Collingwood (1969) calls a "metaphysical presupposition"—puts the two together. An inadequate analogy would be someone seeing a bird sitting on a telegraph wire and, at the same time, hearing birdsong and believing that what is heard comes from the object seen. As the act of comprehension is a creation, so it endows the object observed with this quality. The mind is the constructive organizer, but then the question arises: "Why does this endow the personality with awareness of it-self?" I think it is that the mind can only grasp itself through its activity. Its activity gives, as it were, a peephole into the nature of the mind. If the mind is inactive, then there is no window to its nature. In the ecstatic condition typical of revealed religion the mind is in passive servitude to the tyrant god.

I have mentioned the presence of an exalted power in revealed religion, which, I have suggested, originates in an insulted self that puffs up into a god that paralyses the rest of the personality. It blinds the self to the object and also to awareness of the self's state, as in-stanced in the quote from Marion Milner's autobiographical work. This blindness to the self's nature is therefore always to be found when this ecstatic state is present. As revealed religion is founded upon such ecstatic experiences, the conclusion is that it smothers consciousness of the self.

I said earlier that neither natural religion nor revealed religion ever exist in the pure state. Some further reflection upon this is necessary. As already stated, the origin of natural religion lies in an act in which existence itself is comprehended. This act is ahistorical. There is no taint of the particular in it. Just as this act always becomes conjoined to the sensory input through a metaphysical predisposition, so this a-historical act always accretes to itself historical and cultural forms. So natural religion always exists in a place and time that colour its expres-sion, but this is not central to it—its essence is ahistorical, whereas revealed religion originates in a specific time and place and is therefore historical in its essence. So also, in revealed religion there is some admixture of natural religion. The more the latter is present within it, the less fundamentalist it is, and vice versa. So, for instance, if a sacred text is believed to have been given by God as it is and any scientific exegesis is forbidden, then we have revealed religion in a very pure state. However, if it is held that the meaning of the text can only be elucidated faithfully through textual analysis and historical recon-struction, then there is a considerable presence of natural religion. However, if the core of the religion lies in an ahistorical ontological act in which existence is comprehended and states of mind are judged in relation to that, then we are in the presence of natural religion, which is also the standard from which mental states are judged to be sane or mad, but if that core lies in the ecstatic experience of a particular individual or group at a particular point of time and in a particular place in which a powerful god reveals his message, then we are in the presence of revealed religion, and this form crushes creative insight and therefore consciousness of the self.

I have spoken as if revealed religion were confined to the Judaeo–Christian tradition. It is here, I believe, that we see it in its purest form. A god chose this People; a god revealed himself to this man; god became man. This man was god. It is in the Judaeo–Christian–Islamic tradition that these doctrines have been unashamedly spelt out as official doctrines. However, the same phenomenon is to be found in the Eastern religions. It is said that the Buddha told his followers before he died that they were not to take what he said because he had said it, but to test what he said against their experience of life. However, degeneration set in, and the Buddha became unofficially divinized in many places. Revealed religion begins to emerge as soon as a single person or group of people become divinized and the dictates of this person are substituted for my own creative thinking activity. So these two religious forms exist in the atheist as much as in the theist. They are mental modes existing in all of us. Revealed religion and natural religion exist also in the individual. Consciousness of the self emerges in direct ratio to the extent to which natural religion displaces revealed religion.

It is my contention that natural religion is necessary for the development of awareness of the self. Here lies the true bridge between religion and consciousness.

Notes

1.   All quotes from the Bible taken from *The Jerusalem Bible*, 1966, unless otherwise indicated.

2.   The experience of God as immanent as testified by mystics is in truth existence in all its absoluteness and is the result of ontological reflection.

3.   The British psychoanalyst, Wilfred Bion, called these two modes of presence in the mind "beta elements" and "alpha elements". The former are imprinted and the latter created.

CHAPTER TEN

The true god and the false god

A patient was late one day because snow on the road had delayed her, and she was angry. I mentioned this to Wilfred Bion in supervision, and he said to me: "You must say to her that God has sent down that snow to get between you and her." There is a god that gets in the way of two people coming to know each other. There is a god who interferes with my thinking; there is a god who demands that I follow his instructions; there is a god who punishes me if I think for myself; there is a god who sanctions my sadism, a god who encourages my masochism, a god who fosters my greed, who inflates my envy, who fans my jealousy, a god who possesses me but despises me, a god who solves problems by obliterating them.

You may recognize in this portrait of god, traits with which you are familiar from the reading of the Bible, the Torah, or the Koran. Embodied in these ancient texts are aspects of this god that I have been trying to describe. There are also other aspects that I shall come to later. This cultural expression is manifest in the psychology of the individual. I can find in myself and my patients traces of this god. This god is a narcissistic object seen from one particular angle. The narcissistic object is many-faceted, and it is a part of the self that has been expelled and embodied either in a figure, or figures, outside. The outer figure is then enveloped by this part of the self, in the way that Wilfred Bion describes: "The object, angered at being engulfed, swells up, so to speak, and suffuses and controls the piece of personality that engulfs it (1956, p. 40).

These are the facets of the narcissistic object. The figure, who is an embodiment of the narcissistic object, is extremely sensitive to any hurt. This is the core of the narcissistic object, and is not immediately obvious to external perception. For instance, when a patient installs the analyst as narcissistic object, she perceives him as a god, as an elevated human being in her conscious conceptualization, but unconsciously registers the inner sensitivity to hurt. Patients who are narcissistic are extremely sensitive to hurt, and because they believe that others are the same as themselves, they believe that the analyst is similarly vulnerable to hurt as themselves. In this they may be right or may not be right, but it is a belief that they have that is not put to experimental test.

This narcissistic object gets established in this way: The first thing we infer is that this god is present in the personality as a potential for embodiment. This god never exists as a spiritual reality but always as a god incarnate in a particular person or institution. The prophets whose sayings are recorded in the Old Testament continually chided Israel for chasing after false gods:

> Trouble is coming to the man who says to the piece of wood, "Wake up!"
> to the dumb stone: "On your feet!"
> (And that is the oracle.)
> Plated it may be with gold and silver,
> but not a breath of life inside it.
> What is the use of a carved image,
> or for its maker to carve it at all?
> It is a thing of metal, a lying oracle,
> What is the use of its maker trusting this
> and fashioning dumb idols. [Habbakuk, 2: 19–20]

False gods were gods embodied in statues, trees, rocks, or rivers: a type of religion known as *animism*. The prophets attacked this form of worship unmercifully. The ferocity of their attack might give a psychoanalyst a hint that they themselves were subject inwardly to such a worship or that they were not entirely free of it themselves. It is clear that the prophets were trying to purify themselves and Israel of an embodied god and substitute for this a pure spiritual reality. However, they never managed to cleanse Yahweh of all anthropomorphic elements. He always remained a possession of the Israelites. It was a god who had chosen this race rather than those around as his favourite son

Is Ephraim my dear son?
Is he my darling child?
For as often as I speak against him,
I do remember him still.
Therefore my heart yearns for him;
I will surely have mercy on him,
says the Lord. [Jeremiah, 31: 20][1]

So the god, as part of the narcissistic structure, is ready for embodiment. But how does the embodiment take place? The answer is that the figure or institution has to be a willing host for such an embodiment. The host then has to demonstrate one of the elements of the narcissistic structure. I am going now to sketch just one correlate of the god. God and this correlate are just two elements of the narcissistic structure, though under the *principle of inclusion*,[2] they are one reality with two manifestations.

So this correlate of god is a figure who is hurt by the slightest criticism or neglect. In religious devotion this is seen most clearly in the Christian rite, known as the Stations of the Cross, where the devotee believes that Jesus, who is god, is deeply wounded by every sin. This rests on a theory of redemption whereby the sin of Adam was an infinite offence to the Lord Almighty, who then sent His Son to make reparation to God, His Father, for this infinite offence. We see here a god who is deeply wounded by an insult. This devotional attitude gained great strength in the Middle Ages and still continues today in many Christian communities, particularly within the Catholic Church. The Old Testament is also redolent with the theme of Yahweh who has been offended by Israel's infidelities.

It is not difficult to see how this devotional attitude came about. It is the reification of a fundamental narcissistic attitude. It is typified when I am deeply wounded by the smallest slight and nurse this injury down the years. A man met a friend who said to him: "Good Lord, John, you are looking well today. When I saw you last week, I thought you were a bit off-colour . . ." The man was deeply offended that his friend should have said he was off-colour. "Me . . . off colour"—what an insult. He was so insulted by it that it entirely wiped out the encouraging statement that he was looking well on this particular day. I remember an occasion when a friend of mine asked a Spaniard to carry a letter for him to a friend in Spain, whither the Spaniard was going. It used to be a gentlemanly custom in Spain that if you asked someone to deliver a letter by hand, it was bad manners to seal the envelope. My English friend, not well up in this piece of Iberian etiquette, did not know it. The Spaniard was deeply insulted and would never talk to my English friend again.

The other aspect, already adumbrated, is that the wound is tended and nursed as though it were the greatest treasure. Adam's sin was quite a long time ago now ... but I still hear people beating their breasts about it. Analyst A said to Analyst B,

"Oh, you were analysed by Hanns Sachs, were you ...", and then looking down his nose said, "You know I was analysed by Freud."

Analyst B was still offended thirty years later and took revenge on Analyst A in a specific way. The hurt only makes sense if you put in the idea of a godlike ego:

"Do you not realize that you are insulting a royal personage? Did you not know that you are insulting the Lord Himself?"

So the extreme sensitivity to self-hurt and godhead are included in one another. They are two sides of one coin.

What can be observed as happening in an individual is writ large in the religions of revelation, most particularly Judaism, Christianity, and Islam. I want to make it clear that this god exists in all of us who have a narcissistic structure within us. It is not confined to religious people. I have encountered many patients who are atheists in conscious belief but who are enslaved to an ecstatic god within. Secularization has only changed the external forms, not the inner structure.

The god I have been trying to describe I call a "false god" in that it deceives the believer into trusting his dictates. He believes passionately in what the god directs. As I have tried to illustrate, this passionate belief cannot be shaken by reason, but it is more than that. The presence of this god precludes the possibility of thought. It is intrinsically antagonistic to thought. The inner correlate of the god is a psyche that is gelatinous in nature, with no source of action within and therefore submissive to the god. There is no option other than to capitulate in total submission. The god and gelatinous substance are two parts of an interlocking system. So the action and speech of a person dominated by such a system is false in another sense: that what is said does not represent the thought of a person. It is a pretend person, something standing for a person that could be there but is not. So this is the false god that exists in individuals governed by narcissism; it is also the god that rules all religious observances of a primitive or superstitious kind. As this is death to all thinking, it is completely right that the scientific community has, for the most part, embraced atheism.

I want now to turn to the true god. This is a god who is grasped through a supreme effort of thought—a god who is a triumph of the thinking process. Traces of this god can be found in Judaism, in Christianity, and in Islam, but it is largely overshadowed by the false god. The true god is reached through a deep and sustained reflection on the nature of reality. In our Western tradition, I think the philosopher who best represents this endeavour has been Spinoza. In the East the seers who are responsible for the school of thinking that produced the Upanishads showed the first, and deepest understanding of what I refer to as the true god. God is not a term that is ever used by these seers. They use terms like the THAT, the Absolute, or just Reality. Wilfred Bion called this same Reality "O". Through contemplative thought these seers came to understand the absolute character of reality. They also understood that reality is contingent. How these two can coexist is baffling to the mind, because they are mutually contradictory. Parmenides ran into this problem when he said that all change is illusion. If reality is absolute, then how can there be change? Parmenides, determined that the human mind should not be declared inadequate to any reasoning task, declared that because reality is absolute and because change is incompatible with absoluteness, then change must be an illusion. Yet common sense declares that change does occur in our world. Aristotle believed that he had solved this problem by saying that reality existed in two modes: "pure act" and "potency". By pure act, Aristotle meant what the Seers of the Upanishads meant by the THAT or the Absolute. Potency meant being capable of coming to Absoluteness. However, although Aristotle believed that he had solved this problem, yet he had not. He had given an account of the two horns of the dilemma and refused to deny either aspect, but he had not solved the problem.

We are confronted with this problem: that our minds are not capable of grasping this conceptually. Kant emphasized the limitation of our minds. We do not have the categories necessary to be able to grasp the problem. The progress of evolution may enable our progeny millions years hence to be able to solve this problem. What we need to acknowledge is that the human mind meets here a limitation rather than trying to deny either the absoluteness or the contingency or changeability of reality.

This absoluteness is arrived at through rational reflection and, I believe, probably requires mental discipline and virtue to achieve it. It is entirely different from the revelation of the Judaeo–Christian–Islamic God, which is through an ecstatic experience directly or by faith and tradition indirectly. The absoluteness of being is grasped through a personal act of insight. Although concentrated mental attention is necessary to achieve it, yet there is no experience here of a being outside myself calling me to obedience, submission, or discipleship. It is my own being understood as absolute. The latter is the true god: the former is the false god.

Now, you may ask, does this have any relevance to clinical work? I believe it does, and I approach it in this way: The seers of the Upanishads realized the absoluteness of being *and* that they were part of it. The realization that they were part of it—or, rather, they were IT—turned it from being a philosophical truth into religious one. In other words, it rendered a piece of knowledge about their own selves, and this piece of knowledge had a consequence. As Tolstoy said, religion is concerned with the meaning of life and how we should live. Realization about the absoluteness of the self necessarily has a consequence. I say "necessarily" because the necessary is the essential attribute of the Absolute. This realization led the Buddha, who traced the emotional consequences of this realization, to stress that attachment to what is contingent, to what is passing, is to ignore the central character of our being. It is worth noting, however, that the Buddha also recognized that to ignore or despise the contingent nature of our being was to enact in the religious–moral domain what Parmenides conceptualized philosophically. The famous "middle way" of the Buddha is notoriously difficult to achieve. It requires us to realize the limitations of our minds at the same time as to think continually.

So the absoluteness of being is a truth arrived at through reflection. It is the product of thought. The thinking process has produced an intuition that penetrates through into the nature of being. It is an insight that is grounded in rational processes. I call the Absolute the "true god": I call the god revealed in the religions of Judaism, Christianity, and Islam a false god or, rather, a god who is a mixture of the true and the false. Within this religious tradition it has been the role of mystics to purify the revealed god of its anthropomorphic accretions.

Due to the fact that they bear a loyalty to their religious cult, they only achieve it on the basis of a split.

* * *

The false god is part of the narcissistic system. Other elements in that system are a denigrated object, a state of being merged with the embodied God, a paranoia towards the embodied God, the psyche in a jelly-like state, and absence of creative capacity. As Bion says in his paper "On Arrogance" (1957), this set-up is the living relic of a primitive catastrophe. It is a traumatic event fossilized.

I have referred to the effect of this godly activity within the personality at the beginning. The concept of *embodiment* is central to understanding the effects. There is no thinking process within the personality but only the appearance of such. Embodiment of the thoughts of a god has been substituted for thinking. (Some of these gods have names within the psychoanalytical religion—Freud, Jung, Klein, Bion, Winnicott, Kohut, Balint, and so on; some of you may have heard of them: you can see their statues in those temples belonging to what are known as "psychoanalytic institutes"). The god is embodied within, and his or her thoughts are incorporated in the act of *embodiment*. The embodied god is frequently a person, though it can also be an institution. Due to *coalescence*, person and institution are also frequently fused. The individual in whom this narcissistic structure is operating is then in submissive identification with the god. Through this identification the thoughts and thinking processes of the god are understood, and yet there is always distortion. (Wilfred Bion was once at a group relations conference, and he kept hearing speakers talking about "Bion said . . ." or, "Bion did not think . . .", and so on. He turned to a colleague and said: "this chap Bion sounds as though he was an interesting person").

However, the most important aspect is that the creative capacity in the individual is crushed through this embodiment. We are familiar in the psychoanalytic world with the discipleship of one analyst towards another: Jung towards Freud and Paula Heimann towards Melanie Klein, for example. There is a period of intense submission and then a rebellion. The latter occurs at the moment when the individual is trying to break free from the narcissistic bondage. The rage towards the erstwhile mentor is the projected hatred of the submissive act. It is the submissive act that is hated, but it becomes projected and hypostasized in the outer object. It means that the attempt to achieve freedom has failed. The attempted liberation became perverted. True liberation requires realization that the enslaving principle is the inner submissive act, and total liberation requires an understanding that the enslaving principle is one element in the narcissistic structure.

*   *   *

The realization of the true god in the personality is the product of an inner creative act. This is in direct contrast to the presence of the false god, which is through an act of submission in which the individual psyche is crushed. The realization of the true god lays a foundation in the personality for respect for the Self. I have spelt "Self" here with a capital letter because it is the THAT. I am IT. I am this necessarily so, not through an act of submission. There is no merger here. THAThood is my nature, it is my being. The THAT demands respect. The THAT in me is the THAT in you and demands respect. An act that conforms to that respect has of necessity to be beneficial to me and to you. It cannot be otherwise.

I want to look at just two aspects of the true god: conscience and symbolism. Both of these are extremely relevant to clinical work. Let us take conscience first. Conscience is the subjective evidence of the absolute aspect of our being. We feel conscience to be us, yet not us. We experience it as inviting us. To follow conscience is a free act, not an obligation. Associated with the false god are words such as "driven", "obligated", or "compelled", whereas conscience is an invitation within the personality, and following conscience is a free act. The ontological truth that the Absolute is in the contingent finds its subjective realization in the free acceptance of the invitations of conscience. As the following of conscience is respecting the Absolute in which I and you share, then, if I follow the promptings of conscience, it has to benefit me and you. Similarly, if you follow the promptings of conscience, it has to benefit you and me. It follows, too, that if I say "No" to the prompting of conscience, I harm you as well as myself. What I have said so far about conscience may be categorized as "religious", but what I turn to now has a directly clinical application.

The truth to which I want to draw your attention is this: that every time a person follows his/her conscience, his or her ego is strengthened. You may demand my evidence for this. My answer is that it is a conviction born of clinical observation. I do not want you to believe this because I have said it, however. Go and observe and see whether what I assert is verified. Should your observations not confirm this assertion of mine, then I must ask you to describe the psychological processes that lead to the strengthening of the ego. I shall, however, stick to my assertion until I have evidence to the contrary. If what I assert is true, then it must be crucial that the clinician facilitate the following of conscience. From what I have said, it is clear that the clinician cannot *make* the patient follow conscience. Such a statement is a contradiction in terms, because following conscience is a personal, free act. There are two prescriptions for the clinician that seem to follow from what I have said.

The first prescription is that the clinician be encouraged to follow his own conscience. While listening to the patient, a realization may come to the mind of the clinician. However, I may find what has come to my mind extremely uncomfortable. The truth that has come to mind may make it clear that I have been going up the wrong path for months or perhaps years. I may prefer not to communicate what I have understood to the patient. "I won't", I say to myself, and have almost decided, when conscience pricks me. . . . Alternatively, I may find the truth that has come to mind extremely painful for the patient, wish to protect her from it, and think, "I won't" . . . then conscience pricks me. . . . That we avoid making interpretations because they are disturbing, I am certain. However, if we follow the principle that I have adumbrated above—that is, that if I follow conscience it is mutually beneficial to me and the patient—then it follows that if the clinician follows his conscience, then this strengthens not only his ego but also that of the patient.

The second prescription is that the clinician avoid smothering conscience. The prime way in which the clinician does this is by acting in the persona of the false god. The false god persuades, the false god demands, the false god says, "Do it my way". The patient invites me to be god; the patient installs me as god; the patient puts enormous pressure on me to be god and to act accordingly. It is my job as clinician to avoid this pressure. The more I am able to avoid being a false god, the less is conscience smothered. The extent to which we fail to do this as therapists can, to some extent, be measured by the degree to which in the therapeutic world it is common to find that a therapist follows the doctrinal position of his or her own analyst or the school to which that analyst belongs. I believe that it is extremely difficult to avoid smothering conscience. Following the voice of conscience always means experiencing pain and guilt. This has to mean that it is a path fraught with difficulty and one that all humans fight to avoid. However, it is this difficult path that the clinician is being asked to tread if he is to assist his patient in the job of strengthening her ego.

I want now to turn to the relevance of what I have said about the Absolute to symbolism:

A patient is covertly attacking the analyst, and the analyst points this out. He has made a transference interpretation. The question is "Why?" Is the patient not free verbally to attack the analyst? What is the particular significance that makes the analyst decide to point this out to the patient?

Of one thing I am sure. Very often the implication is, "You have no right to be attacking me". There are two points here. The first is that if this is the analyst's viewpoint, then he is operating from the narcissistic structure within himself. The second is that even if this is not so, from the analyst's point of view, the patient will frequently view it with that viewpoint as her basic assumption. It is a narcissistic principle that I believe that the other is motivated by the same principles as myself; therefore if I the patient would feel entitled not to be accused or attacked, I will also believe that the Other or the analyst is also so motivated. The narcissistic reason, then, for pointing out to a patient that she[3] is subtly attacking the analyst is that she should not be doing this. What, then, is the healthy reason for pointing it out?

We can find the answer to this question if we go back to our fundamental premise about the true god: I am IT or THAT thou art. A patient who is subtly attacking me, the analyst, is subtly attacking herself. In other words, what that person is doing to me is a symbol of what she is doing to herself. The purpose, then, of pointing out that she is subtly attacking me is to bring him to an understanding that she is attacking herself. The other way of reaching this is to realize that her paranoia directed towards the analyst is a primitive hatred against her own submissive activity: that it is the embodying activity, the making of a false god, that is attacking her self. Then, as one looks more closely at the self-damaging activity, it is possible to see the subtle ways in which she attacks her own thinking processes. In fact, it is mentality itself that has been severely damaged—to the extent to which the person is deprived of mentality. It has become so confused and embodied that it is difficult to see that there is a mentality there at all.

"Symbolism" is the name we give to that process whereby we recognize that an activity that is interpersonal, that is outer, represents what is inner. An ontological understanding of the Absolute tells us why this should be so. The true god then becomes not only the rational basis of symbolism but also its creator. The false god, on the other hand, is the destroyer of symbolism, the destroyer of the inner.

* * *

I want to conclude by making some more general reflections about the significance of what has been said for the claim that there exists absolute truth. I will try to illustrate this with a vignette. Many years ago I found myself in this situation:

> A psychotherapist was presenting his work with a patient to a committee that was trying to assess his work. In discussing his work, it was clear that he considered suicide as an evil to be avoided. The chairman of the committee said to him, in a laid-back tone: "But don't you think this patient was free to commit suicide if he wanted to?"

Under a false-god morality the only answer to this question would be to say that God forbids suicide as He does murder, and so on—but for the person who says, "I don't believe in God" (i.e. the false god of revelation), the only arbiter of truth is my subjective feelings. If I want to commit suicide, why shouldn't I? If I want to murder, why shouldn't I? In the latter case you might answer that if I do, I shall go to prison for life. I might answer that I don't care. I can do as I please. My life is my own; it belongs to me. I can contract Aids if I want to; if I have Aids, I can infect someone else with it. I can do entirely as I please. I can destroy my own mind if I want to, it is my business.

This outlook is very pervasive at present in the developed Western world. It is, unfortunately, the degenerate child of the Judaeo–Christian god. It is an outlook shared by most schools of psychotherapy. The chairman of that committee that I referred to was a psychoanalyst of some eminence. Those psychoanalysts and psychotherapists who do not share his outlook are usually not able to ground their position in a convincing set of arguments. There are certain schools of psychotherapy the very basis of which lies in a relativism of values such as this committee chairman espoused. In fact, I believe that it is at present only a small minority who challenge it. In my opinion two consequences follow from this. One is that under such a philosophy there can be no healing of a torn mind, because there is no concept of what a torn mind is; and the other is that psychotherapy itself exists as part of a narcissistic culture and therefore does not have the tools with which to heal narcissism. Without transforming narcissism, any healing that we produce is false coinage. It is not the genuine article. I believe we have a personal and cultural task to address.

Notes

1. Quoted from Revised Standard Version (1962).

2. The *principle of inclusion* states that two psychic elements are one and the same but with two manifestations, or it can be conceptualized that one is contained in the other.

3. In this chapter, for simplicity, the patient is referred to as female.

CHAPTER ELEVEN

Natural spirituality

Religion remains as it always was, the chief motive power, the heart of the life of human societies, and without it, as without the heart, there can be no rational life.

Leo Tolstoy, "What Is Religion?" p. 214

The motivation for action under the influence of revealed religion is that such-and-such should be done and that-other-thing not done because God had so ordained that it shall be such. How do we know that this is the best thing to do? We know because God has ordained that it shall be such. That, in summary, is the position of revealed religion.

Natural religion (see chapter 9, this volume) is arrived at through rational reflection, but how does that throw any light on how we are to live our lives? The answer to this lies in the conditions necessary to achieve such understanding. I cannot engage in a process of reflection upon the nature of reality and of our existence if I am drunk, if I am full of lust, if I am craving food, if all my attention is upon making more money or improving my status. Essential to the process of such reflection is some withdrawal from such pursuits, not out of contempt for them but, rather, in order that *psychic attention* be devoted to this

124

reflection. Could one not say, however, that once this understanding has been reached, then that is that, and no more reflection is necessary? Such a question assumes that an act of understanding is purely an intellectual act, whereas it is both intellectual and emotional and the latter requires months, years, or a whole lifetime for it to permeate the personality. The initial act of understanding needs to be deepened and broadened. Only through continual reflection is the achieved act of understanding taken more deeply into the emotional life. It is that the intellectual act becomes a possession not only of the intellect but of the emotions. When someone dies, this is known intellectually as soon as we are told of the death, but it may take months or years before we know it emotionally. In the same way there is an intellectual act at one moment in time, but in order to know it emotionally considerable time is necessary and not only time, but also concentration of *psychic attention* upon the object.

This is where psychoanalysis comes in. It is not only *psychic attention* that is necessary, but also psychoanalytic investigation. This is because there is *resistance* to reaching such an understanding. We are constantly tempted to avoid personal understanding and to fall back upon the dictate of authority. There is within the personality the presence of cultural authority and the lure of a regression to passive submission. We resist personal understanding because it is painful. Psychoanalysis aids us in recognizing the resistance. When it is recognized for what it is, then it is possible not to follow it. This is based on the principle that if what is self-damaging is known, then it will not be followed. This knowledge, however, has to be not only intellectual but also emotional.

At this point, a judgement comes in. We judge inwardly what is resistance and what is the emotional act through which we deepen and broaden the emotional possession of our understanding. Judgement in this psychic sphere is called *conscience*. Here the individual is judging whether this action rather than that will assist or detract from the emotional assimilation of the ultimate nature of reality.

This position implies that the conditions for emotional understanding are much more far-reaching than those for intellectual understanding alone. If faced with a choice between jumping to the immediate or contemplating the long-term, between acting precipitately or thinking about the consequences, the choice of satisfying what is needful for me as opposed to what is a more general good: the outcome of these decisions determines the extent of my ability to process emotionally the nature of life and reality. But why is this? Why is it that emotional comprehension of the ultimate nature of life and existence requires a discipline that permeates the whole of life, whereas the intellectual act alone does not?

If, for a moment, we follow logic, it would suppose that the emotions are co-extensive with life itself, whereas the intellect refers to only one part of it. Another way of saying this would be that an intellectual act is like a photograph of a moving object taken with a high-speed shutter so that it appears static, whereas the emotional act embraces the continuity of our personal history, both past and future. The fuller the emotional act, the greater is its embrace. It is capable of embracing both the past and the future of the individual, but also the human world that is in connection with that individual. Emotion is not only a living activity within the confines of the individual but also a connectivity with both other human beings in proximity and also of living things and the inanimate world.

* * *

Spirituality is the emotional assimilation by the individual of religious teaching. One particular teaching out of a series of different teachings becomes personally significant for a particular individual. The spirituality of *revealed religion* carries God's precepts into the most subtle sinews of the individual's internal mental processes. Spirituality takes the principles of the religion into the inner forum of the soul. Its essence is to be found in a submissive devotion to God's commands. It will be immediately obvious to psychoanalysts that this is the outer embodiment of a demanding superego. In fact, in my recent writing (Symington, 2002) I have substituted the word *god* for superego. This is because the superego is never purely internal but always embodied in outer figures or institutions, and it is an agent within the personality. The word "god" conjures up better the nature of this agency. I have also used it to indicate that the god of revealed religion is fashioned according to the workings of narcissistic currents within the personality. In fact, in the Bible Yahweh is sometimes a figure fashioned according to such principles, and yet at other times it is equivalent to the *Brahman* reached through contemplative reflection in Eastern mysticism. What is required is a textual analysis, so these different senses of the one word are sorted out clearly. However, a spirituality based upon the commands of this revealed God will always be tinged with an obedience to an outer directive and will ultimately be external in nature. As psychoanalysis aims to free the emotional self from such slavish dependence, any such spirituality will always be inimical to psychoanalysis.

The essence of *natural religion*, however, lies in an active enquiry into the nature of reality, and the spirituality based upon it is by its nature *active, inquiring*, and *devoid of outer endorsement*. I have not found a term for spirituality based upon natural religion in the literature, so I shall call it simply *natural spirituality*.

Let us for a moment suppose that an act of comprehension that encompasses the totality of being in its unity is the foundation stone of natural religion: then a spirituality based upon it recognizes that such an act of comprehension requires certain emotional modes of being in order for this act of comprehension to occur in the first place and then to be deepened and broadened in the second. What we are talking of here is an *askesis*—an ascetic discipline that favours the development of this kind of emotional understanding. Making this a central concern of life turns a mind-set into a *spirituality*.

The very phrase "ascetic discipline" conjures up for many a puritanical regime that many have come to psychoanalysis to be rid of. In most traditional religions the emphasis on asceticism has consisted of restraint in eating and drinking and also restriction, if not total renunciation, of sexual satisfaction. Even here, however, it should be noted that ascetic excesses have always been denounced by the mystics. The Buddha, for instance, achieved Enlightenment just after renouncing the extremes of fasting that had been his habit for six years in the Deer Park and accepting a cake from the Lady Sujata, which he ate. However, with this caution duly noted, it is nevertheless true that the emphasis on ascetic discipline within traditional religions has been upon curbing the senses.

It is the thesis of this enquiry that all the asceticisms of the traditional religions, both East and West, are focused upon the sensual—refraining from eating or drinking too much or lusting after sexual satisfaction—whereas a spirituality based upon the tenets of *natural religion* is focused upon that which is contrary to conscience. Conscience is that sentiment within the individual that invites someone in one direction rather than another. I have used the term "traditional religion", which is a partner of "traditional society"—in other words, a society that is bound together by ties of blood. What differentiates "modern society" from "traditional society" is that the bonds of the latter are emotional and personal. Therefore the ascesis of natural religion in contemporary society is that which promotes love and mitigates hate. The foundation stone for this lies in a process I will call *inner imaging*. I will try to describe what I mean by this.

A woman hated the negativity in her two brothers and sisters and was always spitting abuse at their attitude. One day she got a clear picture of a man on her sofa at home knocking everything she did and said, and she realized that this was a negative presence in herself.

This is an example of *inner-imaging*.

A man hated the self-centredness of a work colleague, but one day this man was talking to him and as he did so, an image of this man as a picture of himself came disturbingly to mind.

Through the process of inner imaging I take possession of what belongs to myself. Rather than hating greed, envy, jealousy, mean-mindedness, self-centredness and, through the hatred, expelling these attributes into others, through inner imaging I own them in myself. Conscience is that voice within that invites me to do just this. The aim of asceticism in natural religion is to convert emotional hatred into emotional love, but this cannot be achieved without that aim mentioned earlier of emotionally grasping the very nature of life itself. Life is not a given; it has to be actively *lived*. Conscience beckons life to be lived. Loving and living are two related realities, but they are both inextricably linked to the contemplation of the ultimate nature of reality. The most detailed way in which this has been worked out has been within the Vedanta philosophy of Shankara. I will try to give a brief exposition of this.

The seers of the Upanishads reflected deeply upon the nature of reality and realized through an act of understanding that it is not as we perceive it through the senses: there is a reality, *Brahman*, which encompasses all that exists, that the individual soul, *Atman*, is inseparable from *Brahman*. The seers knew it must be so, but quite how it is so is beyond our capacity to comprehend. An important component of the Vedanta philosophy was the concept of *Avidya*, or "not-knowing". In this way they prefigured Kant, who stressed the limitations of human understanding. We know through metaphysical reflection that there is only one reality or that reality is one, and yet there is multiplicity and there is one *Brahman* and many *Atman*.

This can be grasped through an intellectual act of understanding, but to become an emotional possession, it is necessary to encompass life stretching into the past and into the future, and not what is just immediate. I am sitting in the country upon a stone admiring the landscape, with my hand at my side. Suddenly I experience a sharp pain in my right hand. I am overcome with rage. I look at my hand and see a red mark on the skin, and I suck it and feel sorry for myself. A friend comes up to me and says, "What was it that stung you?" but I have no idea, and I retort with anger that I don't know and could not care less. I am totally enclosed in myself. My emotional state is divorced from *Brahman*. I am focused on a self (my-self) divorced from reality. The contemplative vision has entirely left me. I have become obsessed with one little piece of the world (my-self) and have actively shut out the rest of reality. The contemplative vision opens me to the whole of reality, and the insect that stung me and myself are it. The spirituality of natural religion requires me to take note of the reality of the insect and its relation to myself. This spirituality is consistent with the scientific spirit. What was this insect that stung me, and why did it do so? This requires a detachment from a self-preoccupation with my own pain. In the example quoted, the pain has flooded experience in such a way that my subjective self has blotted out the object, the other, in this case the insect, altogether. In fact *the* ascesis of natural religion is detachment from self-preoccupation in order to liberate me, leaving me free to contemplate *Brahman*. This perspective has a relevance for a theory of guilt, conscience, and symbolism. As these are all central in the clinical practice of psychoanalysis, I want to consider guilt and conscience, which are so central to spiritual concerns. Symbolism and its importance in human communication and the creation of culture is a subject of its own.

Conscious and unconscious guilt are talked a lot about in psychoanalysis, but I think this is the way it is usually thought about: that guilt is due to damage that I have done to the other. The depressive position of Melanie Klein can, for instance, be described as an awareness of the damage that I have done to the other—often in the paradigmatic form of the damage the infant has done to the mother's body. Yet I believe that this is not correct. If we take the perspective of Vedanta philosophy, then what is damaged is *Brahman*, which means that both *I* and *the Other* are damaged and not only this pair but *Brahman*, which is the whole of reality of which myself and the other are a part. If we link this with chaos theory, then damage in the micro-environment can also be responsible for disturbance in the macro-environment. Therefore guilt is on account of damage done both to myself and the other, and, in fact, damage to *Brahman* implies harm done to each.

If, in the clinical situation, it can be shown that the self is harmed as well as the other, it removes the moralistic taint. It is moralism when I am accused of damaging the other; it is moral when it can be shown that I am doing something that damages myself as well as the other. If I realize that guilt accrues through activity that is self-damaging, it throws a quite different light upon the way it is necessary to proceed clinically. I believe that guilt is a central clinical problem, which arises particularly in this way. Let us say, for instance, that someone has been acting in a way that is damaging to the self and others for many years or since infancy. This is extremely difficult to face. The natural tendency is to push away any knowledge of it with great violence, and much aggressive behaviour can, I believe, be understood as precisely this. One thing is certain: that a person will not come to recognize that of which he/she is guilty by having it pointed out. It only becomes an internal possession through an inner act of realization.

This leads to a very different technique: one of creating an atmosphere within which such a realization can occur. I shall only come into possession of the damaging things I have done through my own inner realization. I believe that this can only come about by the analyst separating himself from the activity of the patient, by each word that the analyst speaks coming out of his own freedom and not because there is some subtle pressure upon him to say something. A man had a realization that he had been enormously controlling, but this was because he tracked in a direction that led him to that conclusion and the analyst had carefully stayed on his own mental path. Now, you have to ask what goal is being pursued when this man realizes that he has been enormously controlling. One has to assume that this realization came about in him because there was a thrust in him to become detached from any such emotional attitudes. This thrust is, I claim, a spiritual aim.

I want now to move on to the question of conscience. Although the psychoanalytic literature is full of the subject of guilt, yet conscience hardly comes into it; yet I believe that conscience is active every time there is an effective interpretation. Let us say the analyst makes the following interpretation to a patient: "I think the chaos you have been talking about is what has driven you to model yourself within the framework of my own personality because you feel held together within it. . . ." and the patient agrees: unless the patient does something, the interpretation is valueless. The supposition is that the patient feels called to a different mode of holding himself together. This feeling is the inner workings of conscience. To take the matter further: in a subsequent session the analyst suggested that to go into himself confronted the patient with such sadness that it led him away from that path and he inserted himself into the analyst instead. Now, conscience operated in this way: it invited him to make the inner journey, despite the sadness that he would encounter. He slowly did this. There is an inference here: that subsequent to that interpretation, conscience invited him in that direction. Good interpretations state not what should be but what is; this allows conscience to operate. The desire for a different emotional mode of operating comes from conscience. Incidentally, if the analyst suggests what the patient should be doing, then he is overriding conscience and depriving the patient of the opportunity of exercising her own inner moral authority. This inner goal of desire which we take for granted functions through the activity of conscience. Conscience is the inner guide, and it is linked to a knowledge of what emotionally fulfils the person's direction of becoming. No one is: we are all in a state of becoming. We are going somewhere. The place to which we are going is dictated by conscience, but there is also a strong resistance to this direction. This is where psychoanalysis comes in.

The road that conscience points to is painful, as it was in the case just mentioned. To go in the direction that conscience invited meant great pain. The virtues that are familiar to all of us are those general demands that we prefer to evade. So, courage, gentleness, humility, compassion, patience, forbearance, tolerance, and so on all require us to confront some obstacle. We resist going in that direction. In old-fashioned religious language we are *tempted* not to go in the direction that conscience calls us to. Resistance and temptation are two different angles on the same phenomenon. Whereas resistance is the force against the beckoning voice of conscience, temptation is the pull towards an objective that is damaging to the self. The damaging objective always has something attractive about it, which makes it into a temptation. So one aspect of temptation is frequently the lure of immediate pleasure. A man felt pulled towards a sexual affair with an attractive woman he met, but he *knew* that it would bring him, her, and his wife trouble and distress; this latter knowledge resulted from viewing matters from a higher perspective, away from the immediate. Conscience therefore beckoned away from this objective, but he was strongly tempted to it.

Repression, then, is that which invites the personality away from the beckoning of conscience, but why? It is because it is safeguarding the personality from pain. It is within the hedonistic system, so conscience is beckoning the individual onto a different plane of action. It is inviting the individual to bear pain not for its own sake, but because it is the path that has to be taken if you want to arrive at the destination. But what is the destination? It is here that we see the connection between conscience and awareness. Conscience invites us into a sphere in which we are able to embrace what has happened to us and our own emotional responses to this. If we answer this invitation, what we receive for our labours is self-awareness or consciousness. In the last analysis, consciousness rests in the contemplation of reality or the ultimate and conscience is the subjective manifestation of this in the personality.

This invites the deeper question: why is there this invitation to human beings to raise themselves above the immediate? I doubt if there is an answer to this question, but what is historically certain is that in what Jaspers referred to as the "axial era" there arose individuals in different cultures teaching the men and women of their time that there was a higher goal for human beings than the immediate. This goal was self-awareness and compassion. These are not two goals but one: they are two manifestations of something that is one. As we become aware of ourselves, so also we become compassionate towards others. And these two dimensions are products of our endeavour to contemplate reality itself, of which we are a part. During the axial era—*Die Achenseit*—which runs from about 800 BC to 400 BC., among the teachers that arose are Lao Tzu, Confucius, the seers of the Upanishads, the Buddha, Mahavira, the Hebrew prophets—Isaiah, Jeremiah, Ezekiel, Hosea, and Amos—Zarathustra, Socrates, and Plato. These teachers in this era invited human beings to embrace self-awareness as a goal. But why? This is the question that cannot be answered, just as it is not possible to answer the question for the individual: "Why follow conscience?"

As conscience is the guiding principle of natural religion, I want to linger longer upon it, especially on how psychoanalysis fits into it. The temptation for all of us are those activities that we would catalogue under the heading of narcissism. So, for instance,

> . . . a woman flew into a terrible rage with a colleague at work, and this was quite a common occurrence for her. The rage would burst out of her without any pause for thought. This colleague's superior

behaviour provoked a hatred in her that was unmitigated by any thinking process. Then a change took place in her: she was about to fly into a rage with one of her colleagues, and she stopped for a moment and allowed into her mind the fact that this fellow was leaving the organization in three months' time. She was angry at the way he had handled some publicity for the organization, and she then thought that there was no point in getting into a rage, because there were no more publicity ventures in the next three months; after that, he would be gone, so the storm in her calmed.

A man on the couch would go into a trance-like state. He realized after a time that this was to anaesthetize him against pain. There was an implication here that it was worth while to bear the pain rather than anaesthetize himself. It was not surprising that he wanted to administer this anaesthetic to himself, because he had had a very traumatic infancy. The greatest pain was to face the fact that much of his subsequent suffering had been the consequence of an accident: the death of his mother. A week after his birth, his mother was killed in a car crash. She had not been driving: her brother was driving, and he was stopped at red lights when a large lorry failed to brake and crashed into the car and killed this man's mother. Many things followed from this. Here was tragedy. No one could be blamed—not even the lorry driver, because the brakes had failed in his lorry. Much of his subsequent sufferings, then, had their origin in an accident—an unkind blow of fate.

What did recognition of this bring? Was there any advantage to him in stopping these trance-like states? How did he change as a result of this recognition? He became more compassionate towards his wife and family. Is this better than being hateful and self-centred? All that can be said is that there is a deep human belief that the former is better than the latter. This was the teaching of those great religious teachers in diverse cultures in the axial era, and belief in what they taught has permeated all the great civilizations of the world: that self-awareness and compassion have a self-authenticating value. There is no proof that that these emotional attitudes are better than hatred and cruelty, but it rests on a deep human conviction. Just as in mathematics there are certain propositions that cannot be proved, so also in the social sciences. The shortest distance between two points is a straight line: this cannot be proved, but it carries a conviction that few would question. So, in the human sciences, there are certain self-authenticating values: that compassion is preferable to hatred and cruelty. What is not immediately realized is that achievement of this value is not possible without pain. Therefore there is an invitation to abandon the pleasure principle in favour of this value, endorsed within by conscience. Socrates (quoted in Plato's dialogue *Gorgias*) said that it is better to suffer pain than to inflict it.

Psychoanalysts have therefore to re-assess Freud's theoretical schema, which was based on the pleasure principle: that human beings seek pleasure and avoid pain. Freud did, however, acknowledge that gratification at this moment in time might be renounced in favour of gratification at a later time. So already here there was a questioning of the principle of immediate satisfaction suggested by the pleasure principle. But the value Socrates enunciates declares that there is a goal that is sought by human beings but one that is not dictated by the pleasure principle at all. Socrates is not a masochist, because he says that he would prefer neither to suffer pain nor to inflict it; but if he had to choose between them, then he would choose to suffer pain rather than inflicting it. His rationale for this is that to choose the former is the greater good. So he has an idea of *the good* that is not defined according to the pleasure principle—that is, that pleasure is good and pain is bad—but, rather, that there is a good that is defined according to a different principle. To reach this principle it is necessary, I believe, to see what follows from our apprehension of the nature of reality itself.

Many, though not all, schools of psychoanalysis do, in fact, base themselves on the firm belief that it is necessary to bear pain in order to develop emotionally, so the underlying philosophy of these schools of psychoanalysis is that of Socrates, of Zarathustra, of the Hebrew Prophets, of the Buddha, and not Freud's pleasure principle. There is a resistance to the idea that it is a religious philosophy that governs the clinical practice of psychoanalysis. I believe that the reason for this resistance lies, very largely, in the fact that nearly all psychoanalysts equate religion with revealed religion, and they are not acquainted with natural religion and its principles.

* * *

As natural religion arises through a deep act of understanding into the nature of reality, so conscience always has to be tested against reasoning—in particular, the observational insight of a third person. If conscience is the repository of reality within the personality, then it is not entirely subjective. It is both an objective fact and a subjective experience, but it is always in danger of being swamped by fits of irrational passion. Psychoanalysis, if practised correctly, does not act according to the techniques of persuasion or suggestion but, rather, promotes a mental attitude of freedom between the two people engaged in the process. It is the interplay of conscience between two people relating to each other that brings the influence of a third term. This third term is reality, which both transcends the pair and yet is inherently within both, through conscience. This reality, this third term, is what Bion referred to as "O". "Father" in the Oedipus complex is, I believe, the anthropomorphic symbol of this.

We all resist the pain that this involves. It is a struggle in which both analyst and patient are engaged. An analyst understood something that was very significant for his early emotional life; he was subsequently able to understand an emotional difficulty in two of his patients. So an emotional realization in one led to a new level of analytic understanding. Was this an emotional development or a spiritual one? Is not an emotional development guided by conscience a spiritual one also? A spirituality based upon natural religion. A natural spirituality.

The conclusion is unavoidable: that psychoanalysis is a process aimed to facilitate natural spirituality, but it is also scientific, because it is based upon clear thinking. The philosopher R. G. Collingwood defined science thus: ". . . a body of systematic or orderly thinking about a determinate subject matter" (1969, p. 4).

In fact, the principles of natural religion require the most orderly and systematic thinking on the subject of emotional development. There is no difficulty in reconciling science and religion as long as the latter is *natural religion* and *not* revealed religion. Natural religion and science are two facets of the one reality.

There is another reason for planting psychoanalysis firmly within the parameters of a *natural spirituality*. It is that, as conscience is central to it, the freedom of the individual is safeguarded through conscience. Cardinal Newman says this about conscience:

> Conscience is a personal guide, and I use it because I must use myself; I am as little able to think by any mind but my own as to breathe with another's lungs. Conscience is nearer to me than any other means of knowledge. And as it is given to me, so also is it given to others; and being carried about by every individual in his own breast, and requiring nothing besides itself, it is thus adapted for the communication to each separately of that knowledge which is most momentous to him individually. [1988, pp. 389–390]

I stress the need to place conscience at the centre of the psychoanalytic endeavour because it is only then that free individual emotional development has some guarantees. There is no doubt that there is a lot of suggestion, persuasion, and hypnotic influence within psychoanalysis. If this were not so, it would not be so common to find analysands following the doctrines of their analyst and adhering so tenaciously to the thought processes of one of the psychoanalytic pioneers, whether it be Freud, Melanie Klein, Fairbairn, Winnicott, Kohut, or Bion. Psychoanalysis seen as a natural spirituality will respect the conscience of each individual. I believe that if this were truly internalized, it would revolutionize psychoanalytic technique in a healthy direction.

CHAPTER TWELVE

An enquiry into the concepts of soul and psyche

This chapter was originally written in 1980, and I gave it as a paper to the Applied Section of Psychoanalysis in that year and then to the Society of Analytical Psychology shortly afterwards.

I would not now agree with the Platonic idea that the self is a non-material reality and that this is implied in Freud. Although at this time I had installed in me the ontological concept of being that I outline in "Religion and Consciousness" (chapter 9, this volume), I had not realized its all-embracing significance, and I had therefore not employed it as an integrating principle. Had I been able to do so, then the duality implied in the following would have been understood as in truth a unity, the duality of which was not a quality of the object but due, rather, to the limitation of the human mind to grasp diversity as compatible with unity.

The main thrust of the chapter, however—that the soul and the psyche are one reality but seen from different perspectives—is something that I still hold.

I want to take one fragment from a more comprehensive endeavour and investigate the ways in which psychoanalysis could be enriched through being open to the influence of certain concepts and goals that are usually considered to be the province of religion. The capacity for love, which is a Christian ideal, is one; the attributes of god as analogues of infantile wishes is another; the psychological significance of the Christian myth yet another; and so on. I think that as a result of taking a rather stand-offish attitude to religion, psychoanalysis has been the loser. It has failed to tap a rich resource and has remained somewhat impoverished thereby. Can we really doubt that religion, which has been such a powerful force in the building up of civilizations in the world, is symbolical of an intrapsychic truth?

I want to try to look at just one aspect of this investigation. Can the religious concept of the soul throw any light on the nature of the psychological entity that we are engaged with every day of our professional lives? I have no doubt that it can, but before I go any further, I want to give you some boundaries that I am setting myself; this may, I think, help to focus on the particular area that I want to consider.

To start with, it is not quite accurate to say that the soul is a religious concept. It is, rather, a philosophical concept, which has been imported into most religious systems as a necessary adjunct to certain religious doctrines. In Christianity, for instance, the crucial revealed truths are few, but they require a great system of philosophical ramparts to support them. The soul is just one such support concept. The finite character of the universe is another. Therefore the soul is not essentially a religious concept. It is a philosophical one that was imported into Christianity and has been carried within it since early days, though not the earliest.

It is worth remarking here that the soul means the whole man in the Old and New Testaments. In recent years Biblical scholarship has pointed more and more to the fact that man was viewed by the Hebrews as a total entity, and that the object of God's salvation was not the soul but the whole human being, the whole living bodily spirit of man and woman—not someone as an individual, but the whole human race. The soul in the Bible means the vital force in man that imparts life. The object of Christian hope is not the soul's escape from the body at death and arrival in heaven but, rather, the *parousia* when all mankind will rise from the dead, body and soul. The in-between period—that between individual death and the Last Day—is hardly referred to in the New Testament. This is probably because Jesus himself and his followers believed that the Messianic Kingdom was on the brink of arrival.[1] Catholic theologians infer heaven, hell, and purgatory as waiting-rooms for the last day from some rather doubtful texts. The soul as having a separate existence emerged certainly very early, but it was an importation from the Hellenistic world into which the Christian faith soon became embedded. It was this import from the Hellenistic world that became part and parcel of our way of thinking about man in the West.[2]

But do the Greek notions of the soul have any connection with the psyche? They are not normally connected in people's minds. When we study psychic reality, we do not really think that it is the same entity as the soul. I think that usually, both in psychoanalytical circles and in religious ones, people consider that the two spheres are quite alien from one another. In support of this view Gregory Zilboorg says in his collection of lectures and essays entitled *Psychoanalysis and Religion*:

> One cannot repeat too many times that psychoanalysis knows and claims to know as little about the soul as the religious opponent knows about the psychic apparatus. These two entities cannot be united and confused with or substituted for one another. Any attempt at such a unity or substitution is an attempt to construct a contentious artificiality, something like a scientific theology or a theological science—which is a contradiction in terms, in concepts, and in basic subject matter. [1967, pp. 41–42]

Something similar was said by E. B. Strauss, a psychiatrist who was also a devout Roman Catholic:

> It is important to assert from the start that the psyche with which the medical psychologist deals is conceptually different from the soul as defined by theologians. By the *psyche* we mean the sum total of what we experience both *actually* and *potentially*—actual experience constituting the conscious, latent and potential experience the unconscious. The soul of theology is conceived of in terms of a different kind of discipline. The soul is that part of man which is aware, individually created, endowed with survival value. It perceives true and real values, not only phenomena, is modified by values and transformed by Grace. The definition of the soul, just given, can be accepted or rejected: and it will strike many of you, doubtless, as arrant nonsense. However, the point I wish to make is that the soul is a theological concept, and hence only understandable in theological and ontological terms, whereas the psyche is a psychological construct. [E. B. Strauss, quoted by White, 1960, p. 16]

This view seems to be universally held by many psychiatrists, psychologists, and psychoanalysts, at least implicitly. I am arguing in favour of a view that is quite opposite to that of Zilboorg and Strauss.

There are, I think, some cogent reasons for rejecting the view that psyche and soul inhabit two quite different domains.

Firstly "soul" and "psyche" are both translations of the Greek word ψυχη. To emphasize the point I will quote some well known passages from the New Testament where the English word "soul" normally means the Greek ψυχη: "My psyche is sorrowful even unto death" . . . "What shall it profit a man if he gains the whole world but suffer the loss of his psyche."

On other occasions the translators have rendered the same word as life: "The good shepherd gives his psyche for his sheep" . . . "The Son of Man is come to give his psyche as a ransom for many." (The Hebrew word in the Old Testament is *nephes*; the Latin is *anima*.)

A psychiatrist is a conjunction of the two Greek words *"psyche"* and *"yatros"*—a soul doctor, psychologist—a soul scientist or a psychoanalyst: one who analyses and studies the soul.

Then both the religious tradition and the psychoanalytic one stress the reality of the soul and psyche. Theologians have stressed the spiritual nature of man's soul. The theological definition of "spiritual" is a reality that is non-material, and both the subject and the complement are stressed—that is, that the soul is *real* yet is non-material. Freud stressed, similarly, that hallucination was a psychic reality. He stressed the reality aspect of that, though he did not examine too closely what he meant by psychic. But both traditions are concerned with a reality that does not have the properties of material reality: that is, extension and tangibility.

Thirdly, if the soul is not the psyche, then do psychoanalysts dismiss the reality that the theologians call the soul—and if not, what name do they give it? What position do they take with regard to it? So, also, if the psyche is not the soul, then what is it, and how is it different from the reality that is the province of a theologian's study?

The only author I have found who did some work trying to establish the identity of the two concepts was the Dominican friar Victor White. In his book *Soul and Psyche* (1960) he holds firmly that the two words describe the same reality, though he concedes that they are *conceptually* different. I do not think that Victor White has expressed himself very happily here. He goes on to explain that in Christianity matters associated with the soul are different: they are those truths that Christians believe through faith in a revelation, like that the soul is the dwelling place of the Holy Spirit. I think it would be more accurate to say that they are associatively different: that "soul" is associated with beliefs that are proper to religion, and that "psyche" is associated with notions that are proper to psychoanalysis, like "schizoid" and "depressed". In other words, the same reality is approached from different universes of meaning, but it is the same reality. When a Christian says that the body is the temple of the Holy Spirit, we would not want to say that the body is an entity that is different from the body to which a medical doctor might refer, but it is being considered from a different perspective.

I now wish to proceed from the assumption that the soul is the psychic reality that Freud studied, and see what truths about it have been formulated, to see whether they are of any use to psychoanalysts.

Within the thinking of the Greek philosophers there were three main views about man's constitution: the materialist one, the Platonic one, and the Aristotelian one. I want now to trace these three views. The materialist one identified existence and matter. Initially matter was understood as a great mass of substance. Heraclitus had said that this was in a constant state of flux and could only be known experientially through the senses; it could not be an object of knowledge. Parmenides, who wanted to safeguard man's knowledge, said that what exists exists, and what does not, does not. What exists cannot pass into non-existence, and what does not exist cannot pass into existence. Therefore all change, all coming-into-being, is an illusion. The philosophers who succeeded Parmenides addressed themselves to this dilemma. It was Aristotle who finally provided the most satisfactory solution.

The most brilliant solution within a materialist conception was that of Democritus of Abdera, who said that matter was, in fact, made up of tiny particles, basic units of matter, which are so minute that they cannot be encompassed by perception. These basic units of matter he called "atomoi", which, ironically, means "unsplittable"—basic irreducible units of matter. The shapes of these atomoi are different, and according to those differences and the way they combine with each other, so we get different types of substance: a metal has a different sort of atom to water, and so on. Now, the human psyche, or soul, is made up of spherical atoms. This was the most thoroughly materialist conception of the soul. With Plato it disappeared from European thought until the advent of Hume in the eighteenth century.

Hume said that there is no such thing as a soul: all we are given is a procession of impressions (or sensations of pleasure or pain), together with echoes or copies of these (images or ideas), and consequently he thought that there was no ego or self (these are incompatible with a materialist conception). Hume said that there was no evidence for the ego, or self. His opponents said that it was not a sensible fact but an intellectual necessity—an object of knowledge (the old debate between Heraclitus and Parmenides had reared its head again). Hume's view gained currency, especially in Britain, where it was taken up by John Stuart Mill and his son, James Mill, the father of associationist psychology, whose basic assumptions have had enormous influence in various spheres of academic psychology. J. B. Watson was deeply committed to such a viewpoint, and it was associated with his vehement rejection of his Baptist upbringing. Freud was also strident in his repudiation of religion and with any notion of a soul that was not material. Freud believed passionately in the scientific stance that was epitomized in the Helmholtz School of Medicine. One of the founders of this school had been Ernst Brücke, whose student and devoted disciple Freud had been. Brücke was a founder member of the *Physicalische Gesellschaft* in Berlin and, together with Helmholtz, Ludwig, and Du Bois-Reymond had pledged the anti-vitalist oath:

> No other forces than the common physical or chemical ones are active within the organism. In those cases which cannot at the time be explained by these forces one has either to find the specific way or specific form of their action by means of the physical–mathematical method or to assume new forces equal in dignity to the chemical–physical forces inherent in matter, reducible to the force of attraction and repulsion. [Jones, 1953, vol. 1, p. 45]

Freud had tried to cast his discoveries in the language and presuppositions of this materialist view. Alongside it, he began to develop notions about the ego, which were incompatible with a materialist conception of the psyche. It is not possible to conceive of an "ego"—an "I" that thinks, perceives, and remembers—unless we posit a non-materialist psyche. Freud specifically stresses that dreams, hallucinations, and delusions are real: they have psychic reality. What can he mean here but that he is talking of something that is real, yet not materially real? I think, therefore, that alongside his materialist conception of man's constitution Freud ran a Platonic one, without, however, re-casting his theory to account for it. It is significant that Freud tended to scorn philosophers.

With mention of Plato I want now to turn to the second notion of the soul that has had such an important place in European thinking. The Platonic idea of the soul has been by far the most influential in European thinking about man. It has pervaded theology, philosophy, and, more latterly, the social sciences. It is so deeply rooted that it is difficult to think in any other mode. Plato was addressing himself to the dilemma that Parmenides had set his frustrated followers. How does motion and change come about? asked Plato, and he would not succumb to the notion that it was an illusion. There must be an invisible force that causes movement. In the human organism this is the psyche—the life—or the soul. Plato was also influenced by the Orphic mystery religions and so subscribed to the doctrine of the transmigration of souls, or what we generally know as reincarnation. The soul's relation to the body is like that of a charioteer to his chariot. The soul has no inherent relation to this or that particular body. As the doctrine of reincarnation implies, the soul can inhabit one body as well as another, just as a charioteer can drive different chariots. The soul's knowledge comes about through contact with eternal "ideas". For Plato, these were existents of which the particular examples in the world of the senses were reproductions. In his famous simile of the men in the cave facing the wall of the cave, they looked at the shadows of people and animals thrown by the sunlight. They only saw the shadows, not the real existents. The soul was imprinted with this knowledge prior to its enslavement to a mortal body, and all knowledge was a process of recollection.

The principal architect of the Platonic point of view in the West was St Augustine of Hippo. Prior to his conversion to Christianity, he was a Manichaean. The Manichaeans believed the world was ruled by two gods—a good god and a bad god. The evil god ruled over matter and the good god over spirit, so that matter was evil and the spirit was good. St Augustine was converted from this belief system to Christianity, and he believed in one God who had created the world, and that it was good. However, patristic scholars have pointed out that Augustine remained tied to his Manichaean past. This is particularly evident in the sphere of sexuality. Of course, he had himself repudiated sex very violently in his own life. What is characteristic of this view is that the soul is what is all-important. The body is just a prison in which the soul has to live out its earthly sentence. In Plato's thinking the person, the "I", or the ego is identified with the soul. The soul's knowledge is from contact with the eternal forms contained in God. The body, then, just becomes a mechanical robot that gets pushed about by the soul. Descartes was a confirmed Platonist. The view that there can be a pure mental sphere, a pure non-material ego, a pure internal object, a psyche that is imprinted with certain concepts like intercourse, or archetypes like anima, is all reminiscent of Platonic thinking. I rather think that whenever a psychic reality is acknowledged but its implications not thought through, then what we end up with is something Platonic. I think that Freud's "psychic reality", Melanie Klein's "internal objects", Anna Freud's "ego" are probably all Platonic. I feel—though I am not sure—that Bion and Winnicott thought about the matter differently.

Aristotle, however, challenged the ideas of Plato and radically recast his theory, but, for reasons that we shall see, his views disappeared from the main current of European thought early in the Christian era, only to reappear in the thirteenth century, by which time Platonic theory was deeply rooted in European consciousness.

So we move to the third view—the Aristotelian one—which, to my mind, is the most satisfying, though the most difficult to conceptualize and perhaps impossible to cathect emotionally with accuracy. For Aristotle, the soul is not like a guest who is staying in one particular hotel but could just as well stay elsewhere, in another hotel. For Aristotle, the soul is the form of the body. Reality is made up of two elements: matter and form. He started with a mental construct of pure formless matter, which can neither exist nor even be imagined, because it is inextricably interwoven with forms. So, for instance, a table is a marriage of wood and tableness, and the two together, which can only be logically separated, become essential constituents of a table. A carpenter needs these two entities in order to construct a table. He needs wood in his workshop and an idea of tableness in his mind. All existence, said Aristotle, is made up of matter, which is shaped by a vast multiplicity of forms. When Aristotle moved from the inorganic world to the organic, he called the forms "souls". Thus the soul is the life of the organism but not as an inhabitant of a pre-existent body, because the soul is the form of the body, just as tableness is the form of the table. The soul is a living form. The individual's minutest characteristics are an endowment from the soul. In his work on the soul—or the psyche in Greek—Aristotle puts it succinctly thus:

> The soul is the principle of vital existence. It animates the frame, and it is a thinking thing besides. Moving the body, then, and showing itself in a manner, to be bodily (as in anger or pain or joy) it pertains, in part, to the province of physics, and in these respects is no more separable from its physical material than snubness is from snub noses.

The soul reaches knowledge not through contact with another world, where forms enjoy some ideal existence, but it grasps the essence or form of things via the senses.

Aristotle believes that the soul has different parts: a vegetative, an animal, and a rational one. There are some ambiguous passages where it is not clear whether the *"nous"* or eternal part is independent of the body, but most passages suggest that Aristotle's overriding conviction was that the soul in its entirety is the form of the body.

Aristotle's theory also gives a much better account of development than does Plato's. Being exists under two modes: in potency and in act. Perfectly actualized being is the unmoved mover, or pure act, and all the rest of being is in potency tending towards pure act or being actualized. This concept allowed Aristotle to account for change without needing to resort to Plato's world of ideas. The soul of man, therefore, was not static but being actualized through space and time according to a preconceived formal cause: the parental figures. There are clearly defects in this view, but I think any scientist today would be much happier with Aristotle's account of knowledge and man's relation to the world than that of Plato. Aristotle was much more of an experimental scientist. His biology was largely built up from acute observation of specimens of animal, plant, and marine life.

Before going on to consider whether Aristotle's view can be of any help to psychoanalysts, I want just to trace a thumbnail sketch of the fate of Aristotelian thought. In fact, in the first centuries of the Christian era, all except Aristotle's logic disappeared from European thought. All his other works were lost to Christendom. The burning in the fourth century of the famous library at Alexandria was responsible for Aristotle's works disappearing from the Hellenic world. However, the works were still known to various Christian sects in Lower Egypt and passed into Islam when these were converted to Muhammadanism in the seventh century. Finally, Aristotle's works were translated back into Latin in the twelfth century through the agency of the Arabian philosopher, Averroes, a native of Cordoba in Spain, which was still Moorish at that time but was re-conquered and brought within Christendom shortly after his death. At that time the Church, which was as indebted to Platonic philosophy as it was to the Ptolomaic system of astronomy, fiercely opposed the innovative ideas of this pagan philosopher, Aristotle (as though Plato was not pagan!). However, this did not deter Thomas Aquinas, the Dominican friar, from building a new theological system on the firm foundation stones of the Christian revelation and the philosophy of Aristotle. Throughout his writings St Thomas says *"Cum dicit Philosophus"* ["as the philosopher says"]—the philosopher being Aristotle. After many battles, the Church accepted the synthesis of Aquinas, whose genius and profundity could not be denied for long. By the time of the Council of Trent in the sixteenth century, the teachings of Thomas Aquinas were laid down as *the* theology to be taught in all seminaries and theological colleges within the Roman Catholic Church. This has continued to be so until the present day. However, this knowledge has remained the preserve of theologians and has not percolated down to the educated public and certainly not to thinkers in the social sciences or to psychoanalysts.

I want now to consider what Aquinas added to Aristotle's thinking about the soul. In the first place, Aquinas was quite certain that the *"principium intellectum"* or intellectual principle is the form—the soul—and he clearly rejects the notion that the intellect is only united to the body *"ut motor"*, like the charioteer to the chariot. He says that those who hold this Platonic view then need to explain how thinking can in any true sense be attributed to John rather than to Paul. Aquinas counters the objection of some of his opponents who said that the soul exists independently after death by saying that eventually the soul becomes the form of the risen body and, in its nature, always tends towards that state.

Closely connected with this point is another. For the Platonists the person was located in the soul, whereas Aquinas stressed that the person is in the *union* of body and soul.

The most cogent objection to St Thomas's position was this: he held that the intellectual act was not bodily in itself, as there were no *specific* bodily organs through which it acted, yet he said that the soul in its intellectual activity communicates through the bodily material. The intellect knows through the *"phantasmata"*, which are in the bodily organs. The intellect can only know through these. The *"phantasmata"* are to the intellect what colours are to vision. The *"phantasmata"* inhabit a world where the senses and intellectual activity are located. Lastly, I want to stress that for Aquinas the soul is the principle of life, the form of the body, the source of the instincts, and the principle of intellectual acts.

Now I want to see whether we can get any mileage out of this concept for psychoanalytic theory and practice. Many may think that all this is abstruse and has no relevance for psychoanalysts. The desire to keep "feet on the ground" is surely a sane sentiment, and yet it is precisely because of this that it is so necessary to avoid the Platonic solution. I think the following points need to be considered:

1. If you take that line, then you need to follow it further and say: "I am a good therapist or want to be, but I leave all matters of theory

to learned experts." But I think we all know that if we want to be therapists, we cannot avoid theory. We are in the business of interpreting, of finding meanings, and this means a theory: about the unconscious, consciousness, the ego, the superego, the self, or other concepts. So all of us have theories, and each of them is underpinned by underlying assumptions about the mind–body problem. Once we start on the journey of theory, we do not go as deep as we can if we avoid the mind–body problem. And our very theories remain confused. I am of the opinion that a great deal of our psychoanalytical theory is impoverished because we have failed to articulate to which of the three theories about the psyche we belong.

2.   Parallel with this is the fact that each of us subscribes to one of the three theories but have not articulated which. In fact, I believe that nearly all psychoanalysts subscribe to both a Platonic theory and a materialist one without reconciling the two.

3.   I am firmly entrenched in an Aristotelian–Aquinian viewpoint. This is so, yet I believe it is extremely difficult, if not impossible, to cathect emotionally the Aristotelian position. Fairbairn stresses that deep down there are splits in all of us. I think this is nowhere manifested more clearly than in the soul–body issue. We all split man into two (and usually into many more than two): body and soul. Following that split, we make one side good and the other bad. I believe that the Aristotelian view is one that intellectually heals the split, and if we attempt to cathect it emotionally (which means altering a lot of our language), the good and the bad come together into an integrated unity. If we remain Platonic, I do not think we carry psychoanalysis to the end-point of its integrative work.

I think the relevance of Aristotle's synthesis can be briefly summarized:

1.   It is clear that Freud started his scientific investigations into the mind in the context of a materialist belief. However, this did not prevent him from affirming the existence of psychic realities like dreams, hallucinations, and the ego. During the early years in psychoanalysis these psychic realities are offered for our attention as discrete elements—how one relates to another is spelt out in terms of the unconscious, the preconscious, and consciousness.

Each of these is seen as a quasi-organic system. In 1923, when he wrote *The Ego and the Id* (1923b), Freud now pulled together the ego in relation to the id and the superego. This was his description of a psychic structure—that is, a psychic entity or soul. But Freud continued to run the homeostatic model alongside this. This version of events is called "psychophysical parallelism" by some (e.g. Ernest Jones): it is what I have called Platonic.

2.   Once this split has been accepted, schools following Freud have tended to emphasize one side or the other. It seems that the classical Freudians get into contortions of language when discussing an issue like the source of motivation. This is the difficulty that is encountered when the soul or the psyche is not the form of the body, and the life of the totality.

3.   Clinically, Kleinians see bodily happenings as part of the psychic entity. An internal object, for instance, is not just psychic but a psychic–somatic entity. That the psychic is always embodied is enormously important clinically. For instance, the superego is usually conceptualized as being purely mental, yet it is always incarnate.

4.   I have a suspicion that an Aristotelian view of man might clear up many misunderstandings between these two approaches.

5.   As we know, Fairbairn re-cast Freud's structural model, banishing the id and replacing it with the libidinal ego. Which is right? I *think* our answer depends on whether we accept an Aristotelian/ Aquinian model or a Platonic one.

6.   For Aquinas, the soul is not in time, though it receives "impressions" or "species". It exists in the past and the present. It contains time. I think if we grasp this firmly, we might avoid these tiresome controversies where one side explains that clinical interpretations neglect the past and the other that they neglect the present. Both are contained in the psychic reality—therefore both sides are expressing the poverty of language to cope with such concepts. Bion never tired of stressing this.

7.   For Aquinas, the soul is the form of the body, but simultaneously it is the life of the whole entity: this means the life, both active and passive. In this way external and internal are not to be separated into separate entities. It is the soul informing matter.

8.   Recently a patient who had been in care as a child for a certain period and was manifesting bodily ailments said to me:

P: "And what makes it worse is that my body should be ill on account of an event that occurred to . . . my psyche."

N.S.:   "Your rage and frustration is that a psychological happening involves the whole of you, from the hair on your head to the soles of your feet."

P: "I am just stuck in the situation. I thought analysis just involved my mind."

Conclusions

1. The "soul" of the Christian tradition is the same entity as the psyche that is the object of study for psychoanalysts.
2. The psychoanalytic tradition is rooted in a Platonic perspective.
3. The Aristotelian–Aquinian view is well worth serious consideration.

Notes

1. This was the view put forward in a scholarly manner by Albert Schweitzer in *The Quest of the Historical Jesus* (1910).

2. Professor G. Lampe, quoted in White (1960, pp. 22–23): "The body in Hebrew thought . . . is neither a tomb nor a prison house for some 'spiritual' or 'intelligible' man buried or imprisoned within the flesh. Man is essentially a unity. His physical aspect is not to be rigidly separated in thought from his intellectual or spiritual character. It is the whole man who is the object of God's dealings, and salvation is concerned with the relation of the whole man to God, not with any triumph of the human 'spirit' over the corrupt and transitory 'flesh'. It is man as a single whole who was created by God. . . . It is the whole man who, as a sinner, is alienated from God, at enmity with him and the object of his wrath: and it is the whole man who is the object of God's grace and is redeemed into the fellowship of a son with his heavenly father."

CHAPTER THIRTEEN

Religion and spirituality

The purpose of detachment is to uncloak spiritual action in all its nakedness. Only when this action is revealed is it possible for the mystic to distinguish good from bad. The founders of the great religious traditions were men who had devoted themselves to this inner scrutiny with the goal of triumphing over the bad and establishing the good. The good was then an internal possession, the light of which they followed, and they were thus able to abandon the religion of the culture in which they had been brought up. However, they never abandoned it completely but retained elements of the religious tradition in which they were socialized. So, for instance, the Buddha maintained the doctrine of reincarnation and built his theory of karma into it.

The internal possession of the good is what guides these mystics who were founders of the great religious traditions. They all founded institutions, and the institution then embodied the good in a scriptural canon, the function of which was to encapsulate the teachings of the founder, and then a responsible body the job of which was to guard the doctrine. The moment the good is made incarnate in these two components, the institution is born, and this marks the transition from spirituality to religion.

A religion, then, is an institution the goal of which is the good. The way the good is conceptualized differs in primitive religion and mature religion. In primitive religion the good is conceived to be the physical survival of the individual and the tribe; in mature religion it is the salvation of the individual members through meaning. In primitive religion the good is articulated through rites, ceremonies, and mythology whereas in mature religion it is through a scriptural canon and an official body the purpose of which is interpret the message of the founder faithfully to the people. Mature religion, in the way in which it is being conceptualized here, always originates in a known founder, whereas primitive religion does not. Between these two categories are transitional religions the best-known of which are Hinduism and Judaism.

A person who is a member of one of the known religions is religious. This membership can be either explicit or implicit. In the case of the former the individual participates in the rites and devotional life of the religion in an identifiable way. Most religions have ceremonies of initiation, which have been called by Lévi-Strauss "rites of passage". There are also, however, implicit members. These are those who belong to a religion through an affective sympathy. They do not hold to all the doctrines, do not attend the ceremonies, but have either been initiated formally or, at some point in their lives, through affective bonds.

However, such membership only exacts commitment at the level of words and sentiments. Adherence to the good can remain merely at the level of external attachment. Tartuffe of Molière's play characterizes a person who displays great religiosity in his expressed sentiments but whose behaviour is at variance with his external declarations. Prince Luzhin in Dostoevsky's Crime and Punishment displays similar hypocrisy. So it is possible to be religious but unspiritual.

A spiritual person is one who, like the founders of the great religious traditions, makes the good an internal possession. For an unknown reason an individual has given priority in his life to this spiritual quest. The quest is to discover the intentional base of his actions and to detach himself from those that are bad and to pursue those that are good. It is possible for someone to be spiritual but not belong explicitly in his sympathies to one or more of the religious traditions.

The person who is in search of the intention that drives his actions is engaged in a spiritual activity. The mystic searches into himself, into the deepest layers of his being whence the power of action emanates. To determine the nature of this action requires reflection. Intentional action in contrast to motor activity is devoid in itself of any bodily constituents. Intentional action has a psychic source and a psychic object, but this can be translated as a spiritual source and a spiritual object. The object has no extension or colour and exists beyond time. It could be called a metaphysical object. But what about the source? The action is determined by the object and receives its structure from it. The object raises the source to its level. Insight into the nature of the action comes about through connaturality.

I have just said that the action is determined by the object. This is not quite so. It is that the source is known through the object. The object is the revealer of the source. The source of action cannot be directly known: it is the *noumenon*. The *phenomenon* is the object. *It* can be known directly. The object can be known directly and the active subject indirectly. The known object is the symbol through which the unknown subject is grasped. The action is connatural to the two. We do not have three entities here but a single reality. The same reality is shared by all three. It is possible to make a logical separation but not a real one. We are looking at a red box. It is possible to separate the boxness from the redness logically but not really. Subject, object, and action are three aspects of one reality.

In analysis we frequently come to a realization that what is said is not real. What do we mean by this? There is the implication that there is something real and something not real. It is possible to ask how much reality is there. What do we mean?

The answer to this question is to be sought in the ascetic's goal of detachment. What is the detachment from? And what does this detach-ment do? It is a detachment from the unreal and attachment to the real. It is this definition of the real that needs some investigation.

The basis upon which the real is separated from the unreal is axiological. (Axiology is the science of values). When you say that this is real and something else is not real, it is a value judgement. This is not so in the natural sciences, where the real is distinguished from the unreal on the basis of whether it does or does not exist. A phoenix has no existence, but a horse does. However, a phoenix has a mental existence, so when it comes to the mind on what basis are we to make this distinction? (This is more fully elaborated in chapter 8.) I will use a clinical example.

A patient complains that her husband bullies her. The analyst has a mental hypothesis that this means that the patient is bullying him and that this is unknown to the patient and, until then, to the analyst. The analyst then remembers that he has been persuaded to believe that an interpretation he made was wrong. He is conscious that he had not truly thought that it was wrong— he had been persuaded against his own better judgement. He then realizes that this has been a pattern.

The analyst then challenges the patient in the later session when she tries again to persuade him that his interpretation of the previous day is not right. He points out that this happens again and again and gives evidence that this is an attempt to persuade the analyst away from his own judgement: that she bullies him, in other words. The patient takes this in and at the following session reports that she has stood up to her husband and was not bullied by him. I do not want here to go into how it is that the analyst's interpretation affects the patient in this way but to concentrate upon something else.

In the analyst's hypothesis there is a value judgement: it is BAD to be bullied and GOOD to refuse to be bullied. However, in the example given there is another element. The analyst might agree with the patient and say, "Yes, I understand that your husband is a bully. I am struck by the fact that it never occurs to you to leave him . . ."

Here the analyst would be saying that it is not good to be bullied, but his value judgement is that it is a good thing to leave the person who is doing the bullying. (I will refer to the two analysts as the "fight analyst" and the "flight analyst"). It needs to be emphasized that these two analysts are in agreement that it is a Bad Thing to be bullied. (A Christian psychotherapist might say that to turn the other cheek is a good thing.) However, they are in disagreement as to the mode of dealing with the bully. The "fight analyst" says that it is a good thing to stand up to the bully, the "flight analyst" says that the best course is to escape from the bully. However, there is more behind this rather crude distinction.

The crucial issue here is that the psychoanalyst has a belief: that the good lies in directing attention towards the inner actions of different parts of the self. If it is asked why the psychoanalyst does this, his answer is that he believes that the good lies in such an endeavour. If you asked a mystic why he directs his attention to inner action, he could only answer that this is his *daimon*. You see, following the example just given, he *might* say that it brings about a better result: that her husband stops bullying her, that it makes her life more comfortable—

yet that is not correct. It is possible that the change in her might have enraged her husband more. The psychoanalyst would say that what she has done was still right. It is an inherent belief of psychoanalysis that to own the different parts of ourselves is a good thing in itself.

In the clinical vignette that I have given the "fight analyst" has said that it is a Good Thing to stand up to the intrapsychic bully, and it is a Bad Thing to identify the bully as a whole entity outside. An analysis in the view of the "fight analyst" is a process that assists the analysand to struggle against inner figures. Now we begin to get near our definition of the Real.

In the clinical example there is real change. The patient is able emotionally not to be bullied. She repels the charge of the bully. She moves from a state where she invites the bully in to one where she repels him. When she invites the bully in she consents to being pushed, to being controlled by another. When she angles her focus towards the management of inner figures (viz. St Augustine: *Intueor intus*), she constructs. The management of inner figures is a euphemism for the owning of a controlling part of the self, a greedy part of the self, an envious part of the self. She constructs a bridge to this disowned part in contrast to disowning a part of herself. It is the difference between these two action structures that separates the real from the unreal. The internal act of owning the part that had, until then, been disowned changes its nature from bad to good.

Every entity in the universe is in relation to every other entity. The same principle applies in the individual psychic world. There are two modes of relating: intentional and anti-intentional. In intentional relating there is a "Yes" to the psycho-ontological structure; in anti-intentional relating there is a "No" to the psycho-ontological structure. The "Yes" that goes with the ontological structure is the real. It affirms reality. The "No" that inwardly repudiates the structure is unreal.

There is, then, an intentional centre that goes with structure or against it. It is a source of action. Going with the structure, the source of action is active; going against the structure, the source is passive. In this case the source renounces its own nature. It is a paradox that in intentional relating the source is active when it goes with structure and passive when it goes against structure. Is the individual inactive, then, in anti-intentional relating? When she goes against structure, it abjures its being, because the intentional source receives its character from its own being. In this case, then, what is the source of action in the personality? The anti-intentional act sets into motion an anti-structure. The puzzle is the how of the anti-intentional act. We have in us the capacity to abjure our own being. This statement brings us into touch with those spiritual leaders who have significantly altered our value systems. They have proclaimed a message in which they have stated "This is our Being", "This is man's nature", "This is the Path to follow." They have not abjured man's being; in their Enlightenment they have enlightened an essential aspect of man's being.

It is implied here that most of us are in darkness: we do not know our own nature or in what direction to find fulfilment. Anti-intentional acts keep us in darkness. It is for this reason that illumination is set in train by an intentional act. The intentional act occurs concurrently with detachment. The Buddha's supreme intentional act, his Enlighten-ment, occurred when he detached himself from the ascetics in the Deer Park. Anti-intentional acts detach *to* and intentional acts detach *from*. It is now a question of examining the way in which the anti-intentional act attaches and to what it attaches. The anti-intentional act is buried in the sensual, the material object. It does not stand on its own. Its anti-intentionality is a life refusal and consequently has to be buried.

Whence comes this life refusal? How does man become endowed with it? We do not know the answer to this. I suspect, however, that it is our way of anaesthetizing pain—but the cost is great. Religions have myths to explain its presence. The spiritual person is he who says that it is possible to become increasingly free of the power of anti-intention-ality and to root active life more and more in intentional action and that this endeavour is eminently worthwhile and endows life with mean-ing. It is in this that life's meaning is to be found. It is a consequence of what we are saying that knowledge of our own intentionality is con-current with the degree of detachment that has been achieved. Contra-riwise, self-knowledge is incompatible with attachment. The core of the self has to be free from any imprisoning structures in order to know itself.

In the writings of the mystics there is a pattern that is something like this: In the initial stages the ascetic's focus is upon the sensual object: sex, food, drink, or sleep, for instance. In the transition from asceticism to mysticism there is a recognition that essentially what needs to be mortified is self-love. An ascetic can abstain from sex, food, drink, and sleep but parade it before men. Jesus went out of his way to condemn the Pharisees for blowing their trumpets when they were giving alms. The implication here is that the self-love we are talking about is a sensual stroking of the self. It is appearance that is the motivating principle. How I appear to others is what motivates me to action. Therefore in this state of affairs I am "in" another. The other's approval is essential, and therefore I am *in* the other. What do I mean by this? I am in the power of the other. I am controlled by the other. But I also have to control the other so that he continues to stroke me. For this reason the other has to be tailored inwardly to this image. The other is scooped into the role of stroking the self. The self then is *in* the other and the other is *in* the self, and this prevents an inner reality because the inner space is occupied by an outer figure.

The endeavour of the spiritual person, then, is to detach the ego not from the desire for food, for drink, for sleep, or for sex, but from that inflation of the ego that needs constant fuel. The fuel for this pseudo-power of the ego does not come from food but from greed, which is taking from others who are inwardly viewed with contempt. Greed consists in taking food that is unnecessary for bodily needs. Therefore it is taken for another motive. It caresses the bodily ego. There is an equation between being powerful and eating from the receptacle for others. That which is over and above the required amount represents "others" who are devoured. This gives the illusion of power. But the contempt of others becomes contempt for the "other-in-the-self". The self is damaged thereby and is then compensated for with illusory power. This is one way of understanding the object from which the spiritual person seeks to detach himself; the other way of looking at it is to see that the mystic's struggle is to detach himself from this refusal of part of himself.

The intentionality of psychic action cannot be ascertained when the intentional object is buried in a sensuous medium, be it sexual, erotic, or sensual. What we have to determine is the nature of the intentional object. The subject is conditioned by the state of the object. If the object is buried in a sensuous object, then the mind's subject is thereby effected. In a real sense, the mind has to be created, or liberated from the sensuous medium. The subject has the capacity for self-awareness, but this is strangled if the intentional object is buried in the sensuous medium. The intentional object can be buried in the body, in a spouse, in two or three people. The subject is in the object and vice versa, so the subject's awareness of self is in proportion to the degree to which the intentional object is free of "in-ness". The state of the subject is determined by the state of the object. When the object is broken into pieces, then this is the state of the subject. It is the state of the being of the intentional structure. If the intentional object is "in" a sensual medium, then self-awareness and free thinking are absent. This is because the object is captive. At the same time the subject is disowning part of his or her own being.

The intentional reality is structured into subject and object with a connection, but the subject is in the object and vice versa, and the connection cannot exist without subject and object. The reality of the subject is in the object and vice versa but it is one being. The intentional structure supports itself. This is the ideal situation achieved only by a few—the Buddha, for example. There is a final battle with evil before this can occur. The great mystics at this point had a great showdown with evil . Evil is the one that personifies annihilation of the intentional structure. It is that when the final detachment occurs and the agent of self-destruction appears in all its nakedness. "Throw yourself down", says Satan to Jesus, "and God's angels will bear you up": in other words, "destroy yourself". As said earlier, the anxiety generated by this powerful agency is so strong that it is too much for normal mortals. This extreme anxiety is defended against by burying the intentional object "in" sensuousness or in auto-generated activity. But it is self-killing, spiritually and bodily.

Then there is a link between this self-killing and being "in" the sensuous self-love. This is a killing. It is a suicide of the sort that Hermann Hesse (1965) describes:

> Among the common run of men there are many of little personality and stamped with no deep impress of fate, who find their end in suicide without belonging on that account to the type of suicide by inclination; while, on the other hand, of those who are to be counted as suicides by the very nature of their beings are many, perhaps a majority, who never in fact lay hands on themselves. [p. 58].

This sensuous self-image is the medium in which the intentional reality buries itself. It is because of its sensuous nature that the mind is clouded. It is therefore a death. Detachment, then, is the liberation of the intentional reality from this imprisoning dungeon. The spiritual person is he whose central goal is this endeavour.

In traditional religion the spiritual person detaches himself from sexual and erotic ties. This is the foundation stone from which he begins his spiritual work. It is therefore a work that is constructed on a base of isolation. This endeavour is undertaken in relation to his own self. This is his reference point. The "other" against which he measures himself are the writings of his spiritual ancestors, the counsel of a spiritual director or a psychoanalyst.

Let us imagine a situation like this:

> A young man has "left the world" and entered a monastery. He prays earnestly, reads the scriptures, performs his spiritual duties,

and examines his conscience each night. In this examination he becomes aware of pride. In the Christian tradition this is the cardinal sin: the sin that poisons all virtues. "If you are proud of being chaste", said St Aelred of Rievaulx, "then it is a vice, because pride is a vice." As our young monk examines his conscience, he becomes increasingly aware of pride. So what does he try to do to overcome it? He prays harder; when feelings of self-exaltation come, he prays harder still and does small acts of penance. He discusses it with his spiritual director. He tries more and more strenuously, and yet he knows that he has made no progress in this endeavour. In a moment of enlightenment he clearly sees that he has made no progress. Our monk is a Christian and prays for the grace to overcome this vice at the centre of him. However, he has a twin, who is a Buddhist monk. He does not pray to a god because he does not believe in a deity. He also has a moment of enlightenment in which he realizes the presence of this pride in himself. He does not have the option of praying to god. What does he do? He strives harder, intensifies his ascetic practices, and consults regularly with his spiritual director. However, in this moment of enlightenment he knows that he is making no progress.

Both of them have reached a deadlock. They both know it. Without a transformation, the situation has no resolution. Acts of restraint, attempts to be humble, and so on are all to no avail, because they feed an exalted self that remains unaffected; the inner disowning remains undisturbed. Gritting the teeth, trying harder, are all signs that the individual is trapped. He had put his core self into these activities. There is a pain to be suffered. The suffering of that pain is the only path to liberation, but to suffer it. . . . How can it be suffered if taking flight into these ascetic activities has been in the service of avoiding pain? What needs to occur in order that the self has the resources to suffer the pain? An act of understanding from another. This is an act of emotional intercourse between two human beings that effects a strengthening of the core self. Then, without gritted teeth, the pain can be suffered. This is the function of psychoanalysis and why it can be considered a spiritual discipline.

CHAPTER FOURTEEN

Is psychoanalysis a religion?

W hen a patient comes for psychoanalysis he does not want to know just why he is depressed. If a patient came to tell me he was depressed, I could give him a little dissertation of this nature:

> "From what you have told me, I think your depression is due to unconscious aggression against your father and that when your father died when you were at the age of eight, you believed that your aggression had killed him. You believed this because of your unconscious omnipotence, and then you felt guilty and bad about what you had done. This guilt and badness is what you experience as depression."

I tell my patient that I have now given him an explanation, and he can go away and rest assured that his depression will vanish.

A wry smile may come to your lips, because you know that I am being absurd. But the question is: in what does the absurdity consist? I have, I believe, given a reasonable scientific explanation for this man's depression. The obvious point is that this patient of mine requires more than a scientific explanation. He needs to know what he has to *do* in order to resolve his depression. He needs, in other words, a prescription for living. He needs to know *how* to live in order to overcome his depression. I might therefore give you another example.

A man comes to a psychoanalyst because he has a drinking problem. As the analysis proceeds, it becomes clear both to the analyst and to the patient that he has no fulfilment from his work or from his marriage, and it is because he has unknowingly alienated himself from close emotional contact. It further becomes clear that he is driving himself in his work, and this drivenness is the method by which this emotional alienation is kept in being. As he becomes aware of all this, he makes decisions that favour the possibility of greater emotional satisfaction in his life.

The question "How am I going to live my life?" is a religious question. It is the ultimate religious question, and the answer to it can solve the problem of how I can live my life so that it will be emotionally satisfying.

It is necessary here to introduce a distinction between two different types of religion: revealed religion and natural religion (see chapter 9, this volume). A revealed religion is based on the belief that God revealed himself and his Law to man. Perhaps Islam is the purest example of a revealed religion. The Prophet Muhammad fell into an ecstatic trance during which God revealed himself and his law. It is part of Mohammedan belief that the full law of God is written on tablets in heaven and through the Prophet the writings in heaven were transcribed direct to man and committed to a definitive text: what is known as the Koran. In Mohammedan belief, therefore, the Koran is the word of God, and to doubt it is a sacrilege. In Judaism and Christianity the principle is the same, though it would be recognized that God's revelation is transmitted through human agents and therefore requires textual criticism, in the same way as any other piece of literature. However, despite this modification, the principle remains the same: that God has revealed himself to man, his submissive receptacle. The essence of such a religion is man's worship of God. God not man is the focus of such a religion. This is what we call revealed religion.

Although some psychoanalysts set themselves up as gods and although psychoanalysis has often been accused of being a religion in this sense, this is not its essential nature. When it is like this, it has been subject to degeneration.

There is another type of religion, less well known but just as truly a religion. This is the kind of religion the focus of which is upon the following questions: How should man live? What is the right path for man? How does man find fulfilment? How is a human being to find satisfaction in his life? What is life's purpose? What is the meaning of life?

Of course, revealed religion has addressed itself to these questions as well, but its authority for its answers rests upon the god who has spoken. There are, however, religions that rely for their authority upon reason. For instance, one of the greatest religious teachers the world has ever seen—I mean the Buddha—spoke emphatically against belief in the existence of God. At least this is the belief that has been carried down through the centuries by the Theravada tradition. In fact, the Buddha said that abstract questions such as whether the universe has always existed are empty questions, questions of no value. For the Buddha the only question that is of interest is *how should man live?*

Another great religious teacher in the same tradition was Socrates. He argued that the pursuit of the good is the true end of man. In this pursuit man will find his happiness. Socrates said that it is a better thing to suffer wrong than to do wrong. He was initially mocked by the Sophists, but by slow argument, by painful logic, step by step, he proved that however unusual this position was in the common opinion of men, yet this was the truth. Socrates established these positions by using his reason. When I use the word "reason", I do not mean disembodied intellectual argument. I mean belief structured through intelligence that carries with it emotional conviction. Socrates lived his life according to this conviction, and for following this path he was put to death. This second type of religion I call "natural religion": in other words, it accords with man's nature. The moral prescriptions that are arrived at through its insights are followed because they make sense.

We need now to come back to the initial question that we have proposed to ourselves in this chapter: Is psychoanalysis a religion? The answer, I believe, is that psychoanalysis is a natural religion but not a revealed one. I gave that first story of the man with the depression who comes to a fictitious analyst in order demonstrate that psychoanalysis is not a natural science. The explanation that the analyst gives to the depressed man is a sort of joke. The man does not want a scientific explanation—he wants to know how to rid himself of his depression; he wants to know how to endure it. In short, he wants to know how to live. Psychoanalysts have a very definite theory about how we live. We believe, for instance, that to blind ourselves to the truth, to deceive ourselves about the way we behave, leads to unhappiness, ill health, and misery. Psychoanalysts say that human beings blind themselves to the truth through the use of psychological means, which we call "defences". We believe that if we pursue the truth and remove these defences through which we blind ourselves, we shall regain—or gain for the first time—a new-found health and a new-found happiness. Psychoanalysis, then, is definitely a religion. It is not, however, a revealed religion. This statement is rather bald, and I shall take up the rest of the space in this chapter in trying to elucidate it further.

* * *

Most patients who come for psychoanalysis today do so because of disasters that have beset them in their human relationships. A man comes for a consultation because suddenly, after five years of marriage, his wife has walked out on him without a word of warning. If he believed that his wife had suddenly become demented, then he would not be consulting a psychoanalyst. He comes to the analyst because he knows, or at least suspects, that he is doing something of which he is not aware. When he comes into analysis, there develops, by slow degrees, knowledge of what he has been doing to contribute to his wife's sudden departure. One of the principles of psychoanalysis is that the ways a person acts emotionally in intimate relationships can be charted according to identifiable pathways. Therefore the way in which this man was behaving towards his wife would in essentials be the same as he was behaving in his childhood towards either his mother or his father, and it continues to be the way he behaves in intimate relations in adulthood.

Although psychoanalysis is a professional relationship, it is nevertheless a relationship of extreme intimacy, and therefore the same identifiable pattern of relating is repeated in the patient's relationship to the analyst. So, for instance, in the case of the man whose wife walked out on him so suddenly, the analyst finds himself thinking, after some months of analysis: "My heavens, I understand why his wife walked out on him." In other words, he begins to feel, sometimes in quite an acute way, an unbearable set of feelings. For instance, he may find himself intensely bored, he may find that everything he says to the patient is sneered at, or that he does all he can to disrupt understanding. It is the analyst's task to elucidate all these matters to the patient. In this process the patient becomes aware of what he is doing, and a realization emerges that these things that he is doing bring a lot of trouble down upon his head. He may discover, for instance, that it has led him to fail in his work, and also he now remembers that he has had strange reactions to him from members of his own family of origin. He begins to get a dawning awareness of a different way of living. When I use the verb "do", "does", or "doing", I am referring to what is done emotionally. These are the things that I do to those with whom I am closely bonded. These are the doings of which I am not aware. These are the activities that I become aware of through psychoanalysis. Psychoanalysis then reveals the way I am behaving towards my wife, my children, my parents, and all those with whom I live in close association. This revelation, however, puts demands upon my conscience.

Socrates said that you do not do wrong at the same time as knowing that you do wrong. Socrates drew the conclusion that once you know that something is wrong, you cannot do it, and therefore you do not do it. There is, however, another conclusion that has been discovered by psychoanalysis: it is that if I am doing wrong, then I am forced not to know it. What psychoanalysis discovered and elucidated is that we all do it, but we manage this by destroying all knowledge of what we are doing. The point, therefore, is that as psychoanalysis reveals these unconscious activities, so the person also transforms the direction of his/her activities. The direction of this attempt constitutes the process of psychoanalysis as a moral struggle. This emotional moral struggle is also closely scrutinized. This scrutiny, called self-analysis by psychoanalysts, changes psychoanalysis from being a morality into a spirituality. A person is spiritual when he examines his motives with the goal of purifying them, and it is an inherent part of psychoanalysis that the individual not only aims to change his emotional structure of relating but also understands it, has insight into it. It is this desire for insight that turns psychoanalysis from being a morality into a spirituality. But is it a religion?

Put at its simplest, the man sees the bad things that he is doing in his intimate human relationships, but does he know positively how to live in a better way? Does he develop a positive philosophy of life? It is the elaborated ethical philosophy that establishes a spirituality as a religion. In fact psychoanalysis embodies a philosophy of life that has its own inner coherence. This philosophy has never been properly formulated. It has not been written down and codified, though it is a coherent system that sustains the psychoanalytic endeavour. It will be the pattern upon which many an analyst constructs his life. This philosophy of life is a natural religion in the making.

You may say that this is just a moral stance—a particular moral stance of this individual. You may want to claim that morality can stand on its own, quite independently of religion; but morality is always rooted in an inner action pattern, and this action pattern, which will have symbolical expression, is what I am calling here a natural religion.

In our Western culture we are so imbued with the idea that religion consists in cultic acts that we dismiss anything that is devoid of this as not being religion. Such a view, for instance, would reject the Buddha as a religious man. On that same narrow definition, Socrates would also be rejected as a religious teacher.

The cultic aspect of religion is concerned with pleasing God or pleasing gods. Natural religion is concerned with the welfare of man; it is concerned with how man should live. Religion has the implicit view that the meaning of life is to be found in a reality that is beyond the tangible. So when I say that natural religion is concerned with the welfare of man, this means something that transcends his material welfare. In other words, it transcends that level of welfare that is contained within the paradigm of pleasure and pain. Pleasure and pain are both hitched to the survival instinct. Natural religion proclaims that there is a purpose that is beyond these narrow confines.

Psychoanalysis has never been established as a natural religion, and I believe this is because it has not had the conceptual tools to enable it to do so. Freud was very anxious that psychoanalysis should be clearly differentiated from revealed religion. For this reason, he insisted that psychoanalysis is a natural science. He also insisted upon the hedonistic hypothesis. It would take a book to demonstrate the fallacy of this position and to show that it is logically inconsistent with the practice of psychoanalysis. It is clear to me that the stuff of psychoanalysis is how the individual treats himself and others. With its concern for the truth, the centrality of love, and the role of guilt in human psychology, it has all the notes of a natural religion. It will not, however, be conceptualized this way until a great deal more philosophical thinking has been directed to this issue.

It is, however, the conviction of this author that psychoanalysis is a natural religion in the making, and that when this is recognized, it will be a considerable enrichment to psychoanalysis and society.

CHAPTER FIFTEEN

The murder of Laius

The story of Oedipus is a myth. A myth functions as a dream in the social group. It also has this function for the individual within the group. Laius, then, represents an inner psychic reality. This is a detective story, but one that is a bit different from the usual format. We know there has been a murder; we do not know who the murdered person is; we want to know why the murder is hushed up.

Setting the scene

When the people of Thebes saw the royal carriage ride past, carrying along their king and queen, Oedipus and Jocasta, all looked well. How fortunate it was that Oedipus, this knightly prince from Corinth, had sallied forth into Jocasta's bedchamber and so had made up for the untimely death of Laius. All looked well in Thebes that day.

The challenge of assumptions

Of course, this knowing reader knows better than did those innocents in Thebes. Yet do we? What was so dreadful about Oedipus being bound in wedlock to his mother? Oh, incest, the reader will say. We all know there is a taboo against that. We all know that is wrong. All societies have condemned it. This is factually not true, however, because there are exceptions—for instance, in the royal house of Hawaii before it was colonized by white Americans. But the question is, "Why is incest wrong?" or, "Is it wrong?" Is it perhaps a taboo that we should long since have abandoned in this scientific age?—in this age of liberal values? Let us address ourselves to the first question: why it is that there has been such a far-reaching taboo on incest and then see whether that answer suggests lines of approach to the other question.

Why is it a crime for the boy growing into a young man to slay his father and sleep with his mother? Why is it that parricide has ever been considered the very worst of murders? Once you get past the expostulations—"Oh, well, it's obvious", and so on—it begins to be more difficult to define satisfactorily why the deed of Oedipus is such a heinous crime. The killing of Laius is an intricate part of the sin of Oedipus. In fact, I think it safe to say that it is because Oedipus can only sleep with Jocasta by first getting rid of Laius that sleeping with his mother becomes a crime. We must remember that Laius is an intrapsychic person.

Imagine an alternative scene at Thebes. Their long-lost son, Oedipus, arrives in the town and is revealed for who he is. So what happens? Tiresias is called, and he removes for ever the curse of the Oracle at Delphi. Oedipus settles down to his princely tasks as heir apparent. He has a long wait before Laius dies and he come into possession of sovereign power. He has to undergo a long apprenticeship. He has to find his own woman and pass along the painful pathway into adulthood.

By killing his father and jumping into bed with his mother, he bypasses all this. He grabs his father's power, yet he remains a child, because he has not done what he needs to do to become adult. Although it looks otherwise, he is, in sorry fact, a child still with his Mummy. The father who is needed to come and say, "Now, now, Oedipus, it is time you left Mummy" is not there. He is absent. What is absent, then? What is the inner reality that is absent, that has been murdered?

Symbolic referent

We are concerned to get hold of the psychic reality to which this myth points. So what is absent intrapsychically? What has Oedipus not done in order for him to be adult? There is no doubt that in any crime, however heinous, the key to the evil is to look at and scrutinize not the dramatic events that have been committed but, rather, what has *not* been done. Paradoxically, it is not easy to see what is not done. The slaying of Laius is easy to see, the sleeping with Jocasta is identifiable. The crowds can shout and scream about these. You cannot scream about a vacuum, an absence, about what is not done. Yet I am sure that it is in the vacuum, in the absence, that we must look for the source of human disaster. In another context (Symington, 1993) I have referred to this as the *principle of omission*. So we have to look at what Oedipus did *not* do.

What we know is that he remained a baby with Mummy, although to the people of Thebes he *looked* a fully grown man. He had slain the sphinx so he looked doubly adult. Surely the slaying of the sphinx was a *rite of passage*, an initiation into adulthood, that no one could gainsay?

I knew a man once who had performed the most valiant deeds as a pilot in the Second World War—deeds for which he was justly decorated. His physical courage was an undoubted fact, but emotionally he was a puny child, a fact of which his wife and family were painfully aware. And so with Oedipus: he had slain the Sphinx and liberated Thebes from its terrors, and yet he was wanting in the essence of manhood. It *looked* as if he was having intercourse with an adult woman, yet he was but a baby with Mummy. He looked an adult and yet was a baby. We must conclude from this that adulthood is not conferred by acts of gallantry that draw the applause of the crowd, not by the fact of marriage, not by the physical ability to have intercourse, not by fathering children, not even by holding the post of king. Positions of high status do not confer adulthood. So in what does adulthood consist? What is its essence?

A conclusion forces itself upon us: adulthood is conferred not by any external act, however valiant, however magnificent in its effects, but only by an *internal act*. Although the internal act has external repercussions, yet it is the internal act that confers adulthood. In the case of Oedipus, the external repercussion would have been to sever the bond with mother, acknowledge his childhood, and take that enormous step of creating a wife. I use the word "creating" deliberately, because he will not find a wife of his pleasing. These, then, are the external repercussions. Had the story been different, Oedipus would have accepted himself as the child of Laius and Jocasta and would have set about the business of becoming a man.

As Freud (1939a) has pointed out, the two royal families—that of Corinth and that of Thebes—are one and the same parents, but divided in the myth. The murderous desires, and the loving ones—the desires to protect the parents—are expressed in the myth by turning the one set of parents into two. Otto Rank, in his book *The Myth of the Birth of the Hero* (1914), shows how frequently heroes are born mythologically of one set of parents but are then reared by another. Often the hero is born of aristocratic parents but is then brought up by humble parents or even sometimes by animals, as with Romulus, for instance. With Oedipus, the myth is similar, except that both families are aristocratic. Freud suggests that this is to indicate more clearly that they are identical.

I think the difference could be to indicate that Oedipus is not a hero, but an anti-hero. Rather than being the father of a glorious dynasty, he begets disaster in his progeny.

Had Oedipus taken the heroic path and set about the business of becoming a man, then one of the external repercussions of this would have been his taking a bride to wed. In the due passage of time his father would have died, and Oedipus could have been seen driving through the streets of Thebes with his lawful wife at his side, to the acclaim of the populace. It would *look* the same as the Oedipus we know riding forth in the carriage with Jocasta, but in reality how different it would be. That terrible catalogue of disaster would have been spared: no suicide of Jocasta, no violent blinding of Oedipus, and none of that pitiful tale that continues in ever-increasing melancholy in *Oedipus at Colonus* and ends with its woeful waste of Antigone and her sister and the final annihilation—that ultimate in evil's potential within the human scene—of Oedipus. This was eventually followed in *Antigone* by that final insult to the human person: the refusal of burial. All this catalogue of disaster is put in train by the action of Oedipus. Yet we have to come back to our question. What is the dread action that Oedipus has perpetrated?

I must remind you again that we must look to what Oedipus has not done. What is the internal action that Oedipus has not performed? To answer this, I want to draw your attention to the fateful voice of the Delphic Oracle: "This child will kill his father and marry his mother." Oedipus is condemned to live out the trajectory of that fateful voice. It is an inescapable fate to which he consents. "You have no choice", it says, "but to live out this appalling destiny." What Oedipus did *not* do was to break the bonds of that appalling sentence. He did not cry from the depths of his soul against so vile a tyranny, against a savagery that robbed him of that very core that makes us human: that kernel of humanness that philosophers from the dawn of civilization have tried inexorably to describe, that transcendent seed in the hearts of human beings. The reader must know that I am talking of that deepest of human mysteries: I mean, of course, freedom. And freedom means choice. Instead, he delivered himself up to Fate. This masochistic submission, this killing of his own soul, was the murder. This was the inner Laius.

I have seen this malign force that had so inexorable a grip upon our Oedipus. I have seen it in myself, I have seen it in friends, I have seen it in patients. It is something that is worse by far than the more sensational manifestations of human depravity. You might say that you cannot get worse than parricide combined with incest, and yet I can state confidently that these are the epiphenomena of a malignancy that is far worse. In fact, the killing of the father is the pseudo-attempt to break free: the delusional belief that Oedipus can set himself free from this malign force by killing the symbol of power rather than transform the power itself. It is what the father symbolizes that requires transformation. To kill the father himself is the maddest madness, yet it is a madness that, I believe, I have witnessed on certain appalling occasions.

There is an action required of Oedipus if he is to break free of this strangling power. It is not an act of gallantry that will be recorded in the annals of the great, but a small, quiet action, the repercussions of which are enormous down the avenues of history. But it is one that goes unnoticed. It is not an action that will have any attraction for those who want fame, no lure for those who long for power. It is an act of faith in the potential of the child, the potential of the seed, to grow. This is followed by an inner resolution to be faithful to that initial pact with truth. All this is within. There is no clapping audience to an action of this kind. There are no badges, no medals, for such an action. It is, however, the action that bit by bit, inch by inch, with undoubted forwardness, drives back the power of that malign force that had so strangling a grip upon the soul of Oedipus.

The malignant power that this would-be action of Oedipus drives back takes the mind into its control. What we are witness to in the Oedipus myth is a mind in the grip of a malign negation. I believe that Oedipus was schizophrenic, and my evidence for this is that the negative fatefulness that ruled his soul is one of the most telltale signs of the schizophrenic condition. Behind the oracle's infernal words, "The Child will kill his father and sleep with his mother", is the implied taunt: "And that's all you're good for"—"You haven't got it in you to grow and come into possession of your own inheritance; to come into possession of your own powers." Another way of saying this is that the child—the child in front of whom a whole world of freedom and possibility expands—this child has been crushed, brutally murdered. The murder of Laius symbolizes the murder of the infant Oedipus. The infant is wounded in the foot, and it is when the wheel of Laius' carriage goes over the adult Oedipus' foot that he goes into a rage and assassinates his father, thereby symbolizing the hurt child who slays Laius. The murder is undertaken as a way of trying to murder the malign child, but with the act is also a murder of the sane child. The negative, malign power is born of the assassination of a wounded child.

It is a terrible thing to have such a malign power within. The human psyche can only flee from it. There are rare cases where an individual turns and stares it in the face and declares war upon it. This is the exception. In most cases we flee it. What we see in the Oedipus myth is the mind in violent flight, with its deceitful substitutes on external display. As I said at the beginning, "It all looks all right." This is the fraudulent mother, Jocasta, to whom Blomfield (1992) refers. Jocasta is a person, an agent–person, in the self—a person so hated, so intolerable, that it is wedded outside. The suicide of Jocasta is another false attempt, just as the murder of Laius is. This psychotic negativism generates a deceitful array of solutions. At that famous junction of the three roads, the voice says: "If you kill him, you will at last be free." And then, when Jocasta's offer beckons, the voice says: "When you sleep with her, you will be freed forever of the bonds of childhood and you will forever be a big man." When he slays the Sphinx, the voice whispers: "And now you can have supreme and kingly power."

When he murders Laius, Oedipus believes that he will be freed. He is deceived into thinking that an external act will deliver him. An act is needed, but it is an internal act. There is something he has to slay, but it is a mental power within, not King Laius riding out in his chariot. He had reason enough to hate Laius, but slaying him did not free him of the inner childhood wound. He does need intercourse with his mother—not sexual intercourse, but an internal intercourse where the child Oedipus can give motherhood to his mother and receive the nurture his child needs, the nurture he needs in order to grow. He needs to exercise power, great power, but an internal power. He is deceived at every point. It looks like the genuine article, but it is so disastrously false, so cunningly fake. It is so fake that the human spirit cannot ultimately bear it; it has to be undone. I believe this is the reason why Oedipus *has* to expose the truth. The appalling deeds that unfurl at the end of Sophocles' play are the external manifestations of this inner evil and, appalling though the external events are, yet the malign power within is worse.

The climax of the corruption sets in with the murder of Laius. What is it that is murdered within? It is this potency, this capacity, to take that small great step: that act of belief in the child's capacity to grow, followed by resolution to follow that path, come what may. At those crossroads, Oedipus murdered his one hope, the one true possession he had, the seed of possibility. He opted for a false route.

Reasons for negativism generating catastrophe

I am making the connection that the submission of Oedipus to the fateful voice of the Delphic Oracle was what generated the awful events with which we are all familiar. I have suggested that the inner malign power that gripped the heart of Oedipus is worse than the catastrophic events that follow. Oedipus has to free himself from the terrible inner curse. Tiresias warns him not to continue with his appalling enquiry, but he cannot heed the warning. He *has* to do it. He can stand the bonds no longer. You might ask, "but why does the enquiry have to lead to such a violent finale?" We have to look back further and ask, "Why does Oedipus fulfil all that was pronounced by the Oracle? Why does he do it so violently?"

We have to ask here what it is that has generated this cruel voice in the heart of Oedipus. I believe the myth is right in suggesting that it is a state of mind implanted in infancy. It is a sour refusal, a bitter hatred of life itself, that takes a grip within the child's mind at the very start of things. The Voice says, "You will kill your father and marry your mother", and with a poisoned mind the child says, "OK, I will."

You may wish to tell me that such a sour intent, such poisonous bitterness, is not common among the ordinary thoroughfares of human decency. Oh, yes, in Thebes perhaps, but not in our civilized twenty-first-century world, not, surely, in our comfortable, developed world that we all know so well. Yet I believe that such complacency is a risky path to take: in the psychoanalytic world we are frequently confronted by appalling events. These events bear all the marks of violence, catastrophe, and psychic murder that the Oedipus legend foreshadowed.

I do believe that in an analysis we need to reach this level where the malign power lies, if we can. If Oedipus were on our couch, we would have great difficulty in keeping him in analysis long enough to reach his sour intent before he went out and slew Laius. The desire for magic is so strong, so violent, that we all fear the transformation of this malign mentality. We all hate the terrible ordeal of looking within. After all, it is a mentality that has been my trusty guardian all these years of my life, from my earliest infancy. Oedipus, by becoming King, believes he can magically banish that inner curse. "If I become an analyst, share the bedchamber with my own analyst, then I shall banish that inner curse: I shall be a big man, a mature woman? What, do you think that *I*, who have slain the Sphinx, cannot banish so fearful an inner voice?" It is so tempting to be deceived that, like Oedipus, we do not even *see* the inner Sphinx, the inner monster. When I am adorned with the grandiose robes of kingship, I do not see. In fact, it is a condition of "turning a blind eye" (Steiner, 1985) that I must be in kingly robes in order to act the blind man. So I believe I am king, yet, despite all appearances to the contrary, I remain a tiny baby with Mummy.

This negative fatefulness is not apparent on the surface. It is so terrible that Oedipus does not bear to look inside and see it. An analysis is a terrible threat to this dark inner blight. An analysis is an offer of hope, an offer of life, but a great threat to one in such a hell as Oedipus. It requires a total reversal—giving up his magical violence and unthinking thrust for power—but, most essentially, it is the murder of the infant self, the emotional core of the personality. It is the core out of which I initiate, the core out of which I create responsiveness in my human environment, the one of creation, the one of freedom. It is this that is killed. It is because it is killed that Oedipus has no source out of which he can with confidence journey along that path from infancy to adulthood, from the seed to the fully grown tree. He leaps hastily *into* the shoes of Laius. But if he is in the shoes of Laius, then where is his own person? The source of personhood is in the crying infant. Herein also lies the source of freedom, and this has been murdered. What we meet is just an absence. The individual lives in the shoes of others, in their phrases, in their language, in their ideas. There is, though, no person. A murder has been done. Like most murders, desperate measures are used to hide it. It is the guilt of discovery that leads Oedipus to blind himself and Jocasta to kill herself, rather than start all over again from the beginning. Such disasters have many manifestations, but they always find their source in a vile murder and a hidden malignity.

Conclusion

We are the people of Thebes. We see the patient riding in his chariot every day for his or her analysis. It all *looks* fine. All the external signs are there; the credentials look impeccable. Are you sure, though, that you are not looking at Oedipus? Has Laius been slain?

CHAPTER SIXTEEN

Psychoanalysis and human freedom

This paper was originally given in Sydney in 1999 as the conclud-
ing lecture of a three-year series on psychoanalysis.

Patients come for psychoanalysis because they wish to be free.
They want to be liberated from those inner forces that limit
their freedom. A psychotic patient is tortured by voices that
castigate her; a patient who suffers from an obsessive compulsive
disorder is prevented from stepping forth into the social world with
confidence; the moods that afflict a borderline patient prevent him
from carrying through some of his most enlightened projects; the psy-
chopath comes for analysis when the world has turned against her and
she can no longer function as a business executive; the schizophrenic is
tortured by all the classic symptoms: belief that he is being watched
through the television screen, that his thoughts are being recorded by
alien powers and so on. The person with a less serious condition wants
to be freed of her depression or of those inner elements that prevent her
from being able to make friends and be loved by people. I say "less
serious", though in terms of human suffering the condition of such
people may be more painful. As every individual who walks into the
consulting-room seeks to rid herself of obstacles to freedom, a psychoanalyst would have to conclude that the desire for freedom must be
one of the deepest human longings.

174

Why freedom is so difficult to achieve is something that has puzzled political theorists since the Enlightenment. Many of us are familiar with Rousseau's famous statement in his *Social Contract* (1792) when he asks himself the question: "Well, what if people do not want to be free?" and his ironical answer is: "Well, they must be forced to be free."

Rousseau, followed by Karl Marx, believed that we were in chains because of the social structures that imprison us, but we have to ask, who set up the structures, and who maintains them? Social theorists like Hobbes and Freud believed that human beings were basically savages who had to be controlled if we were not all to perish in social and political anarchy. We are also all familiar with the situation where those oppressed by a tyranny finally revolt, grab power, and then, in a short time, become as tyrannical as the regime that they have so recently displaced; Stalin used to be referred to as the Red Czar. And the world is divided between dictatorships like those in Burma or Pakistan and democracies like Australia or Switzerland. If there is such deep yearning for freedom within human nature, then why is it so difficult to achieve? Clearly, Rousseau did not have an answer. The only social theorist who approaches an answer in one domain of experience is Max Weber in his famous essay *The Protestant Ethic and the Spirit of Capitalism* (1971), but with the exception of Erich Fromm and Wilfred Bion, I have not seen it given any serious attention by psychoanalysts. It is no good clamouring about political tyrannies like the one recently in Albania, harsh penal codes as in Saudi Arabia, religious fundamentalism as in Iran, political racism, which has raised its head under Pauline Hanson's[1] banner in Australia, and sexism, which still flourishes in some professional groupings, such as in aviation. Shocked horror provides no solutions.

This does not mean that we must accept the inevitable: rather, our task seems to be to look to see why freedom is so fraught with difficulty for human beings. I am aware of only two psychoanalysts who put freedom at the centre of their thinking and conceptualization—Erich Fromm and Wilfred Bion—and of these two, the latter was faithful in a more comprehensive way to his vision. Bion, I believe, saw freedom as being elemental to psychoanalysis and any erosion of freedom within psychoanalysis being a betrayal of its true nature.

I believe that psychoanalysis is able to answer that riddle which has so frustrated social and political theorists over the last 200 years because in our laboratory we are able to see what it is that inhibits free emotional action. Let me summarize the factors that I have been able to observe in my own laboratory:

1. In a free act I see myself.
2. In a free act I see my madness.
3. In a free act I see my "shadow side".
4. In a free act my shameful life confronts me.
5. In a free act I realize my assets.
6. In a free act I return to kindergarten.

An interpretation may free a person from the grip of imprisoning forces but not without anguish of spirit. An effective interpretation brings about this change: before it, I was possessed by madness, but after it I possess it, and at the moment of that transformation I go through a fearful agony.

It may be obvious that I want to disguise from myself the first four of these elements, but why do I not want to realize my assets? Surely, especially with an arrogant person like me, I shall rejoice in them? This is not my experience. When someone "realizes" her assets, she cannot stay as she was. She is a new person and has to leave behind the easy path and embrace those projects that are commensurate with these assets. It means returning to childhood too. I have grown into adulthood in the proficiency of my well-worn roles; now suddenly I have been handed a new qualification, and I have to start all over again. Psychoanalysis teaches that most of us hate being children, stepping forth into the unknown, having to seek the help of those more experienced. The reason for this hatred will divert us from our present project.

One may ask why it is that it is in the free act that we come to see our madness, our shadow side, the waste in our lives, our cruelty, the shocking damage we do to ourselves and our circle. The answer lies in the fact that it is in the creative act that we come to know ourselves, for freedom and creation are inseparable twins—or perhaps the same reality seen from two different perspectives. Unless we are abusing the word, creation means that we produce a new reality out of ourselves. What I am asserting, though, is that knowledge of ourselves accompanies such acts. And the reason for this lies, I believe, in the fact that the creative act proceeds from an ego that has gathered into itself all its parts. An act whereby we disown unwanted aspects of ourselves is the antinomy of the creative act. THE creative act is that one whereby I gather all the disparate parts of myself into a new personal synthesis. Poetry, art, literature, music, scientific invention, the forming of friendships—these are all manifestations of this primordial act of creation. And self-awareness arises through a relation between parts. The pain of the creative act lies in being confronted with those parts of ourselves that we have disowned. Also, when we give birth to this synthesis inside ourselves, we leave behind some of our most cherished attachments; this is why there is no freedom without the pain of detachment. This, I believe, is the reason why Bion recommended analysts to read John of the Cross's *Ascent of Mount Carmel* (1947).

All these things have been known by thinkers, writers, and artists, but what psychoanalysis examines in fine grain are those forces in the personality that keep my infant self from the adult, the shadow from the sunlight, the act from its enjoyment. It examines those forces that prevent freedom, that rob us of our human birthright.

* * *

I am going to repeat what I have said, but from a different angle. We must ask ourselves therefore what the conditions for freedom are. And as soon as I say this, the age-old debate about free will versus determinism raises its head. In his *History of Western Philosophy* Bertrand Russell (1974) says two or three times that any philosophical position that is made to run inexorably to its logical conclusion ends in madness. This is the case with either free will or determinism. The man who tries to argue that we are entirely free ends in mad conclusions: I am free to stop my pulse beating, I can do without sleep for a week, I can live without water. The woman who tries to argue that all her actions are entirely the product of non-willed antecedent causes runs into mad paradoxes also. Why is it that since the axial era human beings in all societies have held their kind responsible for actions? The determinist is forced to argue that all those human institutions based upon the idea that we have choices are founded upon delusion. Logically, the determinist would have to re-cast totally our penal code.

It seems clear that what differentiates living organisms from the "dead" world is that in the latter, movement always has to be explained by the impact upon it of another element that is in motion. The explanation for its movement has to be sought in an outer body impacting upon it, whereas in the case of living organisms the explanation is sought in a combination of outer stimuli and inner responsiveness. The inner responsiveness implies that the organism has a causal element from within. The philosopher Henri Bergson defined life as *the tendency to act on matter*. I prefer Streeter's definition of life as an element the cause of the activity of which is to be found within itself.

Quite how this is possible is difficult for the mind to grasp. There are two ways of approaching such an issue, however. Either we say, "Look, the mind cannot grasp it, therefore we must tailor our data and our theory to what the mind *can* grasp", or we say, "Look, the mind is limited in its capacity to grasp conceptually evident paradoxes." The former formulation is not correct because the way I have phrased it implies that the philosopher knows that the mind is limited, whereas in fact he believes that it has infinite capabilities. The psychologist in her laboratory knows that there are certain dimensions of human experience that she cannot test, so she restricts herself to those that she can test. If you were to meet a psychologist who told you that there was no element of human experience that she could not test, you would say that her estimate of the laboratory's capabilities was wildly exaggerated. So also the belief that the mind can grasp all the contradictory dilemmas that confront it from the universe is, I believe, equally crazy. There are conceptual dilemmas that the mind cannot grasp. This is the true meaning of "mystery" in religious discourse. It is mysterious to our minds how living organisms are able to be causes of their own activity. To refuse this mystery by reducing life to the same restrictions as those that apply to the inanimate world is no better than the solution Parmenides provided to explain oneness and diversity: "Change and diversity must be an illusion." Many contemporary social scientists, refusing mystery, try therefore to restrict life to the parameters that apply to dead matter. They, then, are also the enemies of freedom.

So, human beings are both restricted by the limitations of their organic structure and enjoy a freedom within it. But the area in which there is the potential for freedom is frequently littered with obstruction. Before looking into the soul of the individual, let me first take as an analogy the concept of *negative freedom*. I owe my description of it to Isaiah Berlin's essay, "Two Concepts of Liberty" (1984, pp. 122–134). When I am obstructed by what I want to do by the restrictions of another, then I am not free. If I am kept in prison by an authority, I am not free; if I live in a regime that restricts my movements to within its own national boundaries, I am not free; if I am prevented from practising the religion of my choice, I am not free; if I am not allowed to practise as a psychoanalyst, I am not free; if I am not allowed to accumulate wealth, my freedom is restricted. I do not want to enter into the vexed question of whether my freedom needs to be restricted in order that others may have liberty, as I believe the answer to this lies in a psychological understanding of personal freedom. What Berlin refers to in his essay are the external obstacles to freedom. I am using the same model, but substituting "inner" for "outer". There are inner obstacles to freedom that are, I believe, of much greater importance than the outer ones. However, before it is possible to understand the obstacles, it is necessary to look at what constitutes freedom for me.

It is here necessary to distinguish between freedom and licence. Licence is doing what I want:

"Why shouldn't I light bush fires whenever I want?"

"Why shouldn't I murder if I feel like it?"

"—or kill myself, if I feel inclined, or rape or steal?"

"Why shouldn't I lie and cheat and exploit if I want to?"

What is the answer to these questions? The only way in which it is possible to see why what is being paraded here is not freedom but licence is to look within.

A patient said to me: "Although I have done well in my profession, I have always felt I could achieve greater sense of fulfilment, but it would mean a risk that I have never dared to take."

For some reason he is not free to do what he wishes. There is a sense that there is some obstacle that holds him back from being able to do that which he wishes. To do that which he wishes means overcoming an obstacle. Licence is acting in accordance with the obstacle. So, paradoxically, a sign of freedom is that there is an obstacle to its achievement. Freedom is an emotional achievement; licence is emotional capitulation. To do that which I wish is a risk. What is the step that I wish to take but dare not? It is a step into a void, into nothingness, into a place of no guarantees, of no safety, of no security. In this step the human being *lives* his life; he *lives* rather than being lived. He acts in fidelity to his living being. It is here that the instinct theories so beloved of classical psychology let us down. They dictate the direction in which the organism *must* travel, whereas the very essence of life is that it goes we know not whither.

It is very familiar in the work of an analysis to come across within the personality a menacing figure whose sombre threats discourage the individual from taking a step into the void:

"Play it safe", says the figure.

"You may put yourself in danger", he says.

"Are you sure you are not being foolish?" he cautions.

The menacing figure is a guardian that keeps me close to what is familiar, to what I know, to what I can touch, taste, hear, and see; it keeps me firmly encased within my social grouping. It is to those close familiars that it holds me attached. It dissuades me from stepping forth into alien territory. This figure parades before me all the obstacles; all the reasons for being "sensible" for being "practical".

A living thing, as opposed to a dead thing, has a creative principle within: the source of life is in itself. The exercise of this creative principle is synonymous with freedom. Its exercise expands the horizons of the personality. Every free act deepens and widens the personality; every act performed under pressure, under a directive, shrinks my being. It is the business of psychoanalysis to undo the power of these inner obstacles to freedom.

The exercise of freedom is not to be equated with happiness—or not as that word is usually understood. It is its own end. I do not pursue it so as to obtain happiness or to give me fulfilment. I can never say to myself or anyone else:

"If you take this step, then you will be fulfilled.

If you step into the void, you will find happiness."

Admonitions of this sort betray a radical misunderstanding of freedom. It is very common to come across interpretations of this sort:

"Perhaps you feel that if you do this, I will disapprove . . ."

"You fear to confront this because you fear you will be scorned . . ."

"If you commit yourself, you believe you will be rejected . . ."

There is a reassuring implication that these fears will not be realized. The therapist who made these interpretations does not believe in freedom. He protects his patient from that lonely step into the void, protects him from the terror of freedom.

Freedom is something desired because it is the natural inheritance of a living being. This theme could be looked at from an evolutionary perspective and also historically. The human race, as Teilhard de Chardin (1960) pointed out, is still evolving, but towards what, we do not know. The desire to throw off the yoke of a subjugating power was the motivating principle behind the American War of Independence, the French Revolution, the Second World War, the present turbulence in East Timor, the Republican movement in Australia, and so on. The particular aspect of freedom I want to look at here is that which applies to the emotions.

I once had a patient who used to say that the only way in which he could experience freedom would be by removing himself to a remote place and become a hermit. The presence of other human beings was always a pressure upon him, so the only measure open to him was to remove himself utterly from the precincts of his fellows. I think we can all enter this man's soul with a bond of sympathy: the sense that life is too much, the hurly-burly of the crowd too exhausting, to get away from it all, and so on. Yet the exigencies of life prevent such a solution for the majority. Is it possible to be free in the presence of other human beings, of human beings who bully, who exploit, who treat me as an object of contempt, of humans who expect things of me that I am not able to provide, in the presence of people who hate me? In order to answer this, I need to examine more closely the difference between free and un-free actions.

There are two kinds of activity in human beings: mobile practical action and emotional action. I am examining here freedom of emotional action. No external tyrant, however brutal, can rob me of my emotional freedom, but enormous pressure can be put on me to surrender it. Should I do so, it is a disaster to the human spirit. This is why Otto Rank (1978) emphasized the healthy core that resides in *resistance*.

Very crudely, there are two possibilities: either I surrender my inner autonomy to the energic strength of an outside force, or I let myself be the source and creator of my own action. What psychoanalysis reveals is that the outer force can only exert pressure and rob me of my freedom if it finds within my soul a mirroring echo. In fact, it is the activity of this inner figure or figures that crushes the creative centre in me.[2] To be able to create emotionally, I need all my resources in an integrated state—that is, not dispersed. It is possible to have my emotional resources all gathered into a coherent pattern of interlocking parts through a synthetic creative act. If I have, like an inveterate spendthrift, dispersed my best resources into scam-like projects and filled my domain with unusable goods, and if, furthermore, my inner world is broken up into incommunicable bits, then what I call "I" becomes a clamouring child in a violent sea, totally unable to resist any of the currents of life that bombard me. I am like a paralysed man whose arms and legs are no longer available for use. I am not a person but a hypocrite.

I shall try to elaborate this imagery in greater detail.

The spendthrift who throws away his money on scam-like projects: I have some good resources inside me. Let us say, for instance, that I am able to think imaginatively. That is a gift, and perhaps it is one that I have developed. Then I hear that a very famous philosopher has come to town—perhaps Derrida or Chomsky. I believe that he is the summit of all wisdom and, in a great impulse of admiration, I donate to him all my good inner resources. I am then left empty, and the famous thinker has pocketed a windfall that does not rightly belong to him. The rich get richer and the poor poorer. I have sometimes heard sophisticated adults using a strange word called "idealization": I suspect they may be talking about these violent activities; I cannot make sense of their disembodied language, but I trust that the good practical people in front of me will not have heard of this word or if they have, will have no truck with it. Let us ban once and for all such anodyne language. This language is the armament of the hypocrite who pretends to be a person but is not; who pretends to synthesize but does not; whose activity is hidden behind a facade of passivity.

So I am already in a parlous state because I have got rid of the good qualities inside myself, but now things get worse. I open my ears and drink in indiscriminately everything that is said, so I have my inner domain full of junk. As in all junk, there are some treasures in the junk, but because it has come from god, I believe it all to be good. The situation is even worse than this, because I have drunk in everything with such zealous intensity that I have broken down my protective psychic barriers.[3] I am now victim to every whimsical melody that strikes my ears. My "I" has been drowned.

As if this were not enough, my own soul has now shattered into pieces that are disconnected from each other. It is the zealous ingestion and the spendthrift dispersion that wreaks this havoc and leaves each jig-saw bit of my soul unconnected to every other bit.

You cannot tell someone how to create, because the very essence of creation is a process that lies in each person's interior being.

You come across a man all of whose limbs are broken from a shocking accident, and you say to him: "This is the way to walk." And he rightly says, "Can't you see, you silly fool, that my legs are broken and I need an ambulance?"

Therefore what a psychoanalyst can do is to assist in clearing away those obstacles to the accomplishment of a free act. This is what is meant by analysing. In other words, those processes that prevent the free act are identified and named. Is that all you do, you might ask? What's the good of naming these damaging processes? To answer these questions, we have to make an assumption, and it is in fact an assumption that lies at the basis of all psychoanalytical work: that once someone is aware of self-damaging activity, he remedies it. Just as, if you cut yourself, the white blood cells travel to the spot to start the work of repair, so also when the damaging activity is seen in the personality, the white cells of the psychic system hasten to the place of ill-fortune. The "chrysalis" person is now free to act. She can see the obstacle. She is a free person.

I need here to say what I said about self-damaging activity from a different perspective—the same thing from a different angle. Knowledge and awareness are often equated, but they represent very different states of mind. In the chaotic mix-up where I am dispersed, invaded, and fragmented, I *know* my life is in a mess. It is a knowledge that is piecemeal—a glimpse here, a glimpse there. This is knowledge. Awareness is when the pieces are seen as a whole and in relation to one another. Subjectively it is the difference between a situation where someone says to you, "You are a frightened individual", and you say: "I know", and when you say to yourself one day, "Heavens, I never realized how frightened I am most of the time."

A man started every session saying that he was very guilty about sexual things. The analyst may have believed that this man was aware that he was guilty about sexual matters. One day he came in and said, "A most extraordinary thing happened yesterday. I was shaving in front of the mirror, and I suddenly realized that I am very guilty about everything sexual."

So when the person is aware of self-sabotaging, it is a sign that the damage wrought by this inner activity is already an historical fact and no longer current. Knowledge is now transformed into awareness. A creation has occurred: the creation of my own person, but, because awareness is what it is, it is painful. Knowledge can be free from pain but awareness never.

I am careful these days to distinguish between the word "individual" and "person". By the former I refer to an agglomerative morass of parts, by the latter to a coherent being that has been brought into existence through an inner creative act. Personhood and awareness are correlative attributes. A person is a person to the extent that he or she is a free individual.

* * *

Although these principles are universal, yet their personal embodiment is individual. The way I act, the way I perceive the world, will never be the same as the way you act and perceive it. The minute I suggest, persuade, or cajole, then I have lost freedom. My way is not your way.

It is worth considering why this is so. I believe it is like this: I become a person through owning all parts of myself. My parts can never be matched by another. Even identical twins have a different foetal and infantile history with different inner and outer experiences. The material that is gathered up through the act of ownership is different, and therefore the manufactured compound through the act of ownership is also different. This is so with identical twins, so all the more so with all other individuals.

Before I finish I want to put a puzzling dilemma before you. I have said that the job of psychoanalysis is to transform those elements in the personality that obstruct freedom into ones that enrich it and that therefore the job of analysis is to analyse these obstacles. Yet to do this, I must have some vision against which I can sight these obstacles. Am I therefore subtly imposing a utopian viewpoint? Am I a Rousseau or Marx in disguise after all? I think the answer is both yes and no. I have to have some value that makes me think it is worth while to investigate the workings of my own soul and that of another—some inchoate idea that there is in me a source of life struggling for expression, a life-thrust coming against a frustrating obstacle. This is enough for me to focus my lens upon that inner drama and to investigate its workings. Once given that first push, the scientist sets to work and sees with a newborn clarity those elements that are noxious to our health and sanity. He is able to see how they work, in what they consist, and the process by which they are transformed. I am like Rousseau and Marx in that I have a vision that guides me; I am unlike them in that I only share their thrust but disown utterly the concreteness of their goals. In the former freedom is preserved; in the latter it is destroyed. A thrust into nothingness preserves freedom; an architectural drawing of the end product destroys it.

Science, axiology, and aesthetics come together in this investigation to produce an understanding of these inner elements, which are hidden from the outer gaze of men and women. Any one without the other two renders the investigation null and void; any two without the third also make the endeavour sterile. It is the collaborative effort of this trio that illuminates that baleful assault on our freedom, our supreme treasure.

The goal of psychoanalysis is the transformation of those obstructions to freedom into vehicles for the achievement of it. This is, I believe, the defining characteristic of psychoanalysis; it differentiates psychoanalysis from all other psychotherapeutic endeavours. I do not think I have explained my purpose very clearly, but I hope you will catch the drift of it.

Notes

1. Pauline Hanson was leader of the right-wing "One Nation" party which was anti the aboriginal peoples of Australia.

2. When we speak of inner figures, we make use of a metaphor. I prefer the use of the word "figure" rather than object because the latter is thought of as the object of action, whereas the former suggests the subject of action.

3. Actually what it breaks down are my imaginative processes or, in Bion's terminology, *alpha function*, which processes and therefore can be thought of as a barrier.

CHAPTER SEVENTEEN

Failure of internalization
in modern culture

There are two ways in which an object can be present in the mind. I shall call these two the "photographic" and the "artistic". Two people are facing the same scene. One has in his hands a camera, which he pulls up and points at the landscape and clicks. The other has an easel, a palette, and paints, and after three hours of industry she has a representation of the scene in front of her.[1]

This model is designed to highlight two different ways in which something is present in the mind. In the photographic mode the thing is "taken in" as a whole, and the mind of the individual is like a film upon which the scene is imprinted, like the impression of a seal upon wax. In the artist's mode there is an active engagement with the object. The artist makes a selection; she decides which moment of light she will represent; she will decide what to leave out and what to include. The artist will *know* that scene better a year later than her friend, the photographer.

It is a common dictum that a person learns through teaching. It is something I can personally vouch for. When I have to explain the contents of a book to pupils in a classroom, I come to know and understand the book a good deal better than when I sit back and "drink it in" in my comfortable armchair. I remember Juliet Mitchell saying to me that any serious reading requires note-taking. In other words, there is active engagement with the object. George Orwell complains in "Politics and the English Language" (1971) that the language is being deadened because rather than constructing our own similes and metaphors, we reach for one from the supermarket shelf and put it indiscriminately into our basket.

The point is this: in order for me to know something in the artist's mode, there are two factors that need to be active in me: imagination and curiosity. It is through imagination that we construct our world. I know it when I have constructed it. That remarkable Italian philosopher, Giambattista Vico, who has been made known to the educated English-speaking public through the studies of Isaiah Berlin (1979b, 1980), made the striking statement that we only know that which we have created.[2] This was in direct contradiction to Descartes, who thought that we can only know those things that are already constituted outside ourselves. I only put this in to give a hint that the origins of the modern malaise that I hope to describe has its origins back in the seventeenth century, and, in fact, I believe, it can be traced back to an intellectual *hubris* that goes back much further.[3] We create through our imagination. Three people—Immanuel Kant, Melanie Klein, and Wilfred Bion—have put this at the centre of their theoretical understanding. I would be prepared to ditch everything that Melanie Klein taught as long as I were permitted to keep her fundamental insight that from earliest infancy we construct our human world. The word she uses for this process is *phantasy*. Elliott Jaques told me that he tried to persuade Melanie Klein to use a word that would designate the active constructive process more clearly, but she did not want to do that. I cannot now remember why she repudiated his suggestion, but I regret that she did so.

The other mental component is *curiosity of mind*. Why do I fear death? Why do I need someone else to interpret my state of mind to me? Why was I frightened to speak in public when I was young? Why am I less afraid to do so now? What does it mean when people say that my behaviour is good? What does it mean when they say that it is bad? Why did human beings think, until Copernicus, that the sun went around the earth? Why was it that Copernicus suggested otherwise? Was he the only one, or did he give voice to what many others were thinking? How was it that no one, until Galileo, had thought of measuring speed? Was Galileo the first one? Why did people get upset when Freud suggested that children were sexual? What brought about the Puritan prudishness of the seventeenth century? Why do so many people today read very little? Why is it that principals of schools and academics all complain of the huge increase in paperwork and administration? What brought about secularization? What accounts for the increase in drug-taking? Why is our present age more sexually liberal than that of a generation ago? Is it that now it is just in the open, and in the past it was secret? And if so, why?

Is that enough? When you ask yourself a question, and then one day you suddenly say to yourself "Aha!" then you really know it. Both the question and the answer are self-generated. The question is something of personal concern, and the answer is a convincing echo.

Now here is a problem. You cannot educate someone to have curiosity and you cannot induce imagination. Yet these are the two human features in the absence of which internalization cannot occur. However, I think that a certain maternal ingredient can bring them to life in the developing psyche.

These, then, are the two qualities of soul that are absolutely necessary for internalization to occur. However, something else has to happen if there is to be an internalizing act. We need to stop for a moment to consider the contours of such an event.

Let us see for a moment whether we can abandon latinisms and see what we are talking about. What do I *DO* when something passes from outside into the heart of my mind? I have a very definite job to do: of no lesser status than when I dive into a swimming-pool, drive a car, or write this essay. In fact, it is an act that underlies—or should underlie—all other activities. It is an act in which I grasp the oneness that exists in the multitude; it is an act in which I convert what I can see, hear, and touch into something soul-like. Something has to pass from being touchable stuff into being mind stuff. And how do I do it? I do not know, but I do know that the human mind is the only living thing in the world that is able to do it.[4]

I said at the beginning that we needed to look at the contours of this event. The last bit that needs to be drawn is the mind's act: that which happens when something passes from being touchable stuff into stuff that is untouchable. There is a leap of faith. A moment ago I was in darkness, and suddenly I can see. I was probing, driven on by curiosity; I was imagining this and picturing that, and I am delightedly in possession of a new creation in my mind, but the actual moment of creation I cannot see. This is a limitation of our minds. *Homo sapiens* is able to represent the world in a way that was probably not possible for *Homo erectus*. Perhaps in two million years' time a species will have evolved from us that will be able to comprehend this mystery.

* * *

Is it correct to say that in modern culture there is a failure to achieve this transition—that human beings are failing in the very features that distinguishe us from the rest of the animal kingdom? I want to highlight this question and ask that we keep at the backs of our minds while we look at three features of today's world which, I believe, inhibit the act of understanding.

The first is the information highway with which we are all bombarded. A great deal more of the information that enters our systems comes in a form that does not allow us to *select*. We have to listen to the whole radio programme or not at all. We have to listen to the whole of the television news, even if we only want to hear about one issue. We can, of course, record and then select either through audiotape or videotape, but even with the best modern technology selection is difficult. The written word is much easier to select, either in a newspaper, journal, or book, but the numbers of people who receive their information through reading has decreased dramatically in the last quarter-century. If we follow our principle that you internalize only when the psyche is active, then the inability to select favours a passivity that inhibits internalization. The painter selects from the scene in front of him: the photographer does not.

Some years ago, when people went on holiday, they took photographs and put them into an album and offered these to friends to look at. . . . Today visitors are treated to a video film. The point I am getting at is that the visitor is unable to select, to look at those photographs that catch his attention and pass by those that do not, as is the case when looking at photographs in an album. There is also another aspect to this matter of photography. The point I was getting at in my two models is that the painter, through curiosity and selection, internalizes the scene before her. Rather than look—really look—and take in, the photographer raises his camera and snaps what is before him. The machine has taken in the scene, while the human being remains empty. I hope that you will understand that I am talking of a tendency, an attitude that is captured in the tourist's snapshooting but may not be so in the case of every photographer.

So much more information comes in a form that makes it difficult for the recipient to select than was the case fifty years ago.

Thomas Aquinas said that too much information prevents the act of understanding, and I am certain that this is true. Our present generation is bombarded with information. There is here an analogy with a psychotic situation. A person who is in the grip of a psychotic process is overwhelmed by the stimuli of the moment, is unable to process, and is therefore unable to see any line of continuity between events. The capacity to understand is obliterated. In the consulting-room the reason for this is the presence of a psychotic process, and for this to have any value as an analogy, one needs to posit the presence of such a condition more generally.

This needs to be understood thus: that there is a psychotic process in each of us and that, given sufficient stress, it will break through and overwhelm us. I think the matter needs to be put differently: that we need to be nurtured in a particular way in order that a containing function develops in the personality. This containing function is developed through a caring nurture of a particular kind. We hear a great deal these days about "quality time", and this is the kind of care that I am thinking of. The child needs a contemplative act from either the mother or a mother surrogate. This is more than just nurture or holding. I am talking here of mother and infant, but we can also think of the society in which we live as a mother and of each individual as one of that mother's babies. Psychoanalysis has concentrated its attention upon the influence of the mother (and father) upon the baby. Sociology has focused upon the influence of society upon the individual. If we focus exclusively upon the influence of the mother upon the baby and the effect of this upon the individual's development, we are then squint-eyed and do not see the effect of society upon the individual's development. A pure sociological focus leads to a biased understanding; a purely psychoanalytic focus also blinds us to other influences. Yet this is not quite the right way to describe the matter. In fact, psychoanalysis is not concerned more with the influence upon the individual of his family of origin than with the influence of society. Its objects of study are the mental strategies that the individual employs to deal with both sets of influences. The fruit of a contemplative act is an act of understanding—understanding the mental life of this baby, this individual.

As soon as a person is slave to the pressures of the culture, s/he becomes an object and is depersonalized. Let me tell you of a man, the contours of whose dilemma are typical of a huge number of individuals in modern society:

He could not manage being alone. When he was alone, life seemed meaningless to him. He was a high-profile electronics engineer. He came from a working-class family and was one of five. All five are extremely successful, judged by the criteria of wealth and status. "My life is meaningless", he said, "because I don't create anything",

He went on to say that his father had pushed all five of them into qualifying in either science or technology: "He wanted to make sure that what we did would earn us a good living. I have always regretted not studying Russian literature." "I come home at night and feel a great vacuum. . . . Sometimes I feel like one of those rats psychologists use in their maze experiments."

There was the sense here that he had in him the capacity to create and that this was unfulfilled. It became clear that this was the reason why he had come for treatment.

Because he had not created, or he had created far less than was possible for him, there was a vacuum in his life. This is more than just a metaphor. To have inner possessions that become part of me, I have to create the sensual data into forms that correspond to my own desires. This man had done what his father had pressurized him into doing, and he felt that what he did was inferior to people working in the arts. The reason for this needs to be noted. It is not that being an electronics engineer is inferior to being a Russian historian, but it is that he studied physics and then specifically electronics because he was in submission to his father. There had been no elemental creative act, so that what he did then satisfied his own soul.

This is the difference between ingesting something that sits in the mind like a foreign body and taking something in so that the mind alters it and it alters the mind. An act of understanding achieves the latter.

We live in an age where the acquisition of skills takes the front row of the stalls. How to use a calculator, a computer, a mobile phone, how to send e-mails, to access the internet, and so on. These are skills that can be acquired through the workings of memory and practical intelligence. They can also be encompassed within an act of understanding. Most of us know how to drive a car, but it is the few who understand how the internal combustion engine works, how the power from the engine is transmitted to the axle that rotates the wheels and how the power is differentially distributed through the use of gears and how these work and the difference between combustion that works through a carburettor as opposed to fuel injection. The same principles apply with computers.

We see this tendency most clearly in the field of education. Education means a perfecting of the mind. A subject is studied not for its own sake, but for its capacity to rouse the mind to acts of understanding. Education is from the Latin *"educare"*, meaning "to lead out". Socrates thought of himself as a midwife bringing the mind of his inquirers to birth. The mind has to be roused into activity so that it goes out and grasps the incoming data, transforming it as it does so. The mind searches out and then creates the forms, the principles governing the sensory data. That old debate as to whether the forms are already there or are created is insoluble because the act of understanding creates the forms that are there. There is no analogy that I know of for this, and quite how that can be is mysterious—I mean here "mysterious" in its proper meaning: that there are things that must be so but quite how is not possible to grasp because of the mind's limitation. So the mind needs to be roused out of its slumbers into activity. A nurturing society is one that recognizes that this is its task: to rouse the minds of its people, perfecting and enlarging them. A society that is concerned with filling minds with data, with skills is one that does not nurture the minds of its people. In fact it encourages the mind into a passivity. And here I need to make an aside and explain what is meant by passivity.

I heard a story about the philosopher Alfred North Whitehead. He was lying out in the garden of his house in Cambridge with a newspaper spread over his face. Bertrand Russell arrived and said, "Oh, I'm sorry to wake you". Whitehead replied that he was not asleep but working—thinking. We associate the word "activity" with visible movements. The hardest work is suffering. This word has often become debased and equated with masochism. I mean the active embracing of loss that is the prerequisite for an act of creation. I might give a personal example of what I mean. I admire the philosopher, R. G. Collingwood, and his good down-to-earth language; he calls a spade a spade and so on, and he encourages the use of ordinary language. I was reading his book on metaphysics where he refers to "metaphysical presuppositions". As I read, I thought to myself that this rather pompous phrase is synonymous with a "belief" and possibly even a "religious belief". Then I thought, "Oh no, not Collingwood. He would not embroider an understandable phenomenon with such philosophical pedantry." However, I persevered in my thought that what he was offering was a synonym for belief. I dethroned my hero. It was a loss, but I then gained a new understanding of the way beliefs govern scientific research, and this has been of considerable value to me and has enhanced my understanding quite a bit. The creative act in me was only possible when I had let go of my idol. So this is what I mean by activity. When I was resisting and saying, "Oh no, not Collingwood, he wouldn't use a pompous philosophical phrase for a simple word like 'belief'", I was in a passive mode. Please note that this passive mode is compatible with intense industriousness. I might study Collingwood with fervour, read all his books, become his authoritative interpreter, write books about him, and be in passive mode. People might look on and say, "Heavens, Neville works hard", but I would be in passive mode.

Now back to education. Society entrusts the educational task to institutions: preschool, school, universities. Technical colleges traditionally were for the acquisition of skills, for training. A sign that internalization is not valued in modern society is that there is no longer a clear distinction between training and education. Technical colleges have merged into being universities, and most of them are now called universities. The aim of reading a subject at university is development of the mind. Some subjects have greater educational potential than others. So classics, philosophy, religious studies, history, archaeology, english literature, languages, psychology, sociology, economics, biology, botany, zoology, geography, and astronomy are all educational subjects. There are other subjects, such as medicine, law, chemistry, physics and engineering, that can be educational, depending upon how they are treated. There are others, like accountancy, commerce, media studies, business studies, and environmental studies, the educational content of which is usually minimal. Then there are subjects the educational capacity of which is almost zero: like hotel management, hospitality and hostessing, electronics, flower arranging, and many of the trades that used to be taught through apprenticeship, like the work of a plumber, electrician, or carpenter, which trades are all now taught as "university" subjects. There has been a huge growth in what is called further or tertiary education, but the proportion of this that is actually education rather than training is, I suggest, small.

There is another matter that is implied here: that activities that were traditionally recognized as being trades and skills are now being dignified with "university status". This creates a dichotomy in people between what they are supposed to be and what they are. Inwardly they know that they are not what they are proclaimed to be. This fosters mass inferiority, which leads to drugs, delinquency, gambling, drink-ing, and so on. The basis of psychological inferiority is the failure to generate personal acts of understanding. Labelling theory in sociology has emphasized the damaging effect on the individual of being tagged as "schizophrenic", "alcoholic", or "criminal". It is equally damaging to name someone "a university graduate" or "an educated man" inap-propriately. What differentiates modern society from the society of sixty years ago is that in the latter the carpenter did not believe that he was educated, whereas today he does. (He may be educated, but that will not be through knowing how to carve wood.) It is the age of euphemisms.

The result is that those institutions that were once the custodians of education are no longer so, or at least their function has become very seriously eroded. This bodes ill for our society. Without internaliza-tion, without education, our society can only disintegrate. It is a very dangerous state of affairs—a breeding ground for tyrants. Erich Fromm, in his book *Fear of Freedom,* argues that Nazi tyranny grew up in the soil of a disintegrated society where people were unable to exercise their freedom.

Another manifestation of this failure that I am talking about is in much of the philosophy that underpins what we are calling today post-modernism. In what is known as relativism of values, there is at its heart an incommunicableness. In true relativism my value is my own and bears no relation to yours, and if it does, I don't care about it anyway. As fertile communication lies at the heart of education, at the heart of internalization, then in the presence of such values that legiti-mate isolationism no education can occur. Remember Socrates' image of the teacher as a midwife bringing the mind to a living birth. This requires a trusting communication, but where communication of this sort is inherently denied by the value system, then this reinforces a powerful defiance of internalization. I need to put in here a caution: relativism of values is not the same as cultural pluralism. The former is solipsistic, whereas intrinsic to the latter is inter-communication, which guarantees unity in diversity.

The other dogma is to be found in linguistic philosophy, which has had considerable influence in the post-modern culture. It holds that meaning is to be found according to the place that a word has in a sentence. This confines meaning to the level of intellectual logic and inherently repudiates the emotional. On the other hand, existential philosophy, which also permeates the post-modern culture, does seek meaning in emotional experience but repudiates those forms that arise through acts of understanding.

The whole enterprise of our post-modern culture blends with the technological requirements of this age and is a very strong counter against internalization. Psychoanalysis has very largely submitted to this cultural imperative. Psychoanalysis, which is essentially an uncovering of those emotional currents that are able to transform empty surfaces and invest them with meaning, has instead has gone into submission to those externals stripped of meaning. I want to offer a clarion call to analysts and those sympathetic with this way of viewing life to take hold of the treasure that we have in our midst and become one of the values within a pluralism and to be enriched by fertile contact with others and to enrich in return.

I want to end on this note because nothing is worse to the morale than a prophecy of doom. I note this attitude in quite a number of those warriors of the counter-culture, like Dr Suzuki, perhaps Erich Fromm, and many others. I do think there is a very serious malaise in our contemporary culture, but I ask this question: Has not internalization always been resisted, down through history? Was Socrates not clamouring against unthinking ingestion 2,400 years ago? Were not Thomas Aquinas in the thirteenth century and Kant in the eighteenth clamouring against unthinking acceptance? And what of the uproar when Galileo said no to the accepted laws of motion? And Copernicus? And Kepler? And Freud—was not his whole system geared to showing us that understanding—of which self-understanding is a necessary component—is fearfully resisted by human beings? The process by which we come to understanding is resisted vehemently in every age, and our own is no exception.

The cultural history of the human race is a slow unfolding of potentialities, but each new age presents the culture with a crisis that it is called upon to solve. So what is a malaise can be seen as a challenge. Certain potentialities have lain dormant for centuries and are then called into action in the face of a challenge. There is in this present age a devastating attack against the value of understanding, the value of personal creation, the value of transforming sensory data into new forms. This attack is a challenge to action. Freud's science, psychoanalysis, is a prophecy against this nihilism, against mental blindness. There are other counter-cultures that embody a similar protest. Transcendental meditation, born-again Christians, new-age sects, and numerous other movements, although frequently misguided, are clamouring against the present age's attachment to surfaces. I believe that the present problems of society are too serious for psychoanalysts to remain in isolation from these other groupings. They can stimulate our thinking, and ours will stimulate theirs.

This is an age of great opportunity. The technology available to us is almost miraculous. Its wonders are too evident to be worth listing. This technology can be used to develop our minds enormously. This will only happen if we understand the issues and have a clear outline in our minds of the principles. This is, I believe, the first task for a psychoanalytic society today.

Notes

1. I am aware that photography can be and often is an art. The model I use here is of the "tourist" photographer who pulls out his camera and clicks at the landscape in front of him.

2. I found this a mind-blowing statement when I first read it twenty years ago—because if it were true, then I had to create in order to know and that it must be elemental to psychoanalysis whose aim is self-knowledge.

3. What I am thinking of here is the refusal to acknowledge *mystery*—that is, the mind's limitation.

4. The primates have a limited ability.

CHAPTER EIGHTEEN

Anti-Semitism:
another perspective

This lecture was given at Tel-Aviv University in April 1999.

S o much has been written on this subject that people may justi-
fiably sigh when yet another person launches himself into the
subject. Many of those who have written upon it are more
knowledgeable than I, and they have researched the field far more
thoroughly. Therefore what possible reason could there be for me to
say anything on the matter? My reason is this: I have been developing
a schema that, I hope, can throw light on the nature of madness. This
has developed out of an exploration of narcissism, which, I believe, is
the core of all madness. This exploration has been particularly in
relation to the individual, but it has slowly become clear that certain
elements of madness are always embodied and never purely contained
within the individual psyche, and therefore in such a research social
psychology and individual psychology are inextricably intertwined.
(In fact, I believe that it is a mistake to divide the subject in this way.)
Therefore the principles that have emerged from this study of madness
can and do throw light on some social facts, of which one is anti-
Semitism. My apologetic for this is that I have not seen this explanation
put forward anywhere else. This does not mean that it has not been,

only that I have not come across it. Someone may be able to disabuse me and reveal my ignorance.

I hasten to add that in no way do I think that this is the *sole* explanation. It is just one shaft of light upon a phenomenon that has a bundle of inter-locking causes. I am also confining myself to the anti-Semitism that has been endemic in Christian culture over the centuries. I am obviously thinking particularly of the Holocaust, which, I believe, must be the worst deliberate massacre of a people in the history of the human race. It would be a mistake to think that the Jews are the only people who have been hounded and persecuted over the centuries. The Chinese have been scapegoated on many occasions, the most recent of which has been in Indonesia. The Armenian massacre in 1915, the obliteration of the Tasmanian race of Aborigines by English colonists in the last century, the fearful savagery between the Tutsis and Hutus in Rwanda, the massacre recently of Shi'ite Muslims by the Taliban Sunni Muslims at Mazar-e-Sharif in Afghanistan, and, of course, the crimes against Blacks in South Africa, North America, the whole shocking saga of the slave trade in the last two centuries and what has been named *The Middle Passage*, where it is claimed that a hundred million blacks perished in their passage from Africa to the Americas—all these are glaring evidence that savage violence against racial and religious groups seems to be inseparable from the human condition. However, there has never been anything so deliberate as Hitler's intention to exterminate the Jewish people; I think this was the climax to a long history of hatred of the Jews within that religious political entity known as Christendom. If we can get some understanding of this appalling saga of savagery against the Jews, it may also, in time, throw light upon other massacres, which are, at this very moment, happening around us in different spots on the globe.

And hatred is a good place to start. Why are the Jews hated so by Christians? I feel safe in saying this as a psychoanalyst: that the object of hatred is something within—something that is hated so much that it cannot be borne and is therefore expelled. Even this way of putting it is not quite accurate. It is not that something within my psyche is hated and therefore expelled, as if there were two acts here. The expulsion is what hatred is. Primitive hatred is an expulsion of something within, so it passes from within to without.

There is another closely related psychological factor that needs to be understood. It is that my perception of the outer world is governed by inner emotional acts. Wilfred Bion described how in hallucination a part of the self is projected violently out of the personality into an object, which then, as he says, swells up and assumes a bizarre form. The way the outer object is perceived is governed by this primitive form of expulsion. Bion discusses in some of his papers how an entity is expelled into a physical object like a telephone, a table lamp, or a clock in the room. Distortions of the physical world by such emotional activity are comparatively rare (though even these are less rare than is commonly believed), but expulsions of this sort into human beings living in my own environment is so common that it is part of the very fabric of our perception of the world. The phenomenon of *transference*, which lies at the centre of the psychoanalytical method of treating mental disorders, is nothing other than an expulsion of this kind into the figure of the psychoanalyst. Therefore the way I see the human world around me is governed by the quality of my inner emotional acts. If I expel something from within into outer figures, I see the human world in one way; if, instead, I embrace it within myself, then I see it another way.

When I expel this something from inside myself, I always do so into what I shall call a *corporate personality*. I do not expel it into this individual figure here or that individual figure there. I expel it into an element that is hated, and that element, to borrow Bion's illustrative phrase, swells up and engulfs and becomes embodied—it could be into the Jews, but it could be into lawyers, or Spaniards, or freemasons, or bureaucrats, or the bourgeoisie, or the proletariat, or the Communists, or left-wingers, or right-wingers, or all men or all women. An individual person is made up of many elements. In fact, I would understand a person to be an amalgam of different elements that have been creatively fashioned into a unity in the way a painter fashions the different paints on his palette into a picture. I have said above that the expulsion distorts the perception. So, for instance, brutality within is hated and expelled into men. Men are brutal, and women are gentle. We all know that this is untrue, but I think we all know why the expulsion of brutality is into men rather than women, just as we know that all soldiers are not men but we also know why people's immediate image associated with the word "soldier" is a man. I know that there are women soldiers and remember seeing Wrens marching as a child, yet it takes a moment of reflection to counteract the immediate association "soldier–man". It is this hated element within that is expelled into the image that is associated with Jews, or lawyers, or Spaniards, or freemasons, or bureaucrats, or the bourgeoisie, or the proletariat, or Communists or left-wingers or right-wingers or men or women. It is the image that is associated with the corporate personality. The image has some truth, but only a little. Every race and every culture has its strengths and its deficits. Just as no individual is perfect throughout, so neither is any culture or any grouping.

The reason why I use the term "corporate personality" is that when an element is violently expelled the emotional perception is affected and from that moment the idea of an individual person is not available under the pressure guidance of such an expulsion. Perhaps this is best illustrated in the case of transference.

> A man placed his analyst upon a very high pedestal and refrained assiduously from any criticism of him. The analyst noticed that his attitude was also the same towards all other psychoanalysts. The analyst then realized that he was not differentiated from all analysts. For the patient there was no single, individual analyst, but only a block-entity, which I call a "corporate personality".

Another example:

> A woman hated her male analyst, but it became clear that it was the erect penis that was hated. This was hated so intensely that, to borrow from Bion again, the penis had swelled up and engulfed the individual person of the analyst, so that only the erect penis was present but as a penis and no more. This male was undifferentiated from all other males.

So this is what I mean by "corporate personality". It is that a whole class of objects is merged into a single agglomeration, and a part smothers the other parts. The conjunction of these two processes, which are in fact one process seen from two angles, is what fashions the corporate personality. The act that fashions it is the violent expulsion of an element in the personality that is hated.

Here is an important question: What is it in the personality that is hated so violently? It is that which prevents my freedom. I am going about my business harming no one, and suddenly some ruffians capture me and imprison me. They feed me, give me drink, allow me to sleep, and make sure that I am warm and well cared for, but I am in a compound surrounded by the latest electronic surveillance devices, which make escape impossible. So although my captors look after all my physical needs extremely well, I hate them because they have deprived me of my freedom. We have, I believe, gone astray in our psychological understanding, because most of us are committed to the

Darwinian dogma that the struggle for survival is the motivating force in our lives. I do not want to go off here on a long diversion to argue that desire for freedom is the motivating principle rather than the struggle for survival. Our instincts are the guardians of our survival. In the little fable I have just given you, my captors provide all that the instincts require. Yet I want something more than that. I want to be allowed to go free. The question is: what are those elements in the personality that hold me captive? If I can get some fix on this, I may have the key to interracial hatred, anti-Semitism, and religious intolerance.

So what is it within that prevents my freedom? And what, in essence, is freedom? It is, I believe, my own capacity to create. Crudely speaking, there are two basic options within the field of action. Either I am driven by forces over which I have no control, or I am in command of my ship, and I create out of the raw material that is available to me. Those who have studied the work of Wilfred Bion carefully will know that he saw two alternative modes of action at work in the personality: either the individual is an instinct-driven creature who is the victim of the currents in the river, or she is a person who creates her human environment. No analogy is quite perfect here. I read in a life of Raoul Dufy, the painter, that as a novice painter he attended the studio of a senior artist. He copied and followed the rules laid down. One day, in a life class, he painted a red-haired girl in bright and sunny colours. The master artist came around and told him that he should have selected darker colours. At that moment he was convinced that this mode was not for him, so he went off and forged his own colourful style. He now fashioned something that was his own free creation. What was it that had held him in thrall before? It would be wrong to say it was the master painter. It was, rather, his slavish obedience to him. I had a patient once who was driven by a tyrant within. This tyrant castigated her, told her she was not working hard enough, that she was stupid. If she were late for a session, she believed that I would disapprove of her and write her off as a useless idiot. She could never satisfy this tyrant. She was in no way free. She did what she was told to do. Never could she say that she did something of her own volition. I do not want here to enumerate all those elements in the personality that imprison the soul. There is a constellation of elements, but one of them is god.

It is god who dictates what I should do. For Raoul Dufy, god was installed in the senior painter. For my patient, he was installed both inside her and outside. This was also so for Dufy, though, as related in the biography, he experienced it as outside. My patient had, I believe, a more sophisticated consciousness, but in both cases, if asked, "Why did you act in this way?" the answer would be : "Because I was told to do so." "And why did you obey?" "Because I was ordered to do it by god."

I think you will realize that it would be very rare for someone to answer this last question so candidly. The person would stumble and falter trying to find a convincing reason, but it would not have the ring of truth. It would always ultimately be what philosophers refer to as the argument from authority. In other words, I do it because I was told to do so. It is the presence of god in the personality, that makes me a prisoner. I hate this god with a violent hatred because it thwarts my freedom. You may now have begun to guess where this line of thinking is leading, but let me spell it out in detail.

The central doctrine of Christianity is the belief that Jesus of Nazareth was not just an inspired prophet but was God himself. Therefore as a Christian I believe that I possess the Truth and that all others are barred from it. Christians may object to this as being too extreme a view and that today theologians recognize that those outside the body of Christianity can be saved. Nevertheless those who are outside the Christian fold are saved through the blood of Christ, even though they do not know it. The modern theological view is that all those of good will are by that very act of good will baptized into the blood of Christ by desire. The situation remains that if I am a Christian, I can say to myself: " I am in possession of the truth and I know it. Those of other faiths are not in possession of it as I am."

You may say that for the person who is a Christian, that is a very happy state of affairs. In the 1950s that phrase, which, I think, came from a Peter Sellers film—"I'm Alright, Jack"—is the privileged state of the Christian. Yet we all smile wryly because we know that this is a delusional situation. There is an old joke about a pagan being shown around heaven, and then he is taken past a high Coliseum-type building, and he is asked to stay silent. He asks why and is told that inside are the Christians and they think they are the only people here.

Yet it is not a happy state of affairs because when you think of this truth possessed by the Christian, it is not arrived at through personal thinking and understanding. It is a declared truth. It has been declared to the Christian by the Church, and the Church has been told it by God. So the Christian is not free to come to his conclusions through the efforts of reasoning. "This is what you are to believe" is his inheritance.

In fact, the presence of this god within who declares what he shall believe and what he shall not believe is hated—hated violently. And why? Because it thwarts freedom. In effect, it says: "You are not free to think according to your own lights." "You are my prisoner", says God through his Church, bishops and priests. Therefore the Christian hates this imprisoning god within, and this hatred is in the form of an expulsion. But the question is: Into whom does the Christian expel these hated inner contents? And you all know the answer. It is into the Jews.

When I expel with hatred, I do so into a corporate personality that bears a similarity to myself. So, for instance, if I hold secrets within me that prejudice my freedom, I might expel this mentality with hatred into the freemasons. Their initiation ceremonies with sworn secrets are the perfect candidate for my projection. I can maintain an appearance of sanity if I project into a candidate that bears some of the characteristics of that hated element inside. Now this god who dictates what I should do is almost the defining symbol of the Jewish race and faith. What better candidate for this expulsion than the Jews, then? George Steiner is the only author I know who says something along these lines. He says that the Jews are hated because they introduced the superego into human history (Steiner, 1971). When I read this years ago, I thought it was something of a wry joke, but with the passing of the years I believe he was saying something accurate.

You might ask why the Jews were selected rather than Moslems, for instance? I feel on even shakier ground here, but I believe it must be that since the Diaspora many Jews have lived within the bosom of Christendom and, as it were, defenceless: a minority within the culture, that could be attacked without fear of reprisal. I believe that the reason I have given here is the heart of it. All the other stereotypes with which Jews have been branded are, I believe, not the reason but the reason that Christians give to themselves to justify their attitude. What cannot be admitted is that the god they have been brought up to reverence and worship is so hated. The Christian cannot say, "I hate the Jews" because they worship god, because they brought knowledge of god into the world. It would too quickly bring the retort that it is the same god that he himself worships, so how can he hate the Jews for that? So instead he says he hates the Jews because they crucified Jesus, are ambitious, are money-grubbers, are paedophiles, abusers of children, and so on and so on.

The sort of arrogance typifying the Christian believer that I have been referring to is true of the individual, but is also true of those great Christian bodies, especially the Catholic Church. I believe that wherever this kind of group egoism is found to exist, the Jews living within it or in close proximity to it are in danger. The secular heir to this pride of the denominational group is, of course, national pride. As Isaiah Berlin has pointed out (1979a, p. 337) none of the great social theorists of the last century, from Karl Marx to de Tocqueville, predicted the rise of nationalism and the power it has exercised in this century. They were, to a man, in their very different ways, imbued with the vision of a new universalism that would sweep away the petty boundaries of what Arnold Toynbee has called *The Parochial State* (1962). Yet the horrors that have rent the human race apart and caused such appalling carnage have been due, to a large degree, to nationalism. George Orwell has graphically charted his shock when he realized in the Spanish Civil War that the Russian Communists were turning against other Communist groups because of their universalist perspective. It was also, I think, part of Stalin's detestation of Trotsky. Stalin was a passionate nationalist; Trotsky was a universalist. There were, of course, other factors in that savage enmity, but this was a significant element in it and one that also articulates a whole political stance. Nationalism is to the group what arrogance is to the individual, and the same principle applies. I am going to risk repeating myself in order to emphasize the point here.

I shall put it this way. My thesis is that if I am arrogant, I hate this quality inside me. In order to explicate the matter across boundaries, I say that arrogance is that condition of soul where god is installed in the midst of my psyche. And I hate violently the presence of this god installed within. Now when I describe it like this, it may be somewhat understandable that I should hate it, but when you meet the typically arrogant person, it is not at all evident. Let us take a current example. It is always dangerous to judge public figures by the presentation of them in the press, but with that proviso let us say that Saddam Hussein is an arrogant man. If you examine his statements, his posturing, and his unalloyed provocativeness, you would detect no outward sign that he hates this powerful god installed within his persona. Yet his hatred of America and of Israel is almost intrinsic to the structure of his character. Yet I think you would probably think it was stretching things too far to say that the origin of this hatred lies in a hatred of the god within. Yet, with a certain qualification that I will come to, I believe that this is exactly the case.

Let us for a moment imagine the scenario of Saddam Hussein deciding to enter psychoanalysis, and in the process in the middle of the night he gets a momentary glimpse of the things within that he hates. What is the most likely scenario? Either it will be immediately

suppressed, or he commits suicide. This is one of the reasons why it is
so extremely difficult to conduct a psychoanalysis of someone who, in
their arrogance, has wreaked enormous damage. I personally suspect
that self-knowledge in such a case is too great to be borne by the
psyche. It needs to be remembered that such characters appear strong
and powerful, but this is only how things look to the outsider. Inside,
such bullies are a flabby mess. I know that it is very difficult to believe
this, but I think, even without analysis, a careful study of the details in
the lives of such people reveal it to be so. I am not in possession of any
diaries or intimate correspondence of Saddam Hussein. Such docu-
ments usually only appear when the person is dead and gone but I will
give just two instances from the lives of famous bullies: Stalin and
Napoleon. At a dinner, Stalin's wife criticized him in the presence of
others. She then went out and killed herself. She knew that this was
something he could not tolerate, and he would immediately take savage vengeance upon her. In a biography I read of Napoleon, it said that
he could never reprimand a subordinate unless there was someone
else present to witness it. The god in him got a boost if he were playing
to a clapping gallery, but without it he was no more than a flabby jelly.
So what looks like power is, in fact, something that is extremely dependent upon the audience shouting support.

In the utterly impossible scenario of Saddam Hussein undergoing
an analysis, the result would be either immediate repression or suicide.
In fact, what one witnesses in all these great bullies ruling our political
states, both in the present era—Mobutu, or Suharto—and in past
ones—Hitler, Mussolini, Stalin, or Mao Tse-Tung—is a suicide of the
state. Why I draw on the concept of "corporate personality" is that
there is an interplay between the individual and the state such that the
former becomes totally merged with the latter: there is an equation—
Mobutu/Congo, Suharto/Indonesia, Hitler/Germany, Mussolini/
Italy, Stalin/Russia, Mao Tse-Tung/China. This merged state of affairs
between the individual and the state stood out clearly in the Gulf War,
where one of the declared aims was to kill Saddam Hussein. It would
be a simplification to say that these were a large-scale assassination
attempt, but there is a truth to it. Had Saddam Hussein died two days
before the war began, I am certain that neither war would have been
initiated. It is always dangerous when the individual is entirely sunk
into the group or the mass so that inner personal responsiveness is
eliminated. If one looks at the social group under the sway of the bully,
then one sees that a suicide is in progress all the time in the historical
development of states under a totalitarianism of this kind. It does not

take acute observation to see that the people of Iraq have suffered, that the economy of the Soviet Union was brought to a state of collapse through the administration of Stalin and his tyrant–successors, that Hitler's invasion of Russia, like Napoleon's before him, was a suicidal act, that the Indonesian economy and the institutions of the country were paralysing under Suharto, and so on.

I am trying to draw the parallel between true strength, which lies in inner conviction and essentially requires no outer bolstering, and the false coinage where the emotional flabbiness of the individual requires the excitement and stimulation of the group to sustain it and for whom survival is the over-riding goal. Survival, whatever the cost, is the declared aim of nearly all politicians. Their own individual needs override the true requirements of the people of the country they represent. So I am going to repeat my basic thesis: it is that the god installed within the personality is hated because it obstructs freedom. The further point is that this also applies to nation states. National pride is a group arrogance that inhibits freedom for the same reason. And both in the individual and in the nation state this is hated. It is expelled into a group the identifying feature of which is the worship of this god. The Jews, then, are the chosen vehicle into which this expulsion takes place.

You may ask what I mean by freedom. I will try to expand a bit upon it. I am free when I am capable of a creative act. An artist dips her brush into the different colours on her palette and creates a painting on the canvas in front of her. She can only do this if she has an inner free responsiveness. If she is under direction from within and does what she is "told", she is not free. Bernard Berenson, the art critic, said that from the time of the fourth-century mosaics at Ravenna until Giotto, all artists were illustrators; the Dark Ages were characterized by 700 years of slavish copying. What is meant by creation is when something comes out of the human being that transcends all the environmental stimuli and something is produced that comes from that human being alone. He has not been told what to do, he is not copying a master; he is bringing forth something from his innermost self that no outer stimulation can entirely account for. Numerous stimuli have come in and been processed, but out of them he has created a new reality. This is what I mean by freedom. It applies not only to the arts but also within the sciences and in friendship and political associations. Friendship is a creation. Alliances for the sake of professional or political advantage are not creations: they are manipulated unions, like the royal marriages of a previous era; but friendship is a creation and true political federations are also creations that are freely made and entered into.

As soon as that inner sanctum is invaded and I am under compulsive direction, then I have lost my freedom. I have become a computer. That yearning for freedom has been blocked, and I hate those realities that obstruct it. I hope the link that I have tried to establish above between the individual and the group making for that entity that I describe as "corporate personality" is clear. With the individual that which directs and impels me in a particular direction is embodied in a group identity, so that there is a merged state of affairs between me and the group of which I am a part. I emphasize the word "part" rather than "member". The latter term suggests an individual in free responsive relation to the others, whereas in the former I am just a limb of the whole. There is no clear distinction between me and the group into which I am merged, and a Voice embodied in a dictator is my voice submerged in his. In this situation there is freedom neither for the individual nor for the group. Of course, it is the central doctrine of Christianity that the all-powerful God became embodied first in Jesus then in the Church, which is referred to by St Paul as the Body of Christ or Bride of Christ, alternatively. The nation state is the secular heir to this primary template. The hatred of this is expelled into the Jews. The people of Israel brought into the world a god whose directions were codified in the Ten Commandments and in all the other legislation with which we are familiar. The Christian's hatred of being directed under compulsion to do this and not that and so on is not recognized as such. The hatred of the Jews is a displacement of those inner and embodied realities that imprison the Christian.

However, as I have suggested, this Christian heritage has passed over into that secular horror—the all-powerful nation state. That is its most obvious location, but it is also located in ideological systems of political, scientific, aesthetic, and religious kinds. The tyranny of many left-wing and right-wing movements is too familiar to require any elaboration; the same is the case with many religious fundamentalists, both within and outside the Judaeo–Christian–Islamic tradition. But there is also tyranny within the arts, and the present post-modernist movement has compelled many into its fold against inner individual judgement. But the same treatment has been doled out to members of the scientific community who have espoused unorthodox views, like Rupert Sheldrake and Bob Jahn. The former was vilified as a mischief-maker and mad; the latter was forced to resign from the engineering faculty at Princeton for his "heterodox" views on "psycho-kinesis". But always the scapegoat for this hatred is the Jews who symbolize this submission to a tyranny. What I want to make clear is that it is not the "heterodox" that effect this projection but those that perpetuate a dogma and expel the hated elements in themselves into the "heterodox"; my point is that the ultimate scapegoats in Western Society have been the Jews. What I hate in myself, I expel into the Jews.

That is my thesis, and I have probably already said enough. The very best thing might be for me to draw a line and finish, but it is difficult to resist the question as to whether anything can be done? Let me again take a similar path to the one I have taken already: first to examine the individual and then the group. I believe that there is a fundamental dichotomy in the constitution of the individual. My being is part of something universal, and at the same time I feel I am special. Yet it is the universal in me (what Wilfred Bion called "O") that is responsible for freedom and creativity. For some reason I put great energy into placarding my specialness. I want you to admire me, flatter me, and give me strokes, and yet this is very odd. If we erected statues to Einstein but forgot his theory of relativity, it would be rather absurd. If we know and understand the theory of relativity, it will be helpful in our scientific understanding of our world. If we forgot and did not know that the theory was generated by Einstein, it would matter not a bit. The same goes for the theories of Darwin or Karl Marx or Freud and countless others. If I say something here that you find valuable and you remember that but forget that it was articulated by me, why should it trouble me? That is a serious question. I know, unfortunately, that it does trouble me, but it is a puzzle as to why. What is the self-inflation about? Anyway, that is the dichotomous nature of the individual: there is a universal out of which I am constituted and then an illusory ego that spends a great deal of time in the business of self-inflation.

Then, as with the individual, so with the group. As the anthropologist, Joseph Campbell (1960), says, the world is a unit. Each culture, each religion, each nation has a facet of the truth. It also embedded in mental and emotional attitudes that are false. This is not to say that every religion, for instance, is equal to all others in its access to truth (there are many crackpot religions whose access to truth is very restricted) but it is to say that those great religious traditions—Hinduism, Taoism, Buddhism, Zoroastrianism, Judaism, Christianity, and Islam—are each facets of a diamond reflecting the truth; and when I say "truth", I mean practical wisdom as a guiding light in our dark and complex world. But each has its limitations. The value of each is in the truth that it conveys, but it does require human individual responsiveness to sift truth from falsity. Hinduism has endowed the world with a contemplative understanding of the unifying structure of the world, yet it failed in the field of practical action. Buddhism, on the other hand, triumphed in its understanding of human responsibility and action but regretfully repudiated the value of intellectual contemplation. The same kind of exegesis could be made of Judaism, of Christianity, and of Islam, but my aim is not to embark on such an examination but only to point out that facets of the truth are contained in each, but each has also limiting factors. I would also like to say that just as I think the wisdom contained in each of these traditions is a pearl of great price, so also there are serious falsities in each. Just as my own self-inflation is a barrier to understanding the truth, so religious or cultural self-inflation is a massive blockade that prevents our grasp of the truth.

The time has come for rooting ourselves in a universal perspective. This requires a major revolution in consciousness. It requires persevering work on the part of the few and the many. There is no other solution now for our world. Only when this has been achieved will the Jews be safe from persecution.

REFERENCES

Abraham, K. (1925). *Selected Papers of Karl Abraham*. London: Hogarth Press & the Institute of Psycho-Analysis, 1973.

Arendt, H. (1964). *Eichmann in Jerusalem: A Report on the Banality of Evil*. New York: Viking Press.

Berlin, I. (1979a). *Against the Current*. London: Hogarth Press.

Berlin, I. (1979b). The divorce between the sciences and the humanities. In: *Against the Current*. London: Hogarth Press.

Berlin, I. (1980). *Vico and Herder*. London: Chatto & Windus.

Berlin, I. (1984). *Four Essays on Liberty*. Oxford/New York: Oxford University Press.

Bion, W. R. (1956). Development of schizophrenic thought. In: *Second Thoughts*. London: Heinemann Medical Books; reprinted London: Karnac, 1993.

Bion, W. R. (1957). On arrogance. In: *Second Thoughts*. London: Heinemann Medical Books, 1967; reprinted London: Karnac, 1993.

Bion, W. (1974). *Brazilian Lectures, Vol. 1*. Rio de Janeiro: Imago Editora.

Bion, W. R. (1977). *Two Papers: The Grid and Caesura*. Rio de Janeiro: Imago Editora.

Blomfield, O. H. D. (1992). "Fantasy and Shock in Phocis." Unpublished paper.

Boring, E. (1950). *A History of Experimental Psychology*. New York: Appleton-Century-Crofts.

Brentano, F. (1973). *Psychology from the Empirical Standpoint*. London: Routledge & Kegan Paul.

Campbell, J. (1960). *The Masks of God: Primitive Mythology*. London: Secker & Warburg.

Chardin, T. de (1964). *Le Milieu Divin*. London: Collins Fontana Books.

Chardin, T. de (1960). *The Phenomenon of Man*. London: Collins.

Collingwood, R. G. (1969). *An Essay on Metaphysics*. Oxford: Clarendon Press.

Ellenberger, H. (1970). *Discovery of the Unconscious*. London: Allen Lane/ Penguin

Fairbairn, W. R. D. (1976). *Psychoanalytic Studies of the Personality*. London/ Henley/Boston, MA: Routledge & Kegan Paul.

Freud, S. (1895d) (with Breuer, J.). *Studies on Hysteria. S.E., 2.*

Freud, S. (1900a). *The Interpretation of Dreams. S.E., 4–5.*

Freud, S. (1905d). *Three Essays on the Theory of Sexuality. S.E., 7.*

Freud, S. (1907b). Obsessive actions and religious practices. *S.E., 9.*

Freud, S. (1912–13). *Totem and Taboo. S.E., 13.*

Freud, S. (1914c). On narcissism: An introduction. *S.E., 14.*

Freud, S. (1914d). On the history of the psycho-analytic movement. *S.E., 14.*

Freud, S. (1915b). Thoughts for the times on war and death, I: Our attitude towards death. *S.E., 14.*

Freud, S. (1915f). A case of paranoia running counter to the psycho-analytic theory of the disease. *S.E., 14.*

Freud, S. (1916d). Some character-types met with in psycho-analysis, II: Those wrecked by success. *S.E., 14.*

Freud, S. (1917e [1915]). Mourning and melancholia. *S.E., 14.*

Freud, S. (1920c). *Group Psychology and the Analysis of the Ego. S.E., 18.*

Freud, S. (1920g). *Beyond the Pleasure Principle. S.E., 18.*

Freud, S. (1922b). Some neurotic mechanisms in jealousy, paranoia and homosexuality. *S.E., 18.*

Freud, S. (1923b). *The Ego and the Id. S.E., 19.*

Freud, S. (1924c). The economic problem of masochism. *S.E., 19.*

Freud, S. (1926d). *Inhibitions, Symptoms and Anxiety. S.E., 20.*

Freud, S. (1926e). *The Question of Lay Analysis. S.E., 20.*

Freud, S. (1927c). *The Future of an Illusion. S.E., 21.*

Freud, S. (1928b). Dostoevsky and parricide. *S.E., 21.*

Freud, S. (1930a [1929]). *Civilization and Its Discontents. S.E., 21.*

Freud, S. (1933a). *New Introductory Lectures on Psycho-Analysis. S.E., 22.*

Freud, S. (1933b [1932]). Why war? *S.E., 22.*

Freud, S. (1939a). *Moses and Monotheism. S.E., 23.*

Freud. S. (1940a). *An Outline of Psycho-Analysis. S.E., 23.*

Freud, S. (1950 [1892–99]). Extracts from the Fliess Papers. *S.E., 1.*

Freud, S. (1950 [1895]). A project for a scientific psychology. *S.E., 1.*

Gay, P. (1988). *Freud—A Life for Our Time.* London/Melbourne: J. M. Dent.

Guillaume, A. (1976). *Islam.* Harmondsworth, Middlesex: Penguin Books.

Hampson, N. (1971). *The Enlightenment.* Harmondsworth, Middlesex: Pelican Books.

Hesse, H. (1965). *Steppenwolf.* Harmondsworth, Middlesex: Penguin Books.

Husserl, E. (1979). *Experience and Judgment.* Evanston, IL: Northwestern University Press.

Jahoda, M. (1977). *Freud and the Dilemmas of Psychology.* London: Hogarth Press.

Jerusalem Bible (1966). London: Darton, Longman & Todd.

John of the Cross, St (1947). *Ascent of Mount Carmel.* In: *The Complete Works of St. John of the Cross, Vol. 1.* London: Burns, Oates & Washbourne.

John of the Cross, St (2000). *Poems: Coplas del Alma que pena por ver a Dios,.* transl. R. Campbell. London: Harvill Press.

Jones, E. (1953). *Sigmund Freud—Life and Work* (3 vols.). London: Hogarth Press.

Kipling, R. (1970). *The Light that Failed.* Harmondsworth, Middlesex: Penguin Books.

Klein, G. (1976). *Psychoanalytic Theory.* New York: International Universities Press.

Lecky, W. E. H. (1913). *History of European Morals.* London/New York/Bombay/Calcutta: Longmans, Green & Co.

Macmurray, J. (1932). *Freedom in the Modern World.* London: Faber & Faber.

Macmurray, J. (1936). *The Structure of Religious Experience.* London: Faber & Faber.

Milner, M. [J. Field] (1987). *An Experiment in Leisure.* Los Angeles, CA: Jeremy P. Tarcher. [Originally published under the pseudonym "Joanna Field"—London: Chatto & Windus, 1937.]

Newman, J. H. (1888). *An Essay in Aid of a Grammar of Assent.* London: Longmans, Green & Co.

Orwell, G. (1971). Politics and the English language. In: *Inside the Whale and Other Essays.* Harmondsworth, Middlesex: Penguin Books.

Rancurello, A. C. (1968). *A Study of Franz Brentano: His Psychological Standpoint and His Significance in the History of Psychology.* New York: Academic Press.

Rank, O. (1914). The myth of the birth of the hero. In: *The Myth of the Birth of the Hero and Other Writings*, trans. F. Robbins & S. E. Jelliffe, et al., ed. P. Freund. New York: Vintage Books/Random House, 1964.

Rank, O. (1978). *Will Therapy*. New York/London: W. W. Norton.

Ricoeur, P. (1970). *Freud and Philosophy*. New Haven, CT: Yale University Press.

Rousseau, J. J. (1762). *The Social Contract*. Amsterdam: Marc Michel Rey.

Russell, B. (1974). *History of Western Philosophy*. London: George Allen & Unwin.

Saint Exupéry, A. de (1940). *Wind, Sand and Stars*. London: Readers' Union Ltd/Heinemann.

Sales, Francis de (1608). *Introduction to the Devout Life*. London/New York: Longmans, Green & Co., 1956.

Schweitzer, A. (1910). *The Quest of the Historical Jesus*. London: A. & C. Black.

Steiner, G. (1971). *In Bluebeard's Castle*. London & Boston: Faber & Faber.

Steiner, J. (1985). Turning a blind eye: The coverup for Oedipus. *International Review of Psychoanalysis*, 12: 161–172.

Sulloway, F. (1980). *Freud, Biologist of the Mind*. London: Fontana.

Symington, J. (1985). The survival function of primitive omnipotence. *International Journal of Psycho-Analysis*, 66: 481–487.

Symington, N. (1993). *Narcissism: A New Theory*. London: Karnac.

Symington, N. (2002). *A Pattern of Madness*. London: Karnac.

Thompson, F. (1913). The hound of heaven. In: *The Works of Francis Thompson, Vol. 1*. London: Burns & Oates.

Thornton, E. M. (1983). *The Freudian Fallacy*. Garden City, NY: Doubleday/Dial.

Tolstoy, L. N. (1899). What is religion? In: *The Complete Works of Lyof. N. Tolstoi*. New York: Thomas Y. Crowell.

Toynbee, A. (1962). *A Study of History, Vol. 4*. London: Oxford University Press.

Vereecke, L. (1997). La conscience: Jalons d'histoire. *Revue d'ethique et de theologie morale*: 75–101.

Webb, C. C. J. (1915). *Studies in the History of Natural Theology*. Oxford: Clarendon Press.

Weber, M. (1971). *The Protestant Ethic and the Spirit of Capitalism*. London: Unwin University Books.

Webster, R. (1995). *Why Freud Was Wrong*. London: Harper Collins.

White, M. (1986). *The Greening of Gondwana*. Sydney, NSW: Reed.

White, V. (1960). *Soul and Psyche*. London: Collins/Harvill Press:

Whitehead, A. N. (1925). *Science in the Modern World*. London: Macmillan.

Winnicott, D. W. (1958). A note on normality and anxiety. In: *Collected Papers*. London: Tavistock Publications.

Zilboorg, G. (1967). *Psychoanalysis and Religion*. London: George Allen & Unwin.

INDEX

Abraham, 38
Abraham, K., 39, 57
accountability, 51, 52
action, emotional, 62, 81–82, 175, 181
addiction, 76
Adeodatus, 19
Adler, A., 17, 23
Alexandria library, burning of, 145
alpha:
    elements, 6, 111
    function, 185
American War of Independence, 181
Amos, 132
analytic neutrality, 94
Anglican Church, 43
anthropomorphism, 86, 87
Antigone, 168
anti-Semitism, 197–209
anxiety, as dread of conscience, 32
apodictic certainty, 28
Aquinas, Thomas, 27, 145–146, 190, 195
Aquinian conception(s), 147
Archimedes, 103, 106, 107

Arendt, H., 42, 43
Aristotelian conception(s):
    Brentano, 23, 25, 26
    of soul, 141, 144–149
Aristotle, 23, 25, 27, 97–98, 116, 141, 144–147
artist's mode, 186–196
askesis, 127
associationist psychology, 27, 142
assumptions, challenge of, 165–166
Atman, 128
attachment to narcissistic self-image, 9
Augustine, St, of Hippo, 19, 143, 154
Averroes, Ibn R., 145
Avidya, 128
awakening from psychological blindness as stage in development of religious leader, 2, 5–9
    Freud's, 14–15
awareness:
    vs conscience, 132
    and creative action, 87
    of guilt, 31, 34, 51, 60

awareness (*continued*):
  vs knowledge, 183–184
  obliteration of, 60, 65
    see also unawareness
  of self, 109–111, 132, 156, 177
    and compassion, 132, 133
axial era, 98, 132, 133, 177
axiology, 152

Balint, M., 118
Beethoven, L. van, 64
being:
  obliteration of, 76
  participated, 77–84
    obliteration of, 77
Benedict, St, 9
Berenson, B., 206
Bergson, H., 177
Berlin, I., 86–88, 99, 142, 178–179, 187,
    204
Bernays, M., 14, 20
Bernheim, H., 14, 26
beta elements, 6, 111
Bion, W. R., 69, 93, 112, 118, 136, 144,
    148, 175, 177, 187, 198–201
  alpha elements, 6, 111
  alpha function, 185
  beta elements, 6, 111
  Grid, 58
  "O", 116, 135, 208
bipolar disorder, 107
blindness, psychological, as stage in
    development of religious
    leader, 2–5
  Freud's, 11–13
Blomfield, O. H. D., 65, 170
Boring, E., 24
Brahe, T., 108
Brahman, 126, 128, 129, 130
Brentano, F., and Freud, 22–29
Breuer, J., 12, 25, 31
British School, 69
Brouardel, P. C. H., 12, 13
Brücke, E. W. von, 1, 14, 15, 24, 26, 49,
    142
Buddha, the (Siddhartha Gautama),

    20, 73, 99, 111, 117, 132, 134,
    150, 157, 161, 164
  enlightenment of, 127, 155
  stages in development of as
    religious leader, 2–11
Buddhism, 208, 209
  Mara, the evil one, 10
  primordial vision, 81
  revealed religion, 81, 111
  Theravada School of, 21

Calvin, J., 19
Campbell, J., 208
Cannon, W. B., 66
castration by father, fear of, 35, 37
categorical imperative, 38
Channa, 1, 3, 8, 15, 20
Chantal, J. F., 19
chaos theory, 129
Charcot, J.-M., 12, 13, 14, 26, 46
Chardin, T. de, 2, 8, 181
Cheshire, L., 3–5
Chomsky, N., 182
Christianity, 86, 102, 104, 106, 111–
    118, 122, 140, 153
  and anti-Semitism, 198
  arrogance of, 203
  chastity, vow of, 18
  concept of soul, 138–141, 149
  conversion experience, 3, 4, 7
  Devil, 10
  and existence, 104
  "fuga mundi" mode of religious
    life, 21
  fundamentalism in, 207
  god of:
    false, 116–117
    hated, 203, 207
    inflated self as, 103, 115, 203
    offended by sin, 114
  love as ideal, 138
  pride as sin, 73, 158
  and Reformation, 19
  revealed religion, 81, 100, 111, 160
    vs rational reflection, 117, 202
  revelation, 101, 138, 145

Pentecost experience, 102
Roman Catholicism:
    arrogance of, 203
    and Reformation, 18
    St Augustine of Hippo, 143
    St Paul, 3, 4
    and truth, 202
    facets of in, 208, 209
    vision of compassion, 81
Chrobak, R., 12, 13
Clark, R. W., 15
Collingwood, R. G., x, 109, 135, 192,
    193
compassion, 131–133
Confucius, 132
connaturality, 152
conscience, 95–99, 125, 127–136, 158,
    163
    anxiety, 37
    vs awareness, 132
    bad, 40, 42, 43
    and ego-ideal, 35
    ego-dystonic nature of, 32
    ego-syntonic, 44
    exegesis of in Freud's works, 30–44
    good, 42–44
    and guilt, 130–134
    as internalization of external
        authority, 32–33
    moral, 35
    and participated being, 77–80
    pathological, 43
    persecuting, 36
    as repository in personality of
        group's authority, 35
    St Paul's use of, 44
    and superego, 78, 96
        equation of, 33–44
    taboo, 31
    and true god, 119–121
conscious (Cs) system, 29
consciousness and religion, 100–111
constancy theory, 68–70
conversion hysteria, 14
Copernicus, N., 108, 187, 195
core neurosis, 59

corporate personality, 199–200, 203,
    205, 207
Council of Trent, 146
creative principle, 80, 180
Crews, F., 46
Cs (conscious system), 29
curiosity of mind, 187

Darwin, C., 208
Darwinian theory, 63, 81, 201
day residues, 56
death:
    fear of, 37
    instinct, 10, 41, 62
        and disintegrated mind, 62
Delphic Oracle, 20, 166, 168, 171
delusion(s), 83, 142, 177
    paranoid, 33
Democritus of Abdera, 141
depressive position, 51, 80, 129
Derrida, J., 182
Descartes, R., 87, 143, 187
detachment, 150, 152, 155, 157, 177
    from self-preoccupation, 129
determinist model of mind vs
        religious model of mind, 48–
        53
disintegrated parts of the mind, 62
Dostoevsky, F., 99, 151
dream(s), 56, 57, 65, 142, 147, 165
    censor, 33
    Freud's:
        "my friend R", 25
        work on, 16
        and unfulfilled wishes, 56–57
drive(s), 48
du Bois-Reymond, E., 24, 49, 142
Dufy, R., 201
Durkheim, E., 38

education, 192
ego (passim):
    broken, 37
    -ideal, 33, 34
        loved object as, 35
    psychology, 29

Eichmann, K. A., 42, 43
Einstein, A., 106, 208
Eliot, G., 99
Elizabeth von R (Freud's patient), 46
Ellenberger, H., 15–16, 45–47
embryo mind, 59, 61, 69, 71
emotional action, 62, 81, 82, 175, 181
enlightenment:
    inner, state of, 10, 16, 73, 158
        Buddha, 9, 10, 127, 155
        Freud, 17
    as stage in development of
        religious leader, 2, 10
        Freud, 16–17
Enlightenment era, 30, 42, 44, 86–87,
        107, 108, 175
    post-, 43
envy, 20, 73, 112, 128
epistemology, 26, 103
Eros, 62
evil, inner structure of, 59–61
external reality, 5, 26, 34
Ezekiel, 98, 132

Fairbairn, W. R. D., 10, 50–52, 66–67,
        93, 136, 147–148
false god vs true god, 112–123
false self, 93
Fechner, G., 16, 26, 28, 66
Ferenczi, S., 17
"fight analyst", 153, 154
Fliess, W., 15, 30
"flight analyst", 153
freedom:
    human, and psychoanalysis, 174–
        185
    negative, 178
French Revolution, 181
Freud, A., 144
Freud, S., x, 136, 137, 168, 195, 208
    and Brentano, 22–29
    creative illness, 15
    development of as religious leader,
        11–21
    "Elizabeth von R", 46
    homeostatic model, 148

humans as savages, 175
infantile sexuality, 11, 16, 187
instinct theory, 10
libido theory, 66
making the unconscious conscious,
        x
and Martha Bernays, 1, 14–15
materialist view, 142, 147
mental topography, 29
pleasure principle, 134
psychic reality, 141, 144
    hallucination as, 140, 142
psychoanalysis as natural science,
        164
rejection of belief in God, 5, 20, 142
self-analysis, 16, 17
structural model, 148
on successful analysis, 9
superego, role of, 30–44
theory of, defects of, 65–70
works, exegesis of conscience in,
        30–44
Fromm, E., 175, 194, 195
Fuchs, K., 93

Galileo, 108, 187, 195
Gandhi, M., 99
gathering of followers as stage in
        development of religious
        leader, 2, 10–11
    Freud, 17
Gay, P., 15, 17
Giotto (di Bondone), 206
Gomperz, H., 25
Gomperz, T., 25
Graf, M., 17
greed, 20, 112, 128, 156
Groddeck, G., 52, 84
Guillaume, A., 101
guilt, 65, 75, 164, 172
    and conscience, 31–34, 37, 39, 130–
        134
    and anxiety, 32, 34, 40, 120
    and death instinct, 62
    and depression, 159
    and depressive position, 51, 129

displaced, 78
neurotic, 78
psychotic, 78
and self-mutilated mind, 62–64,
    130, 184
sexual, 183
and suicide, 37, 56
unconscious, 129
    and conscience, 31
    and conversion, 5

hallucination, 69, 74, 85, 140, 142, 147,
    198
Hamlet, 30, 64
Hampson, N., 42
Hanson, P., 175, 185
Heimann, P., 118
Helmholtz, H. L. F. von, 24, 49
Helmholtz School of Medicine, 142
Heraclitus, 97, 141–142
Hesse, H., 157
Hinduism, 81, 151, 208
Hitler, A., 198, 205–206
Hobbes, T., 175
homeostatic theory, 10, 66
hominization, 79, 106
Hopkins, G. M., 81
Hosea, 132
Hume, D., 106, 141–142
Hussein, S., 204–205
Husserl, E., 24, 51, 90
hypnotism, 14
hysteria, 46, 107
    conversion, 14

Ibsen, H., 34
idealized self, 33
identification:
    narcissistic, 36
    projective, 51
incest taboo, 166–173
induction, 13, 28
inductive metaphysics, 28
inert reality, 4–6, 8–10
infantile sexuality, 11, 16
inner reality, 5, 69, 75, 156, 166

instinct(s), 36, 38, 48–50, 59, 67, 70, 84,
    146, 179
death, 10, 41, 62
survival, 40, 164, 201
theory, 10
institution, founding of, as stage in
    development of religious
    leader, 2, 11
Freud, 17–18
intentional inexistence, 26, 27
intentional reality, 157
internal object(s), 22, 26–29, 143–144,
    148
ego's relation to, 27
internal reality, 34
internalization, 36
    and communication, 194
    of death instinct, conscience as, 41
    of external authority, 36, 43
        conscience as, 32–33, 40, 43–44
    failure of in modern culture, 186–
        196
    narcissistic, 36
International Psychoanalytical
    Society, 18
interpretation, role of, 61
introjection, 51
Isaac, 38
Isaiah, 98, 101, 102, 132
Islam, 101, 145, 160
    and existence, 104
    fundamentalism in, 207
    god of:
        false, 116, 117
        inflated self as, 103, 115
    revealed religion, 81, 100, 111
        vs rational reflection, 117
    and truth
        facets of in, 208, 209
    vision of compassion, 81

Jacob, 38
Jahn, B., 207
Jahoda, M., 49
Jainism, 3, 4, 18
James, W., 24, 62

Janet, P., 47
Jaques, E., 91, 187
Jaspers, K., 98, 132
jealousy, 20, 36, 112, 128
Jeremiah, 98, 102, 114, 132
Jesus, 3, 6–11, 18, 73, 102, 105, 114, 138, 155, 157, 202–203, 207
Jocasta, and murder of Laius, 165–173
John of the Cross, St, 11, 108, 109, 177
jokes, significance of, 16
Jones, E., 14–17, 25, 45, 47, 142, 148
Judaism, 122, 151
    and existence, 104
    "fuga mundi" mode of religious life, 21
    fundamentalism in, 207
    god of:
        false, 116, 117
        inflated self as, 103, 115
    revealed religion, 81, 100, 111, 160
        vs rational reflection, 117
    revelation, 101–102
    and truth, facets of in, 208, 209
    vision of compassion, 81
Jung, C. G., 16, 17, 23, 47, 118

Kahane, M., 17
Kant, I., 26, 28, 38, 105–106, 116, 128, 187, 195
karma, theory of, 150
Kepler, J., 108, 195
Kierkegaard, S., 99
Kipling, R., 80
Klein, G., 66, 88
Klein, M., 10, 50–52, 62, 80, 93, 118, 136, 187
    depressive position, 129
    internal objects, 144
    paranoid–schizoid position, 81
knowledge:
    vs awareness, 183–184
    nature of, 64–65
    obliteration of, 55–57, 61–64
Kohut, H., 118, 136
Koran, 101–102, 112, 160

Laertes, 30, 31
Laius, murder of, 165–173
Lampe, G., 149
Lao Tzu, 99, 132
Lecky, W. E. H., 43
Lévi-Strauss, C., 151
libido, 50, 51, 67
    object-related, 50
    object-seeking, 50, 93
    theory, 66
Ludwig, K. F. W., 24, 49, 142
Luther, M., 19

Macmurray, J., x, 95–96
Mahavira, 3–4, 18, 99, 132
Manichaean, 143
Mao Tse-Tung (Zedong), 205
Mara, the Evil One, 9
Marx, K., 175, 184, 185, 204, 208
masochism, 40, 112, 192
masturbation, 50, 66
materialist view in Greek philosophy, 147
    of soul, 141
mathematical certainty, 28
mathematical symbols, 57
mathematics, 86, 133
mature religion, 150–151
mental topography, Freud's, 29
metaphysical presuppositions, 192
metaphysics, 28, 192
    inductive, 28
metapsychology, 49, 54
Michelangelo, 64
Michelet, J., 87
Mill, James, 27, 142
Mill, John Stuart, 25, 27–28, 142
Milner, M. [J. Field], 108–110
mind:
    embryo, 59, 61, 69, 71
    model of:
        determinist vs religious, 48–53
        intentional, 50
        structural, 29, 31, 37, 50, 84, 93, 148
        topographical, 29, 49, 50

Mitchell, J., 186
Mobutu Sese Seko, J. D., 205
modern society, 127, 190, 193, 194
Molière, 151
Mona Lisa, 63
Moses, 101, 105
Muhammad, 18, 101–102, 105, 145, 160
Muller, J., 24
Mussolini, B., 205

Nagasaki, bombing of, 3
Napoleon Bonaparte, 205, 206
narcissism, 35, 37, 44, 73, 80, 116, 123, 132, 197
    and moral conscience, 35
narcissistic identification, 36–37
narcissistic self-image, attachment to, 9
narcissistic structure, 33, 36, 114–115, 118–119, 121
natural religion, 124, 127–129, 132, 134–135, 160–161, 164
    vs revealed religion, 80–84, 100–111
natural science(s), 54, 65, 85–87, 99, 152, 161, 164
    Brentano's methodology, 28
    psychophysics as, 26
natural spirituality, 124–136
negative freedom, 178
neurosis, 76, 77
    core, 59
neurotic symptoms, 46
    Freud's work on, 16
Newman, J. H., 43, 135
Newton, I., 106, 108
Newtonian physics, 86
Nietzsche, F., 26
noumenon, 152

object(s):
    internal: see internal object(s)
    relations theory, 29, 50–52
obsessive compulsive disorder, 107
oedipal drama, 35, 70

Oedipus:
    complex, 16, 35, 38, 59, 135
    and murder of Laius, 165–173
omnipotence, 73–80
ontology, 76, 103
Orwell, G., 187, 204
Oxford Movement, 43

paranoia, 73, 118, 121
paranoid delusions, 33
paranoid–schizoid position, 81
Parmenides, 97, 116–117, 141–143, 178
parricide, 166–173
participated being, 77–84
Paul, St (Saul), 3, 4, 42, 44, 102, 207
Pcs (pre-conscious system), 29, 56
perception, obliteration of, 74
persecuting conscience, 36
personality disorder, 77
perversion, 76, 77
phenomenology, 25, 29
photographic mode, 186–196
Physicalische Gesellschaft, 14, 29, 49, 142
Plato, 23, 25, 98, 132, 134, 141–149
Platonic conception(s), 141–149
    of soul, 137, 142
pleasure principle, 29, 69, 134
Polanyi, M., 13
post-modernism, 194, 207
pre-conscious (Pcs) system, 29, 56
primitive religion, 81–82, 84, 150–151
Princeton University, 207
principle:
    of constancy, 29
    of inclusion, 114, 123
    of omission, 167
projection, 36, 41, 51, 203, 208
projective identification, 51
prophecy, 98, 99, 195
psyche, concept of, vs soul, 137–149
psychic activity, nature of, 57–59
psychoanalysis (passim):
    and freedom, 174–185
    as religion, 159–164
    religion and science in, 72–84

psychology, 10, 22–28, 43, 66, 88, 142, 164, 179, 193, 197
   associationist: *see* associationist psychology
psychopathy, 76–77, 107
psychophysical parallelism, 148
psychophysics, 16, 26
psychosis, 57, 76, 77
Ptolomaic system of astronomy, 145

Rancurello, A. C., 23, 25, 27, 28
Rank, O., 168, 181
reality:
   external, 5, 26, 34
   inert, 4–6, 8–10
   inner, 5, 69, 75, 156, 166
   intentional, 157
   nature of, 85–99
   testing, 88, 98
realization, vital: *see* vital realization
reincarnation, 143, 150
Reitler, R., 17
relativity, theory of, 106, 208
religion (*passim*):
   and consciousness, 100–111
   mature, 150–151
   natural, 124, 127–129, 132, 134–135, 160–161, 164
      vs revealed religion, 80–84, 100–111
   primitive, 81–82, 84, 150–151
   in psychoanalysis, 72
   psychoanalysis as, 159–164
   revealed, 124, 126, 134–135, 160–164
      vs natural religion, 80–84, 100–111
   and spirituality, 150–158
   traditional, 19, 21, 65, 82, 127, 157
religious leader, development of, stages of, 2–11
religious model of mind vs determinist model of mind, 48–53
repression, 16, 69, 87, 132, 205
resistance, 16, 87, 90, 125, 131

   healthy core in, 181
   and vital realization, 8
revealed religion, 124, 126, 134–135, 160–164
   vs natural religion, 80–84, 100–111
Ricoeur, P., 46
"Rosmersholm" (Ibsen), 34
Rousseau, J. J., 42, 175, 184, 185
Rushdie, S., 18
Russell, B., 42, 177, 192

sadism, 112
Saint Exupéry, A. de, 54
Sales, Francis de, 18, 19
Schelling, F. W. J. von, 23
schizophrenia, 33, 103, 107, 169, 170, 174
Schweitzer, A., 149
science(s):
   natural, 54, 65, 85–87, 99, 152, 161, 164
      Brentano's methodology, 28
      psychophysics as, 26
   in psychoanalysis, 72
Second World War, 3, 167, 181
self-analysis, 8, 163
   Freud's, 16, 17
Sellers, P., 202
sexuality, infantile, 11, 16
Shakespeare, W., 30, 47, 99
Shankara, Vedanta philosophy of, 128
Sheldrake, R., 207
Siddhartha Gautama (the Buddha), 1, 2, 13–15, 18, 20, 132
   development of as religious leader, 2–11
   see also Buddha, the
social anxiety, 34, 40
society:
   modern, 127, 194
   traditional, 82, 127
Socrates, 42, 61, 70, 81, 97–98, 132–134, 161–164, 192–195
   principle of moral action, 54–56, 60, 163

Socratic religion, 81
Solzhenitsyn, A., 99
Sophism, 161
soul, concept of, vs psyche, 137–149
Spanish Civil War, 204
Spinoza, B., 116
spirituality:
    natural, 124–136
    and religion, 150–158
Stalin, J., 175, 204–206
Steiner, G., 203
Steiner, J., 172
Stekel, W., 17
Strachey, J., 34
Strauss, E. B., 139
Streeter, B. H., 177
structural model, 29, 31, 37, 50, 84, 93,
    148
struggle, as stage in development of
        religious leader, 2, 9–10
    Freud, 15–16
sublimation, 38
subliminal perception, 26
Suddhodana, 2
Suharto, T., 205, 206
suicide, 73, 82, 122, 157, 168, 170, 205
    of Beata in "Rosmersholm", 34
    and guilt, 37
Sulloway, F., 11, 46
superego, 29, 50, 74, 126, 147, 148, 203
    and conscience, 30–44, 78, 96
        equation of, 33–44
    functions of, 41
    and identification with parents, 38
    sadism of, 38
    tyrannical, 70
survival instinct, 164
symbolism, 16, 119, 129
    and true god, 121–122
Symington, J., 75

taboo conscience, 31
Taj Mahal, 64
talking cure, 72
Taoism, 208
Thanatos, 62

theory of relativity, 106, 208
Theravada School of Buddhism, 21,
    161
Thompson, F., 7
Thornton, E. M., 46
time, 99
Tiresias, 166, 171
Tocqueville, A. C. H. C. de, 204
Tolstoy, L. N., x, 47, 99, 105–106, 117,
    124
topographical model of mind, 49
Torah, 112
Toynbee, A., 204
traditional religion, 19, 21, 65, 82, 127,
    157
traditional society, 82, 127
transference, 16, 76, 79, 199, 200
    interpretation, 121
Trotsky, L., 204
true god vs false god, 112–123
true self, 93

Ucs (unconscious system), 29, 56, 61,
    69
    amoral construction of, 54–71
unawareness, 61, 62, 64
unconscious (Ucs) system, 29, 56, 61,
    69
    amoral construction of, 54–71
unconscious guilt, 5, 129
unpleasure, 67, 70
    principle, 69
Upanishads, 76–79, 81, 116–117, 128,
    132

Vedanta philosophy, 128, 129
Vereecke, L., 44
Vico, G., 86, 87, 88, 99, 187
Vienna Psychoanalytical Society, 18
Vienna University, 22, 23, 24
vital realization, 4–10
vitalism, 24

Wandsworth Prison, 56
Watson, J. B., 142
Webb, C. C. J., 105

Weber, M., 16, 18, 175
Webster, R., 45–47
Wednesday Psychological Society,
    17–18
Wessel, E., 25
White, M., 58
White, V., 139–140, 149
Whitehead, A. N., 62, 192

Winnicott, D. W., 6–7, 93, 118, 136, 144
wish fulfilment, hallucinatory, 68
Wittgenstein, L. J. J., 16
Wundt, W., 24, 26–28

Zarathustra, 99, 132, 134
Zilboorg, G., 139
Zoroastrianism, 81, 208